THE BRICK BIBLE

THE BRICK BIBLE
A NEW SPIN ON THE OLD TESTAMENT

AS TOLD AND ILLUSTRATED BY
BRENDAN POWELL SMITH

Skyhorse Publishing

CONTENTS

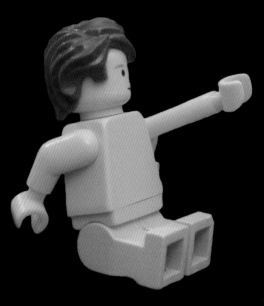

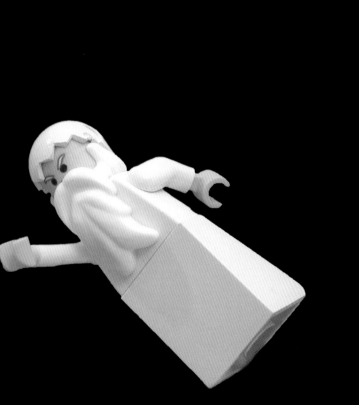

I have spent the past ten years on a one-man project to illustrate the entire Bible in LEGO ® building blocks. I have been inspired to do this for one reason: people should really know what's in the Bible. For a book that so many of us consider our ultimate moral guide and the very word of God, it can be shocking to consider how few people ever actually read it.

My goal is to present the Bible's content in a new, engaging, and fun way, and yet also to remain faithful to the way the Bible itself tells these stories. To this end, all of the text in this book is drawn from direct quotes of scripture. Chapter and verse numbers have been suppressed for stylistic reasons, but can be referenced at this book's accompanying website: **www.thebricktestament.com**

It has truly been a pleasure and a labor of love building and photographing all 1,400 of the illustrations collected here, and I do hope you enjoy the result.

—Brendan Powell Smith

IN THE BEGINNING, WHEN GOD CREATED THE HEAVENS AND THE EARTH, THE EARTH WAS FORMLESS AND EMPTY WITH DARKNESS COVERING THE DEEP, AND THE SPIRIT OF GOD WAS HOVERING OVER THE SURFACE OF THE WATERS.

GENESIS

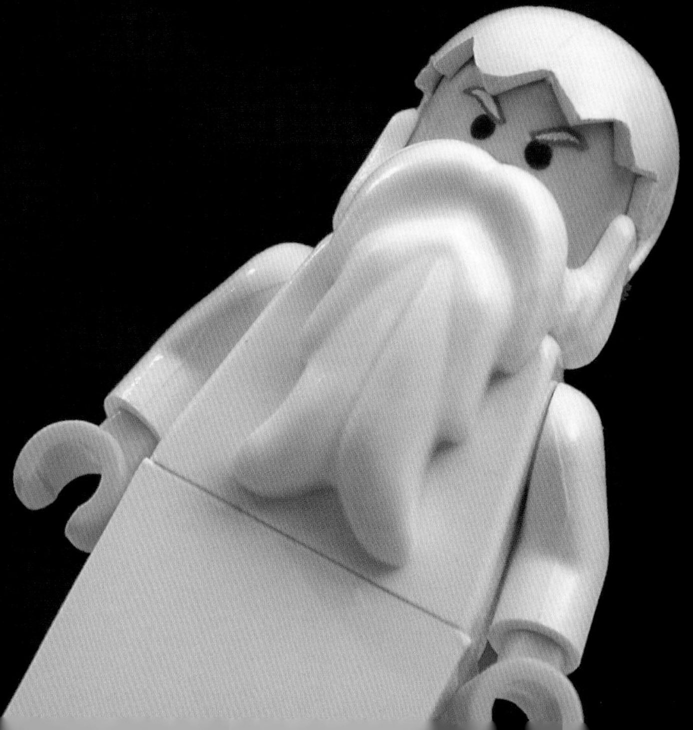

AND GOD SAID, 'LET THERE BE LIGHT.' AND THERE WAS LIGHT. AND GOD SAW THAT THE LIGHT WAS GOOD.

GOD SEPARATED THE LIGHT FROM THE DARKNESS. GOD CALLED THE LIGHT 'DAY' AND CALLED THE DARKNESS 'NIGHT.' AND THERE WAS EVENING, AND THERE WAS MORNING: THE FIRST DAY.

THEN GOD SAID, 'LET THERE BE A VAULT TO SEPARATE THE WATERS UNDER THE VAULT FROM THE WATERS ABOVE THE VAULT.' AND GOD MADE THE VAULT AND CALLED IT 'SKY.' AND THERE WAS EVENING, AND THERE WAS MORNING: THE SECOND DAY.

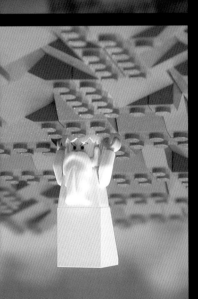

THEN GOD SAID, 'LET THE WATERS UNDER THE SKY BE GATHERED TO ONE PLACE, AND LET THE DRY GROUND APPEAR.' GOD CALLED THE DRY GROUND 'LAND' AND THE WATERS 'SEAS.' AND GOD SAW THAT IT WAS GOOD.

GOD SAID, 'LET THE LAND PRODUCE PLANTS AND TREES OF EVERY KIND.' AND THE LAND PRODUCED PLANTS AND TREES OF EVERY KIND. AND GOD SAW THAT IT WAS GOOD. AND THERE WAS EVENING, AND THERE WAS MORNING: THE THIRD DAY.

THEN GOD SAID, 'LET THERE BE LIGHTS IN THE VAULT OF THE SKY TO SEPARATE THE DAY FROM THE NIGHT. AND LET THEM BE SIGNS TO MARK SEASONS, DAYS, AND YEARS.' AND IT WAS SO: GOD MADE THE GREATER LIGHT TO RULE OVER THE DAY.

AND GOD MADE THE LESSER LIGHT TO RULE THE NIGHT AND THE STARS. AND GOD SAW THAT IT WAS GOOD. AND THERE WAS EVENING, AND THERE WAS MORNING: THE FOURTH DAY.

THEN GOD SAID, 'LET THE WATERS SWARM WITH SWARMS OF LIVING CREATURES, AND LET BIRDS FLY ABOVE THE EARTH ACROSS THE VAULT OF THE SKY.'

AND IT WAS SO: GOD CREATED THE GREAT SEA MONSTERS AND CREATURES OF EVERY KIND WITH WHICH THE WATERS SWARM AND WINGED BIRDS OF EVERY KIND. AND GOD SAW THAT IT WAS GOOD.

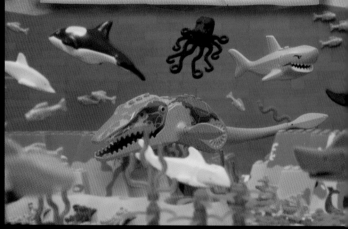

GOD BLESSED THEM, SAYING, 'BREED AND MUL-TIPLY. FILL THE SEAS. AND LET BIRDS MULTIPLY ON THE EARTH.' AND THERE WAS EVENING AND THERE WAS MORNING: THE FIFTH DAY.

THEN GOD SAID, 'LET THE LAND PRODUCE LIVING CREATURES: LIVESTOCK, CREEPING THINGS, AND WILD ANIMALS OF EVERY KIND.' AND IT WAS SO: GOD MADE WILD ANIMALS, LIVESTOCK, AND CREATURES THAT CREEP ALONG THE GROUND OF EVERY KIND. AND GOD SAW THAT IT WAS GOOD.

AND GOD CREATED HUMANS IN HIS IMAGE. IN THE IMAGE OF GOD, HE CREATED THEM. MALE AND FEMALE, HE CREATED THEM.

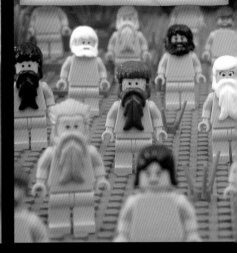

THEN GOD SAID, 'LET US MAKE HUMANS IN OUR IMAGE, IN OUR LIKENESS. AND LET THEM RULE OVER THE FISH OF THE SEA, THE BIRDS OF THE AIR, THE LIVESTOCK, AND ALL THE CREATURES THAT CREEP ALONG THE GROUND.'

GOD BLESSED THEM, SAYING, 'BREED AND MULTIPLY. FILL THE EARTH AND SUBDUE IT. RULE OVER THE FISH OF THE SEA, THE BIRDS OF THE AIR, AND EVERY CREATURE THAT MOVES ON THE GROUND.'

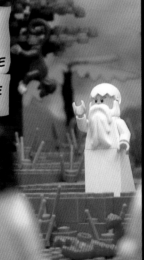

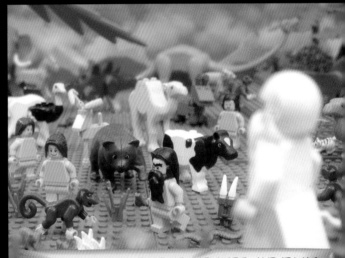

AND GOD SAW ALL THAT HE HAD MADE, AND IT WAS VERY GOOD. AND THERE WAS EVENING, AND THERE WAS MORNING: THE SIXTH DAY.

THUS THE HEAVENS AND THE EARTH WERE FINISHED. AND ON THE SEVENTH DAY, GOD RESTED FROM ALL THE WORK THAT HE HAD DONE.

ON THE DAY YAHWEH GOD MADE THE EARTH AND THE HEAVENS, NO PLANT OR SHRUB HAD YET SPRUNG UP BECAUSE YAHWEH GOD HAD NOT CAUSED IT TO RAIN, AND THERE WAS NO MAN TO WORK THE GROUND.

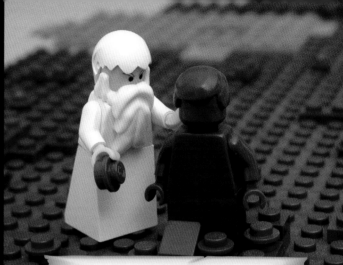

AND YAHWEH GOD FORMED MAN FROM THE DIRT OF THE GROUND.

AND HE BREATHED INTO HIS NOSTRILS THE BREATH OF LIFE.

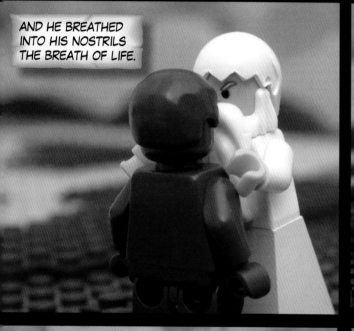

AND MAN BECAME A LIVING BEING.

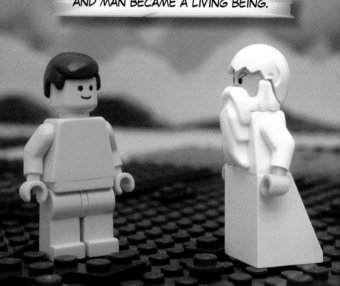

YAHWEH GOD PLANTED A GARDEN IN EDEN WITH THE TREE OF LIFE IN THE MIDDLE OF THE GARDEN AND THE TREE OF KNOWLEDGE OF GOOD AND EVIL.

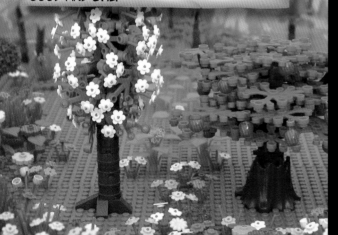

YAHWEH GOD TOOK THE MAN AND PUT HIM IN THE GARDEN OF EDEN TO LOOK AFTER AND MAINTAIN IT.

YAHWEH GOD COMMANDED THE MAN, 'FROM EVERY TREE OF THE GARDEN YOU MAY FREELY EAT, BUT FROM THE TREE OF KNOWLEDGE OF GOOD AND EVIL, YOU MAY NOT EAT. FOR THE DAY THAT YOU EAT FROM IT, YOU WILL SURELY DIE.'

THEN YAHWEH GOD SAID, 'IT IS NOT GOOD FOR THE MAN TO BE ALONE. I WILL MAKE HIM A HELPER, HIS COUNTERPART.'

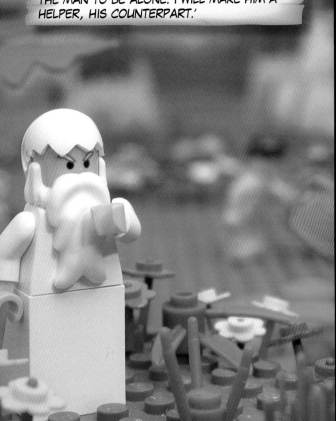

SO FROM THE DIRT YAHWEH GOD FORMED EVERY ANIMAL OF THE FIELD AND EVERY BIRD OF THE SKY.

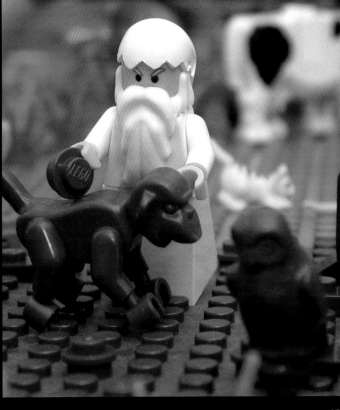

HE BROUGHT THEM TO THE MAN TO SEE WHAT HE WOULD CALL THEM. WHATEVER THE MAN CALLED THEM, THAT WAS ITS NAME. BUT NO SUITABLE HELPER WAS FOUND FOR THE MAN.

THEN YAHWEH GOD CAUSED A DEEP SLEEP TO FALL ON THE MAN. AND WHILE HE SLEPT, HE TOOK ONE OF HIS RIBS AND CLOSED UP THE FLESH IN ITS PLACE.

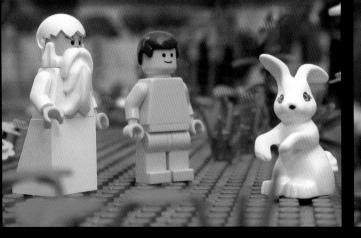

AND FROM THE RIB YAHWEH GOD HAD TAKEN FROM THE MAN, HE MADE A WOMAN.

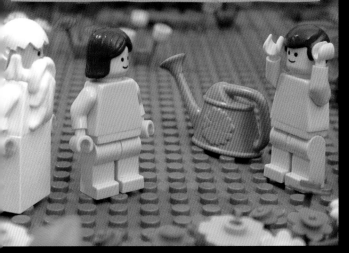

HE BROUGHT HER TO THE MAN, AND THE MAN SAID, 'THIS, AT LAST, IS BONE OF MY BONES AND FLESH OF MY FLESH! SHE WILL BE CALLED WOMAN BECAUSE SHE WAS TAKEN OUT OF MAN.'

THIS IS WHY A MAN LEAVES HIS FATHER AND MOTHER AND CLINGS TO HIS WIFE, AND THEY BECOME ONE FLESH.

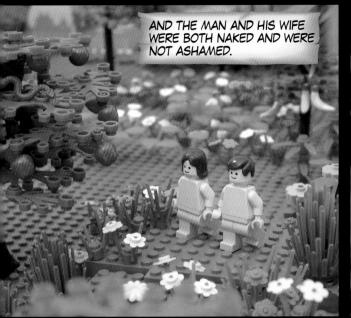

AND THE MAN AND HIS WIFE WERE BOTH NAKED AND WERE NOT ASHAMED.

NOW OF ALL THE ANIMALS OF THE FIELD THAT YAHWEH GOD HAD MADE, THE SNAKE WAS THE MOST CLEVER. HE SAID TO THE WOMAN, 'HAS GOD REALLY SAID, "YOU SHALL NOT EAT FROM ANY TREE OF THE GARDEN"?'

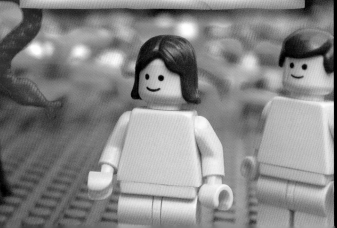

THE WOMAN SAID TO THE SNAKE, 'WE MAY EAT FROM THE TREES OF THE GARDEN, BUT OF THE FRUIT FROM THE TREE IN THE MIDDLE OF THE GARDEN, GOD SAID, "DO NOT EAT FROM IT, AND DO NOT EVEN TOUCH IT, OR ELSE YOU WILL DIE."'

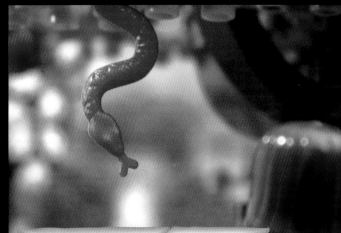

THE SNAKE SAID TO THE WOMAN, 'SURELY YOU WILL NOT DIE! FOR GOD KNOWS THAT ON THE DAY YOU EAT FROM IT, YOUR EYES WILL BE OPENED, AND YOU WILL BE LIKE GODS, KNOWING GOOD AND EVIL.'

THE WOMAN SAW THAT THE TREE WAS GOOD FOR FOOD, PLEASING TO THE EYES, AND DESIRABLE FOR THE KNOWLEDGE IT COULD GIVE.

AND SHE TOOK FRUIT FROM IT AND ATE IT.

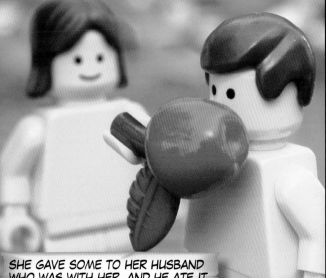

SHE GAVE SOME TO HER HUSBAND WHO WAS WITH HER, AND HE ATE IT.

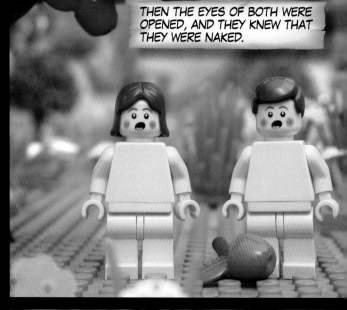

THEN THE EYES OF BOTH WERE OPENED, AND THEY KNEW THAT THEY WERE NAKED.

THEN THEY HEARD THE SOUND OF YAHWEH GOD WALKING ABOUT IN THE GARDEN IN THE BREEZE OF THE DAY. THE MAN AND HIS WIFE HID THEM-SELVES, AND YAHWEH GOD CALLED TO THE MAN, 'WHERE ARE YOU?'

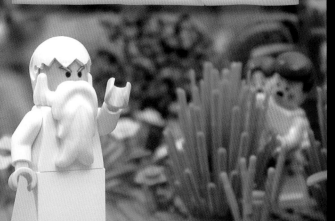

THE MAN SAID, 'I HEARD YOUR VOICE IN THE GARDEN, AND I WAS AFRAID BECAUSE I WAS NAKED, SO I HID MYSELF.'

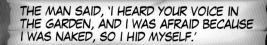

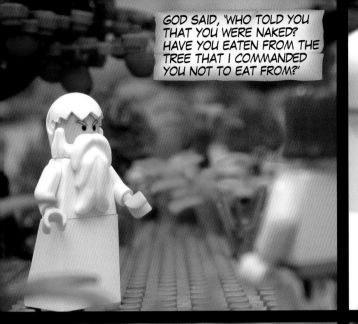

GOD SAID, 'WHO TOLD YOU THAT YOU WERE NAKED? HAVE YOU EATEN FROM THE TREE THAT I COMMANDED YOU NOT TO EAT FROM?'

THE MAN SAID, 'THE WOMAN YOU GAVE ME, SHE GAVE ME FRUIT OF THE TREE, AND I ATE IT.'

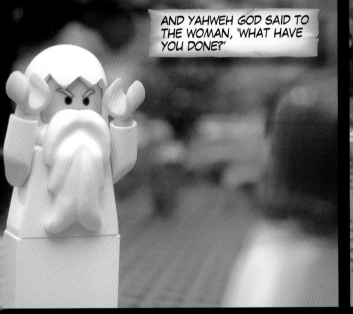

AND YAHWEH GOD SAID TO THE WOMAN, 'WHAT HAVE YOU DONE?'

THE WOMAN SAID, 'THE SNAKE CONVINCED ME, AND I ATE.'

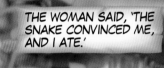

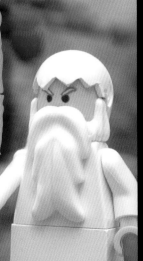

YAHWEH GOD SAID TO THE SNAKE, 'BECAUSE YOU HAVE DONE THIS, YOU ARE CURSED! ON YOUR BELLY YOU SHALL GO AND EAT DIRT ALL THE DAYS OF YOUR LIFE. I WILL PUT HOSTILITY BETWEEN YOU AND THE WOMAN. HER OFFSPRING WILL STRIKE AT YOUR HEAD, AND YOU WILL STRIKE AT HER OFFSPRING'S HEEL.'

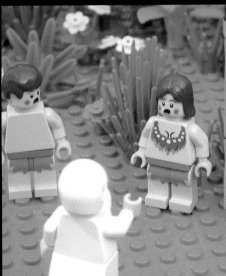

TO THE WOMAN HE SAID, 'I WILL GREATLY INCREASE YOUR SUFFERING DURING CHILD-BIRTH. IN AN-GUISH WILL YOU BRING FORTH CHILDREN. YOU WILL DESIRE YOUR HUSBAND, AND HE WILL DOMINATE YOU.'

TO THE MAN HE SAID, 'CURSED IS THE GROUND BECAUSE OF YOU! IT WILL YIELD YOU THORNS AND THISTLES. IN PAINFUL TOIL WILL YOU EAT FROM IT ALL THE DAYS OF YOUR LIFE UNTIL YOU RETURN TO THE GROUND FROM WHICH YOU WERE TAKEN. FOR YOU ARE DIRT, AND TO DIRT YOU WILL RETURN.'

YAHWEH GOD MADE LEATHER GARMENTS FOR THE MAN AND HIS WIFE AND CLOTHED THEM.

THEN YAHWEH GOD SAID, 'THE MAN HAS BECOME LIKE ONE OF US, KNOWING GOOD AND EVIL. HE MUST BE PREVENTED FROM REACHING OUT HIS HAND TO TAKE FROM THE TREE OF LIFE, LEST HE EAT FROM IT AND ALSO LIVE FOREVER!'

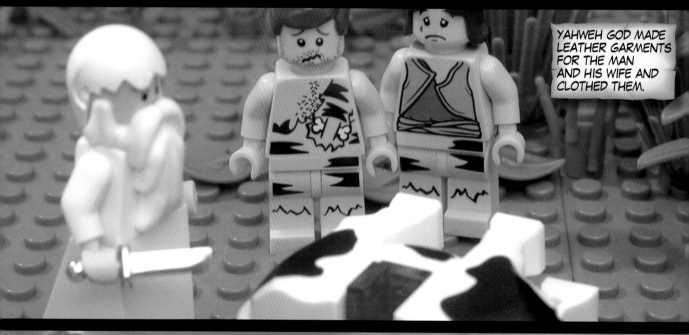

SO HE DROVE THE MAN AWAY AND STATIONED CHERUBS AT THE EAST OF THE GARDEN OF EDEN AND A WHIRLING FLAMING SWORD TO GUARD THE WAY TO THE TREE OF LIFE.

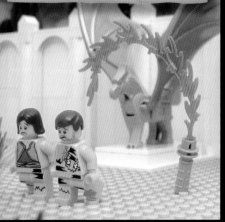

YAHWEH GOD SENT HIM AWAY FROM THE GARDEN OF EDEN TO TILL THE GROUND FROM WHICH HE WAS TAKEN.

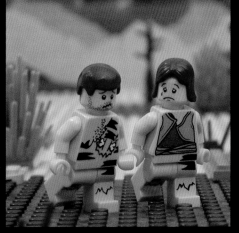

THE MAN LAID WITH HIS WIFE, EVE, AND SHE BECAME PREGNANT AND GAVE BIRTH TO CAIN. SHE GAVE BIRTH AGAIN TO CAIN'S BROTHER ABEL.

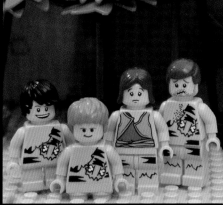

ABEL WAS A SHEPHERD OF THE FLOCKS.

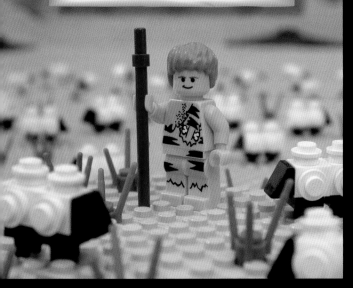

CAIN WAS A WORKER OF THE SOIL.

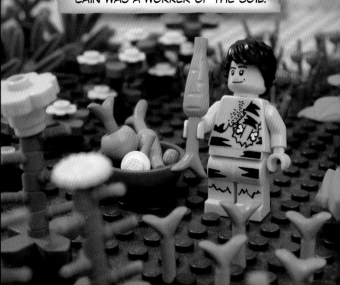

AFTER SOME TIME, CAIN BROUGHT SOME OF THE PRODUCE OF THE SOIL AS AN OFFERING TO YAHWEH.

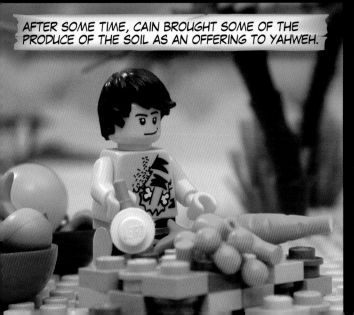

AND ABEL, HE ALSO BROUGHT SOME OF THE FIRSTBORN OF HIS FLOCK, THE FAT ONES.

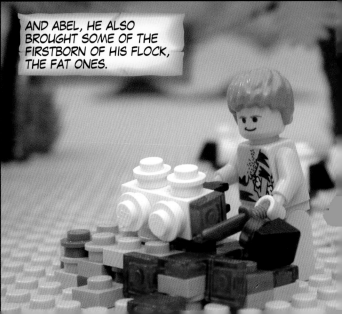

YAHWEH LOOKED WITH FAVOR ON ABEL AND HIS OFFERING.

BUT YAHWEH DID NOT LOOK WITH FAVOR ON CAIN AND HIS OFFERING. THIS WAS UPSETTING TO CAIN, AND HIS FACE WAS FALLEN.

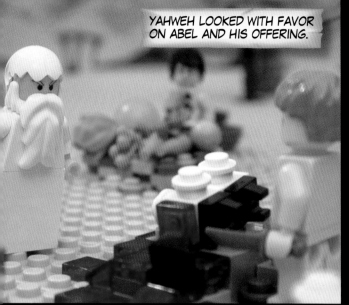

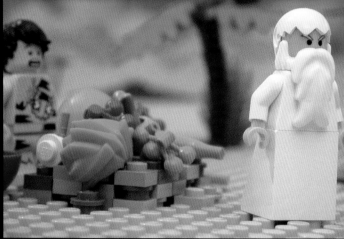

YAHWEH SAID TO CAIN, 'WHY ARE YOU UPSET, AND WHY IS YOUR FACE FALLEN? IF YOU DO GOOD, ISN'T IT LIFTED? IF YOU DO NOT DO GOOD, ERROR, SHE IS CROUCHING AT THE OPENING. HIS DESIRE IS TO YOU, AND YOU WILL DOMINATE HIM.'

CAIN SAID TO HIS BROTHER ABEL, 'LET'S GO INTO THE FIELD.'

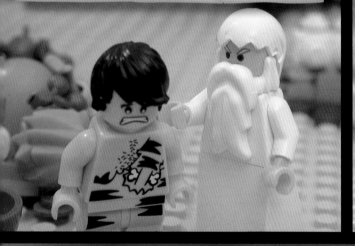

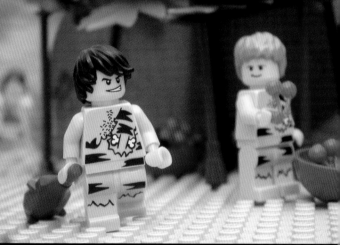

AND THEY WERE OUT IN THE FIELD. AND CAIN ATTACKED HIS BROTHER ABEL AND KILLED HIM.

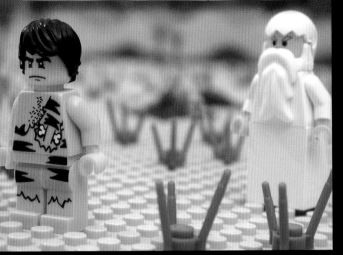

'WHERE IS YOUR BROTHER ABEL?' YAHWEH SAID TO CAIN. 'I DON'T KNOW,' REPLIED CAIN. 'AM I MY BROTHER'S KEEPER?'

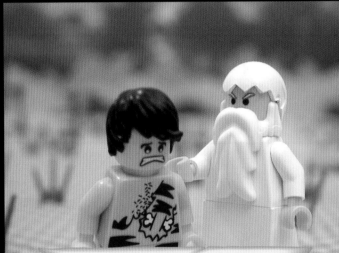

YAHWEH SAID, 'THE VOICE OF YOUR BROTHER'S BLOOD CRIES OUT TO ME FROM THE GROUND! NOW YOU ARE CURSED FROM THE GROUND WHICH HAS OPENED ITS MOUTH TO RECEIVE YOUR BROTHER'S BLOOD. WHEN YOU TILL THE GROUND, IT WILL NOT YIELD ITS STRENGTH TO YOU. YOU WILL BE A DRIFTER AND A WANDERER ON THE EARTH.'

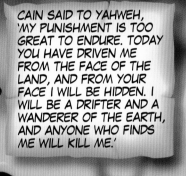

CAIN SAID TO YAHWEH, 'MY PUNISHMENT IS TOO GREAT TO ENDURE. TODAY YOU HAVE DRIVEN ME FROM THE FACE OF THE LAND, AND FROM YOUR FACE I WILL BE HIDDEN. I WILL BE A DRIFTER AND A WANDERER OF THE EARTH, AND ANYONE WHO FINDS ME WILL KILL ME.'

YAHWEH SAID TO CAIN, 'IN THAT CASE, WHO-EVER KILLS CAIN, A SEVENFOLD VENGEANCE WILL BE TAKEN ON HIM.'

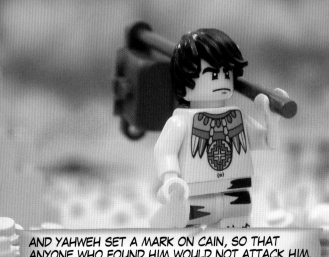

AND YAHWEH SET A MARK ON CAIN, SO THAT ANYONE WHO FOUND HIM WOULD NOT ATTACK HIM. THEN CAIN WENT AWAY FROM THE PRESENCE OF YAHWEH AND SETTLED IN NOD, EAST OF EDEN.

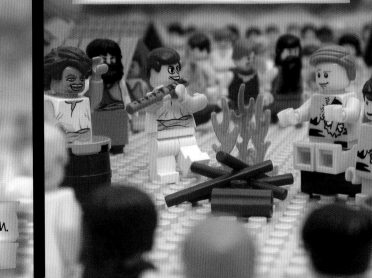

HUMANKIND BECAME ABUNDANT ON THE EARTH.

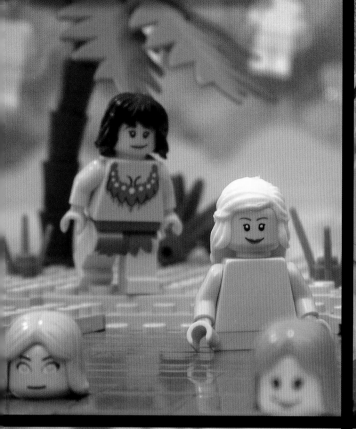

DAUGHTERS WERE BORN TO THEM, AND THE SONS OF GOD SAW THAT THE DAUGHTERS OF HUMANKIND WERE GOOD.

AND THEY TOOK FOR THEMSELVES ANY WOMEN THEY CHOSE.

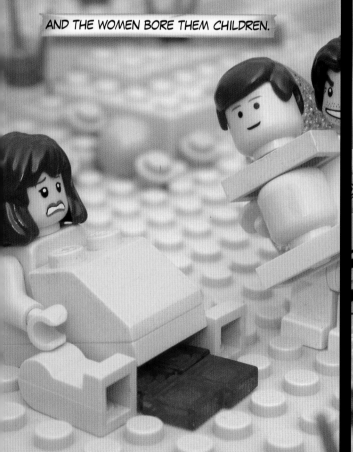

AND THE WOMEN BORE THEM CHILDREN.

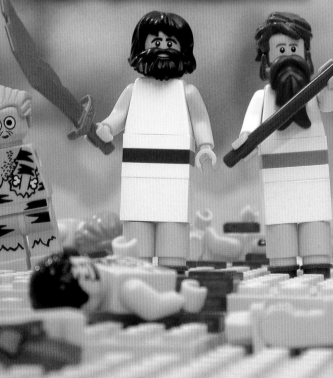

THERE WERE GIANTS ON THE EARTH IN THOSE DAYS AND AFTERWARDS, TOO. THESE WERE THE FAMOUS, MIGHTY MEN OF OLD.

NOW GOD LOOKED AT THE EARTH, AND IT WAS COR-
RUPTED, FOR ALL FLESHLY BEINGS HAD BECOME
CORRUPT. AND THE EARTH WAS FULL OF INJUSTICE.
AND HE REGRETTED HAVING MADE HUMANKIND ON
EARTH, AND IT PAINED HIS HEART.

AND YAHWEH SAID, 'I WILL WIPE OUT
HUMANKIND FROM THE FACE OF THE
EARTH - HUMANS, ANIMALS, CREATURES,
AND BIRDS - FOR I REGRET HAVING
MADE THEM.'

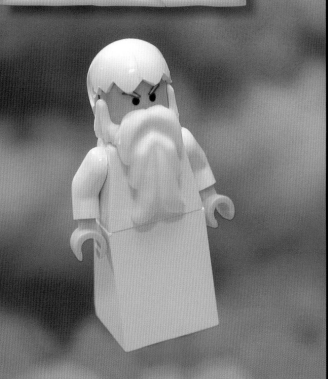

BUT NOAH FOUND FAVOR IN YAHWEH'S EYES.
NOAH WAS A JUST MAN AND PERFECT AMONG
HIS GENERATION. HE WALKED WITH GOD.

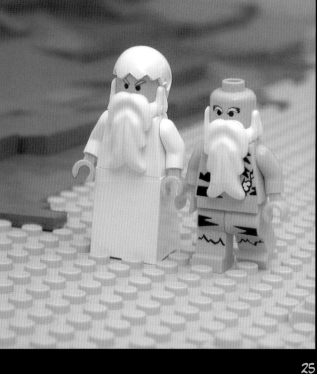

GOD SAID TO NOAH, 'I AM ABOUT TO BRING WATERS TO FLOOD THE EARTH AND DESTROY EVERY LIVING CREATURE UNDER THE HEAVENS. EVERYTHING ON THE EARTH WILL DIE. I WILL SEND RAIN FOR 40 DAYS AND 40 NIGHTS, AND I WILL WIPE OUT EVERY LIVING THING FROM THE FACE OF THE EARTH.'

'BUT I WILL MAKE MY PACT WITH YOU. MAKE YOUR-SELF AN ARK OF GOPHER WOOD.' NOAH DID ALL THAT GOD COMMANDED HIM TO DO. GOD SAID, 'HERE IS HOW YOU SHOULD MAKE IT: 450 FEET LONG, 75 FEET WIDE.'

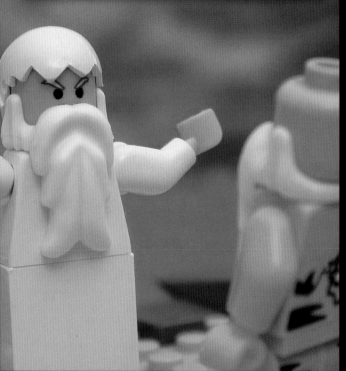

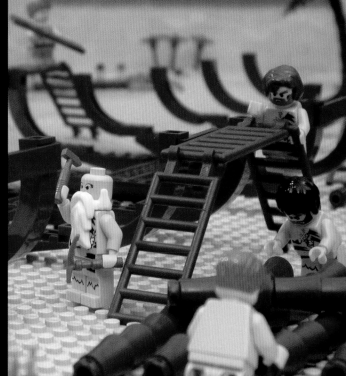

'MAKE IT 45 FEET HIGH, WITH A LOWER, MIDDLE, AND UPPER DECK. MAKE A ROOF EXTENDING TO 18 INCHES ABOVE THE SIDES, AND PUT A DOOR IN THE SIDE.'

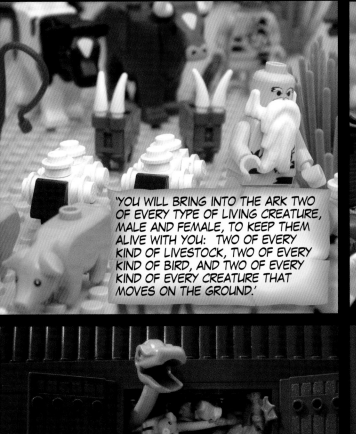

AND PAIRS OF CLEAN AND UNCLEAN ANIMALS ENTERED THE ARK.

'YOU WILL BRING INTO THE ARK TWO OF EVERY TYPE OF LIVING CREATURE, MALE AND FEMALE, TO KEEP THEM ALIVE WITH YOU: TWO OF EVERY KIND OF LIVESTOCK, TWO OF EVERY KIND OF BIRD, AND TWO OF EVERY KIND OF EVERY CREATURE THAT MOVES ON THE GROUND.'

THEN YAHWEH SHUT HIM IN.

YAHWEH SAID TO NOAH, 'COME INTO THE ARK, YOU AND ALL YOUR FAMILY.' AND NOAH ENTERED THE ARK WITH HIS SONS, HIS WIFE, AND HIS SONS' WIVES.

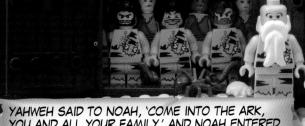

IN THE 600TH YEAR OF NOAH'S LIFE, IN THE SECOND MONTH, ON THE SEVENTEENTH DAY OF THE MONTH, ALL THE FOUNTAINS OF THE GREAT DEEP BURST FORTH. THE WINDOWS OF HEAVEN WERE OPENED AND RAIN FELL ON THE EARTH FOR 40 DAYS AND 40 NIGHTS.

THE WATERS ROSE AND GREATLY IN-CREASED ON THE EARTH AND THE ARK FLOATED ON THE SURFACE OF THE WATER.

AND THE WATERS INCREASED MORE AND MORE, AND ALL THE HIGH MOUNTAINS WERE COVERED. THE WATERS ROSE 20 FEET ABOVE THE MOUNTAINS.

AND ALL THE LIVING THINGS ON EARTH DIED: THE BIRDS, LIVESTOCK, WILD ANIMALS, ALL SWARMING CREATURES THAT SWARM ON THE EARTH, AND ALL HUMANKIND.

YAHWEH WIPED OUT EVERY LIVING THING ON THE FACE OF THE EARTH: HUMAN AND ANIMAL, CREATURES THAT MOVE ALONG THE GROUND, AND THE BIRDS OF THE SKY. EVERYTHING ON DRY LAND WITH THE BREATH OF LIFE IN ITS NOSTRILS DIED.

AND THE WATERS DOMINATED THE EARTH FOR 150 DAYS.

THEN GOD REMEMBERED NOAH AND ALL THE LIVING THINGS AND THE LIVESTOCK THAT WERE WITH HIM ON THE ARK.

THE WATERS GRADUALLY RECEDED FROM THE EARTH, AND THE ARK CAME TO REST ON THE MOUNTAINS OF ARARAT.

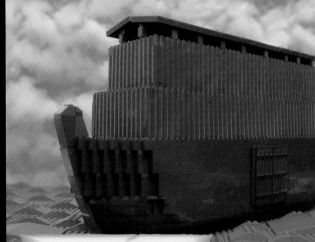
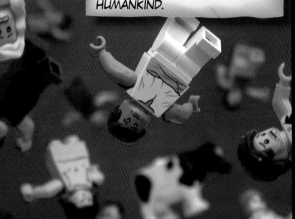
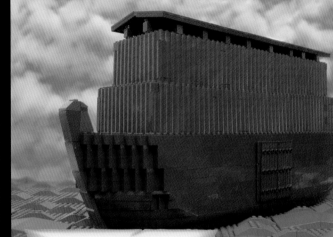
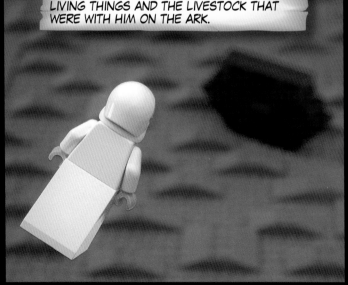

GOD SAID TO NOAH, 'COME OUT OF THE ARK!' AND NOAH WENT OUT ALONG WITH HIS SONS, HIS WIFE, HIS SONS' WIVES, AND EVERY LIVING THING.

AND NOAH BUILT AN ALTAR TO YAHWEH AND TOOK SOME OF EVERY CLEAN ANIMAL AND EVERY CLEAN BIRD AND OFFERED THEM AS BURNT SACRIFICES ON THE ALTAR.

AND YAHWEH SMELLED THE SOOTHING SMELL AND SAID IN HIS HEART, 'NEVER AGAIN WILL I CURSE THE SOIL BECAUSE OF HUMANKIND. NEVER AGAIN WILL I KILL EVERY LIVING THING AS I HAVE DONE.'

'LOOK, I AM MAKING MY PACT WITH YOU, YOUR DESCENDANTS, AND EVERY LIVING THING THAT CAME OUT OF THE ARK. NEVER AGAIN WILL ALL LIFE BE WIPED OUT BY A FLOOD. THIS IS THE SIGN OF THE PACT: I HAVE SET MY BOW IN THE CLOUDS.'

'WHENEVER THE BOW IS SEEN, I WILL REMEMBER MY PACT BETWEEN ME AND YOU AND EVERY LIVING FLESHLY CREATURE ON THE EARTH.'

THE SONS OF NOAH WHO WENT OUT FROM THE ARK WERE SHEM, HAM, AND JAPHETH. FROM THESE THREE, THE WHOLE EARTH WAS POPULATED. AND HAM WAS THE FATHER OF CANAAN.

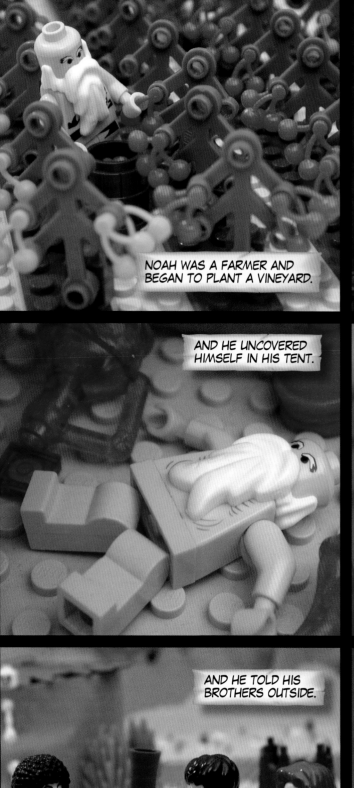

NOAH WAS A FARMER AND BEGAN TO PLANT A VINEYARD.

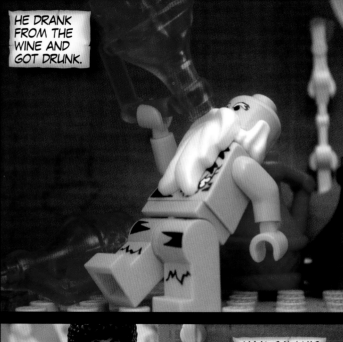

HE DRANK FROM THE WINE AND GOT DRUNK.

AND HE UNCOVERED HIMSELF IN HIS TENT.

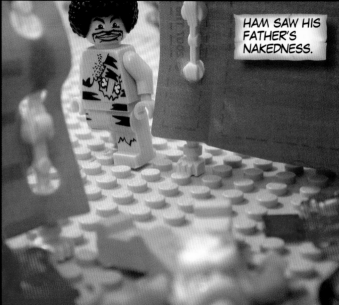

HAM SAW HIS FATHER'S NAKEDNESS.

AND HE TOLD HIS BROTHERS OUTSIDE.

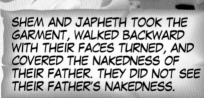

SHEM AND JAPHETH TOOK THE GARMENT, WALKED BACKWARD WITH THEIR FACES TURNED, AND COVERED THE NAKEDNESS OF THEIR FATHER. THEY DID NOT SEE THEIR FATHER'S NAKEDNESS.

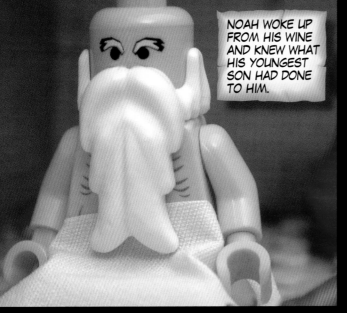

NOAH WOKE UP FROM HIS WINE AND KNEW WHAT HIS YOUNGEST SON HAD DONE TO HIM.

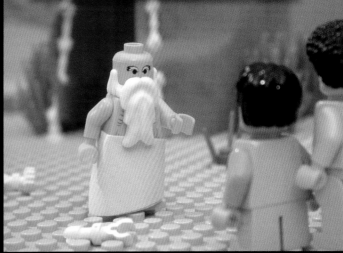

AND HE SAID, 'CURSED IS CANAAN! A SERVILE SLAVE HE WILL BE TO HIS BROTHERS!'

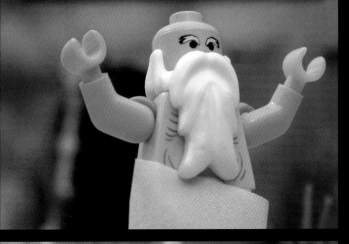

AND HE SAID, 'BLESSED BE YAHWEH, GOD OF SHEM, AND CANAAN WILL BE SHEM'S SLAVE! GOD WILL ENLARGE JAPHETH, AND HE WILL DWELL IN THE TENTS OF SHEM, AND LET CANAAN BE JAPHETH'S SLAVE!'

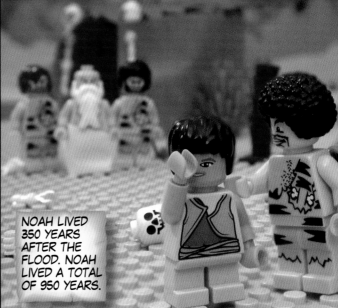

NOAH LIVED 350 YEARS AFTER THE FLOOD. NOAH LIVED A TOTAL OF 950 YEARS.

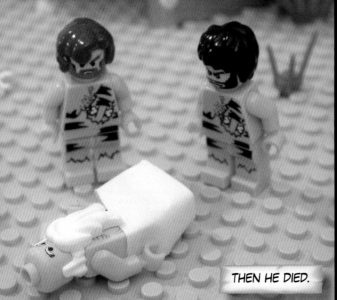

THEN HE DIED.

NOW ALL THE EARTH HAD ONE LANGUAGE AND SPOKE THE SAME DIALECT. WHEN THEY MOVED TO THE EAST, THEY FOUND A VALLEY IN THE LAND OF SHINAR.

THEY SETTLED THERE AND SAID TO EACH OTHER, 'LET'S FORM BRICKS AND BAKE THEM. LET'S BUILD OURSELVES A CITY AND A TOWER WITH ITS TOP IN THE SKY. LET'S MAKE A NAME FOR OURSELVES, FOR OTHERWISE WE'LL BE SCATTERED ACROSS THE FACE OF THE EARTH.'

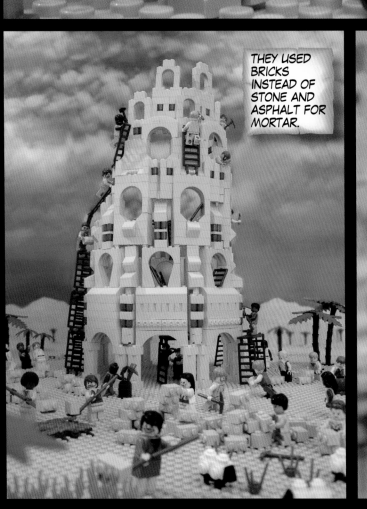

THEY USED BRICKS INSTEAD OF STONE AND ASPHALT FOR MORTAR.

AND YAHWEH WENT DOWN TO SEE THE CITY AND THE TOWER THAT THE SONS OF HUMANKIND WERE BUILDING AND SAID, 'LOOK! A SINGLE PEOPLE WITH A SINGLE LANGUAGE, AND THIS IS WHAT THEY START TO DO! NOW NOTHING THEY PLAN WILL BE IMPOSSIBLE FOR THEM!'

'COME, LET'S GO DOWN AND CONFUSE THEIR LANGUAGE, SO THAT THEY WILL NOT UNDERSTAND ONE ANOTHER.'

AND YAHWEH SCATTERED THEM FROM THAT PLACE ACROSS THE FACE OF THE EARTH.

AND THEY STOPPED BUILDING THE CITY.

THAT IS WHY IT WAS CALLED BABEL, BECAUSE THERE YAHWEH CONFUSED THE LANGUAGE OF ALL THE EARTH. AND YAHWEH SCATTERED THEM FROM THAT PLACE ACROSS THE FACE OF THE EARTH.

NOW TERAH TOOK HIS SON ABRAM AND HIS WIFE SARAI AND HIS GRANDSON LOT, AND THEY SET OUT FROM UR TOWARD THE LAND OF CANAAN. SARAI WAS INFERTILE AND HAD NO CHILDREN.

WHEN THEY REACHED HARAN, THEY SETTLED THERE. AND TERAH DIED IN HARAN AFTER HAVING LIVED FOR 205 YEARS.

THEN YAHWEH SAID TO ABRAM, 'LEAVE YOUR FATHER'S FAMILY FOR A LAND THAT I WILL SHOW YOU. I WILL MAKE YOU INTO A LARGE NATION. I WILL BLESS YOU AND MAKE YOU FAMOUS. I WILL BLESS THOSE WHO BLESS YOU, AND THOSE WHO MOCK YOU, I WILL CURSE!'

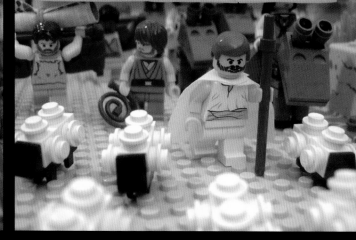

AND ABRAM LEFT AS YAHWEH TOLD HIM TO. ABRAM WAS 75 YEARS OLD WHEN HE LEFT HARAN, TAKING WITH HIM HIS WIFE SARAI, HIS NEPHEW LOT, ALL THE POSSESSIONS THEY HAD ACCUMULATED IN HARAN, AND ALL THE PEOPLE THEY HAD ACQUIRED.

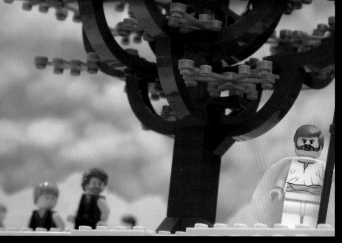

WHEN THEY CAME TO CANAAN, THE CANAANITES WERE LIVING IN THE LAND AT THAT TIME. ABRAM WENT AS FAR AS THE OAK TREE OF MOREH AT SHECHEM.

AND YAHWEH APPEARED TO ABRAM AND SAID, 'I WILL GIVE THIS LAND TO YOUR OFFSPRING.'

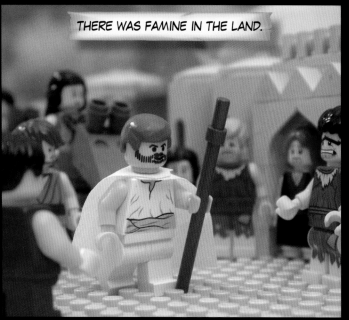

THERE WAS FAMINE IN THE LAND.

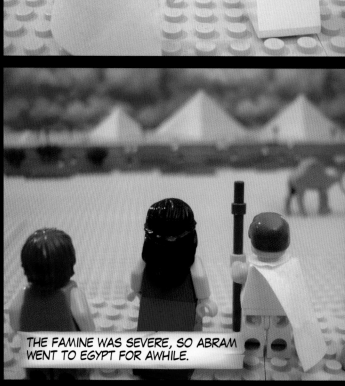

THE FAMINE WAS SEVERE, SO ABRAM WENT TO EGYPT FOR AWHILE.

34

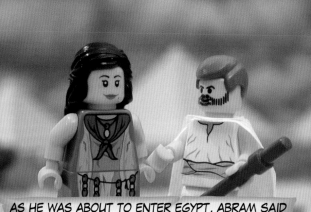

AS HE WAS ABOUT TO ENTER EGYPT, ABRAM SAID TO HIS WIFE, 'YOU ARE A BEAUTIFUL WOMAN, AND WHEN THE EGYPTIANS SEE YOU, THEY WILL SAY "THIS IS HIS WIFE", AND THEY WILL KILL ME. SAY YOU ARE MY SISTER SO MY LIFE WILL BE SPARED.'

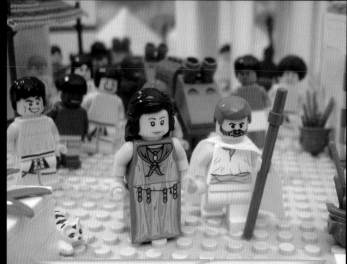

ABRAM ENTERED EGYPT, AND THE EGYPTIANS SAW THAT THE WOMAN WAS VERY BEAUTIFUL.

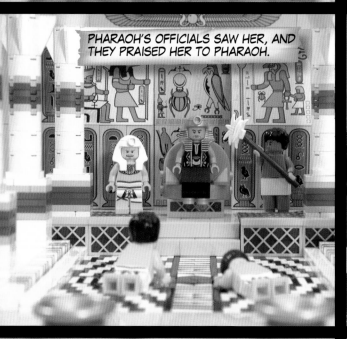

PHARAOH'S OFFICIALS SAW HER, AND THEY PRAISED HER TO PHARAOH.

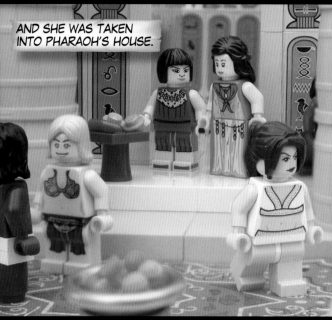

AND SHE WAS TAKEN INTO PHARAOH'S HOUSE.

ABRAM WAS TREATED WELL BECAUSE OF HER AND WAS GIVEN SHEEP, CATTLE, DONKEYS, CAMELS, AND MALE AND FEMALE SLAVES.

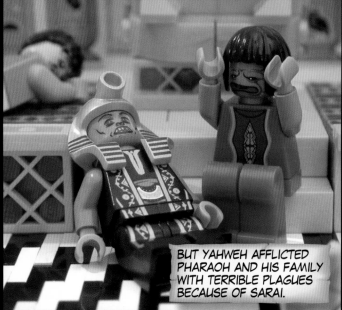

BUT YAHWEH AFFLICTED PHARAOH AND HIS FAMILY WITH TERRIBLE PLAGUES BECAUSE OF SARAI.

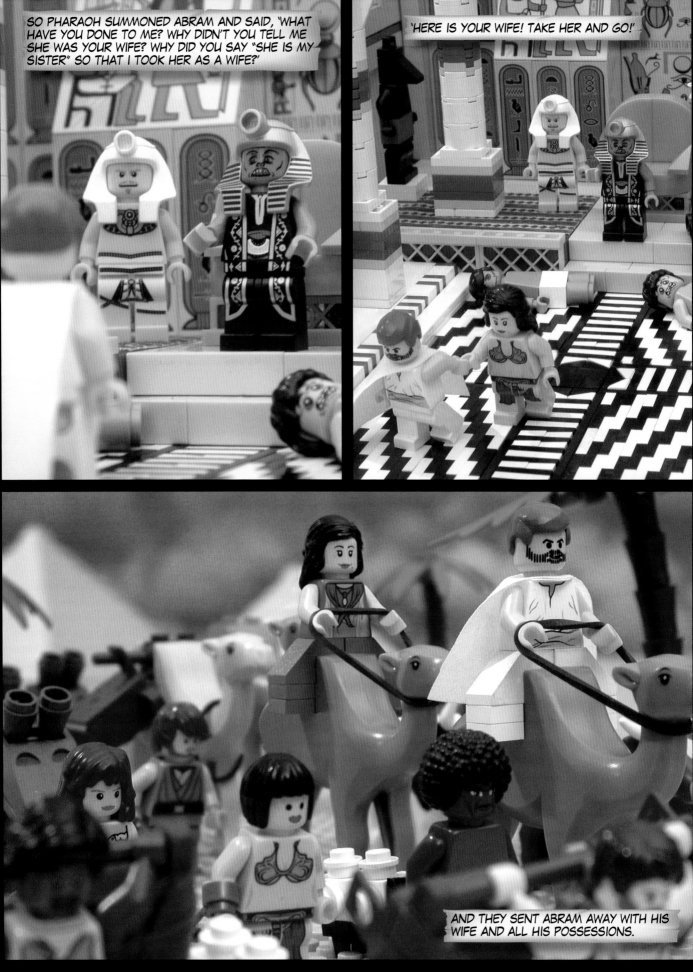

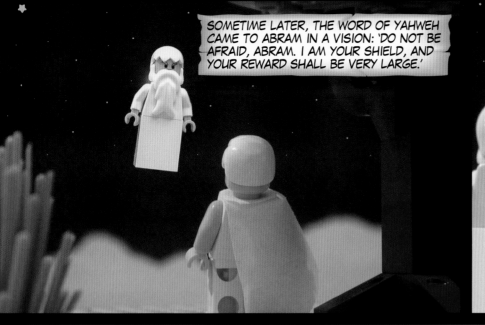

SOMETIME LATER, THE WORD OF YAHWEH CAME TO ABRAM IN A VISION: 'DO NOT BE AFRAID, ABRAM. I AM YOUR SHIELD, AND YOUR REWARD SHALL BE VERY LARGE.'

'LOOK UP AND COUNT THE STARS IF YOU CAN. SO SHALL YOUR OFFSPRING BE.'

'I AM YAHWEH WHO BROUGHT YOU OUT OF UR TO GIVE YOU THIS LAND TO POSSESS, FROM THE RIVER OF EGYPT TO THE EUPHRATES RIVER—THE LAND OF THE KENITES, KENIZZITES, KADMONITES, HITTITES, PERIZZITES, REPHAITES, AMORITES, CANAANITES, GIRGASHITES, AND JEBUSITES.'

YAHWEH SAID TO HIM, 'BRING ME A 3-YEAR-OLD COW, A 3-YEAR OLD SHE-GOAT, A 3-YEAR-OLD RAM, A TURTLE DOVE, AND A YOUNG PIGEON.'

ABRAM SAID TO HIM, 'LORD YAHWEH, HOW CAN I KNOW I WILL POSSESS IT?'

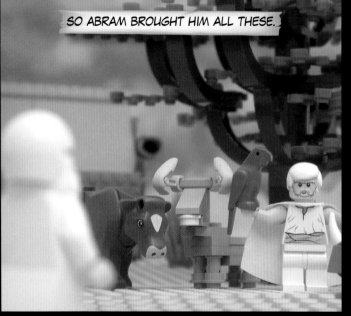

SO ABRAM BROUGHT HIM ALL THESE.

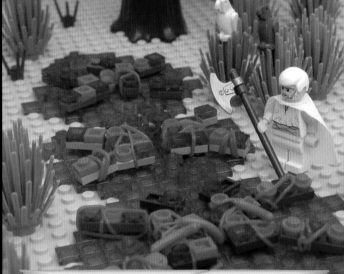

AND HE CUT THEM IN HALF, PUTTING EACH HALF OPPOSITE THE OTHER. BUT HE DID NOT CUT THE BIRDS.

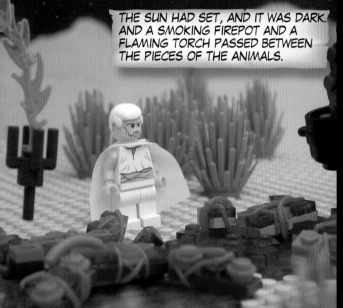

THE SUN HAD SET, AND IT WAS DARK. AND A SMOKING FIREPOT AND A FLAMING TORCH PASSED BETWEEN THE PIECES OF THE ANIMALS.

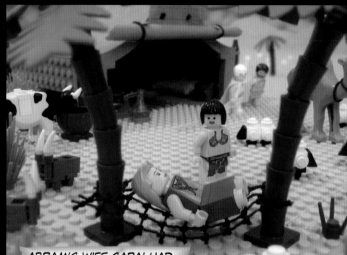

ABRAM'S WIFE SARAI HAD BORNE HIM NO CHILDREN, BUT SHE HAD AN EGYPTIAN SLAVE-GIRL NAMED HAGAR.

AND SARAI SAID TO ABRAM, 'LOOK, YAHWEH HAS PREVENTED ME FROM BEARING CHILDREN, SO LAY WITH MY SLAVE-GIRL. MAYBE I CAN BUILD A FAMILY THROUGH HER.'

WHEN ABRAM WAS 99 YEARS OLD, YAHWEH APPEARED TO HIM AND SAID, 'NO LONGER WILL YOUR NAME BE ABRAM, BUT "ABRAHAM," FOR YOU WILL BE THE ANCESTOR OF MANY NATIONS. I WILL ESTABLISH MY NEVER-ENDING PACT WITH YOU AND YOUR DESCENDANTS.'

ABRAM DID WHAT SARAI SAID, AND LAY WITH HAGAR. SHE BORE HIM A SON AND ABRAM NAMED HIM ISHMAEL. ABRAM WAS 86 YEARS OLD.

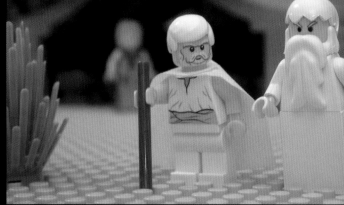

'FOR YOUR PART, YOU MUST CUT OFF THE FLESH OF YOUR FORESKINS. THROUGHOUT THE GENERATIONS, EVERY MALE AMONG YOU MUST BE CIRCUMCISED ONCE HE IS 8 DAYS OLD, INCLUDING SLAVES BORN IN YOUR HOUSE AND ANY PEOPLE PURCHASED WITH MONEY.'

GOD SAID TO ABRAHAM, 'YOU SHALL NO LONGER CALL YOUR WIFE SARAI. "SARAH" WILL BE HER NAME, AND I WILL GIVE YOU A SON THROUGH HER.' ABRAHAM FELL ON HIS FACE AND LAUGHED, THINKING, 'CAN A SON BE BORN TO A MAN WHO IS 100? CAN SARAH GIVE BIRTH TO A CHILD AT 90?'

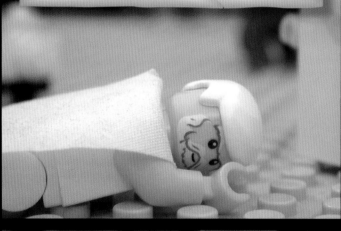

ABRAHAM WAS 99 YEARS OLD WHEN THE FLESH OF HIS FORESKIN WAS CUT OFF.

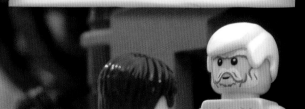

ISHMAEL WAS 13 YEARS OLD WHEN THE FLESH OF HIS FORESKIN WAS CUT OFF.

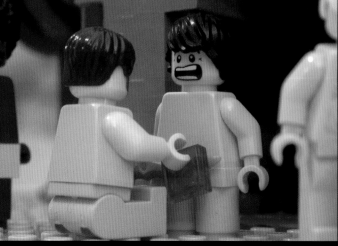

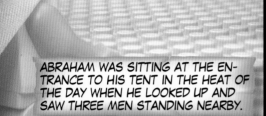

ABRAHAM WAS SITTING AT THE ENTRANCE TO HIS TENT IN THE HEAT OF THE DAY WHEN HE LOOKED UP AND SAW THREE MEN STANDING NEARBY.

ABRAHAM RAN TO MEET THEM AND SAID, 'DO NOT PASS BY. LET SOME WATER BE BROUGHT SO YOU MAY WASH YOUR FEET. LET ME BRING SOME BREAD, AND AFTER THAT YOU MAY PASS ON.' AND THEY SAID, 'VERY WELL, DO AS YOU SAY.'

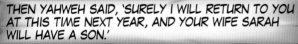

ABRAHAM TOOK SOME CURDS AND MILK AND THE CALF HE HAD PREPARED AND SET IT BEFORE THEM. HE STOOD NEARBY WHILE THEY ATE UNDER A TREE. AND THEY ASKED HIM, 'WHERE IS YOUR WIFE SARAH?'

THEN YAHWEH SAID, 'SURELY I WILL RETURN TO YOU AT THIS TIME NEXT YEAR, AND YOUR WIFE SARAH WILL HAVE A SON.'

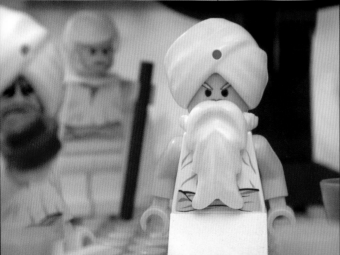

SARAH WAS LISTENING AT THE ENTRANCE TO THE TENT, AND SHE LAUGHED TO HERSELF, SAYING, 'AFTER I HAVE GROWN OLD AND MY MASTER IS OLD, SHALL I HAVE PLEASURE?'

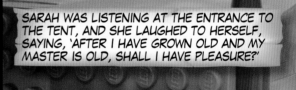

YAHWEH SAID TO ABRAHAM, 'WHY DID SARAH LAUGH? IS ANYTHING TOO AMAZING FOR YAHWEH?'

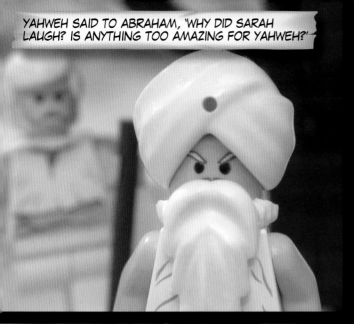

SARAH WAS AFRAID AND LIED, SAYING, 'I DIDN'T LAUGH.'

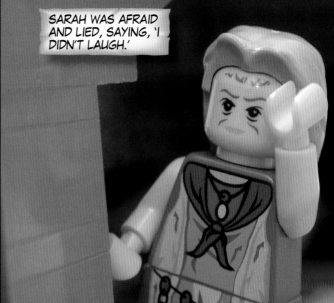

BUT YAHWEH SAID, 'YES, YOU DID LAUGH.'

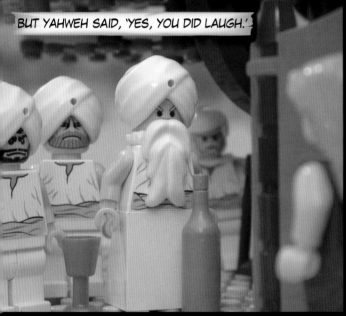

WHEN THE MEN SET OUT FROM THERE, THEY LOOKED TOWARD SODOM. AND YAHWEH SAID, 'SHALL I HIDE FROM ABRAHAM WHAT I AM ABOUT TO DO? THE OUTCRY OVER SODOM AND GOMORRAH IS GREAT, AND THEIR SIN IS WEIGHTY.'

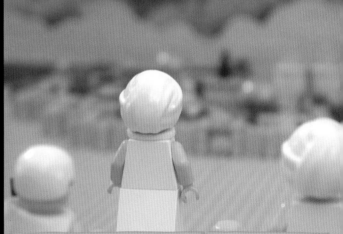

THEN YAHWEH SAID, 'I WILL GO DOWN AND SEE IF WHAT THEY HAVE DONE IS TRULY IN ACCORDANCE WITH THE OUTCRY.' AND THE MEN TURNED FROM THERE AND WENT TOWARD SODOM, WHILE ABRAHAM REMAINED STANDING BEFORE YAHWEH.

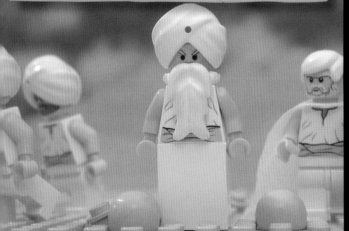

THE TWO ANGELS CAME TO SODOM IN THE EVENING, AND ABRAHAM'S NEPHEW, LOT, WAS SITTING AT THE CITY GATE.

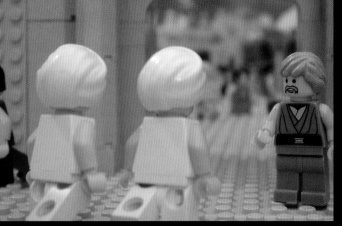
LOT SAID, 'MY LORDS, PLEASE TURN ASIDE TO YOUR SERVANT'S HOUSE. WASH YOUR FEET AND SPEND THE NIGHT, AND THEN WAKE UP EARLY AND GO YOUR WAY.'

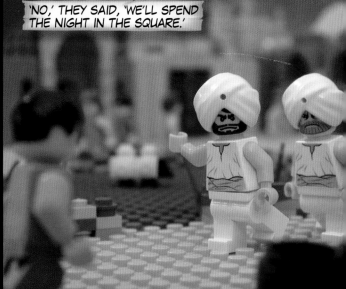
'NO,' THEY SAID, 'WE'LL SPEND THE NIGHT IN THE SQUARE.'

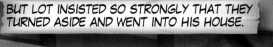
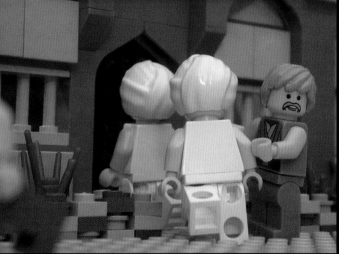
BUT LOT INSISTED SO STRONGLY THAT THEY TURNED ASIDE AND WENT INTO HIS HOUSE.

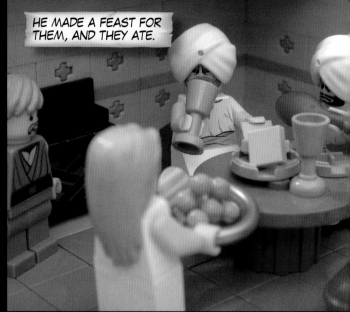
HE MADE A FEAST FOR THEM, AND THEY ATE.

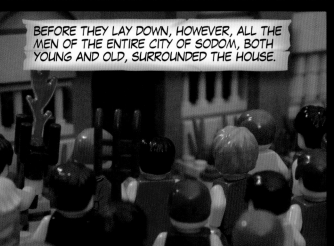
BEFORE THEY LAY DOWN, HOWEVER, ALL THE MEN OF THE ENTIRE CITY OF SODOM, BOTH YOUNG AND OLD, SURROUNDED THE HOUSE.

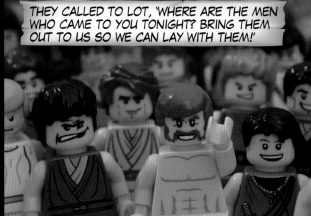
THEY CALLED TO LOT, 'WHERE ARE THE MEN WHO CAME TO YOU TONIGHT? BRING THEM OUT TO US SO WE CAN LAY WITH THEM!'

LOT WENT OUTSIDE AND SHUT THE DOOR BEHIND HIM. HE SAID, 'NO, MY BROTHERS, DO NOT BE SO WICKED! LOOK, I HAVE TWO VIRGIN DAUGHTERS. LET ME BRING THEM OUT TO YOU, AND YOU MAY DO TO THEM WHATEVER YOU WISH!'

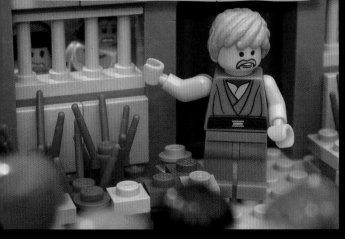

'JUST DON'T DO ANYTHING TO THESE MEN, FOR THEY HAVE COME UNDER THE PROTECTION OF MY ROOF!' SAID LOT. BUT THEY SAID, 'STEP ASIDE!'

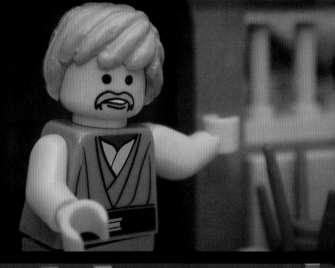

AND THEY SAID, 'THIS MAN CAME HERE AS A FOREIGNER, AND NOW HE WANTS TO JUDGE US? NOW WE'LL TREAT YOU MORE WICKEDLY THAN WE TREAT THEM!'

THEY PRESSED HARD AGAINST LOT AND MOVED IN TO BREAK DOWN THE DOOR.

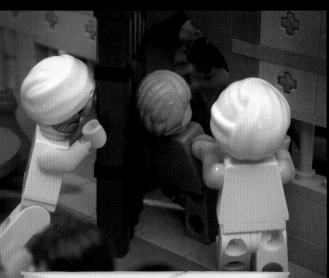

SO THE MEN REACHED OUT AND PULLED LOT INSIDE THE HOUSE AND SHUT THE DOOR.

THEN THEY STRUCK WITH BLINDNESS THE MEN WHO WERE AT THE DOOR, YOUNG AND OLD, SO THAT THEY COULD NOT FIND THE DOOR.

AND THE MEN SAID TO LOT, 'DO YOU HAVE ANYONE ELSE HERE? ANYONE IN THE CITY WHO BELONGS TO YOU? GET THEM OUT, FOR WE ARE GOING TO DESTROY THIS PLACE. YAHWEH SENT US TO DESTROY IT.'

SO LOT WENT OUT AND SAID TO THE MEN BETROTHED TO HIS DAUGHTERS, 'HURRY! GET OUT OF THIS PLACE, FOR YAHWEH IS ABOUT TO DESTROY THE CITY!'

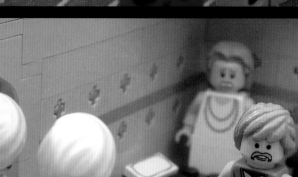

BUT THE MEN BETROTHED TO HIS DAUGHTERS THOUGHT HE WAS KIDDING THEM.

WHEN DAWN CAME, THE TWO MEN URGED LOT, SAYING, 'GET UP! TAKE YOUR WIFE AND YOUR TWO DAUGHTERS OR YOU WILL BE DESTROYED ALONG WITH THE WICKEDNESS OF THE CITY!' BUT LOT HESITATED.

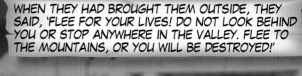

SO THE MEN GRABBED THE HANDS OF LOT, HIS WIFE, AND HIS TWO DAUGHTERS, AND TOOK HIM OUT OF THE CITY.

WHEN THEY HAD BROUGHT THEM OUTSIDE, THEY SAID, 'FLEE FOR YOUR LIVES! DO NOT LOOK BEHIND YOU OR STOP ANYWHERE IN THE VALLEY. FLEE TO THE MOUNTAINS, OR YOU WILL BE DESTROYED!'

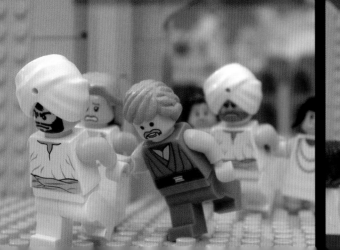

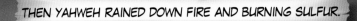
THEN YAHWEH RAINED DOWN FIRE AND BURNING SULFUR.

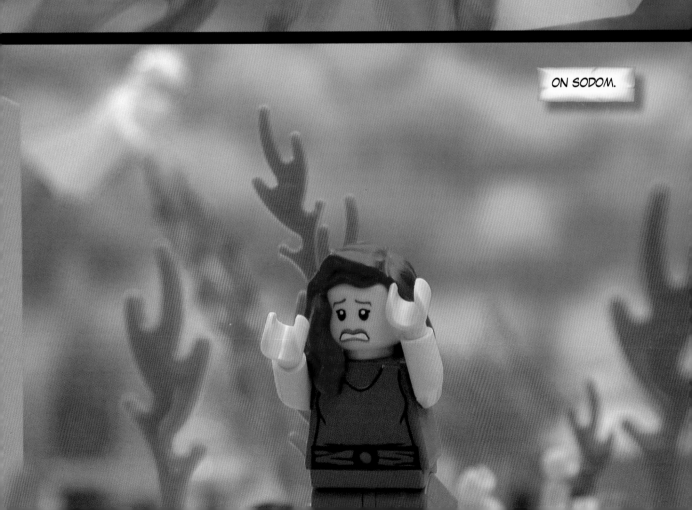
ON SODOM.

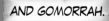

AND GOMORRAH.

HE VANQUISHED THOSE CITIES AND ALL THE INHABITANTS OF THE VALLEY AND EVERYTHING THAT GREW ON THE GROUND.

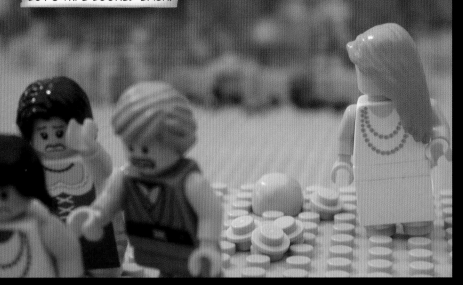

LOT'S WIFE LOOKED BACK.

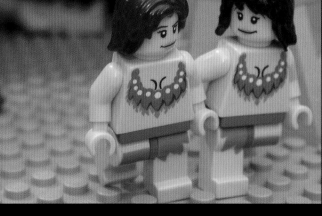

AND SHE BECAME A PILLAR OF SALT.

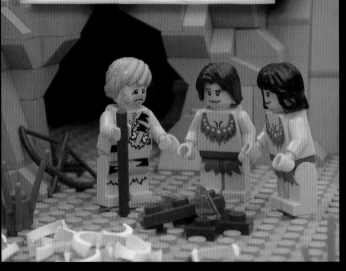

LOT SETTLED IN THE MOUNTAINS AND LIVED IN A CAVE WITH HIS TWO DAUGHTERS.

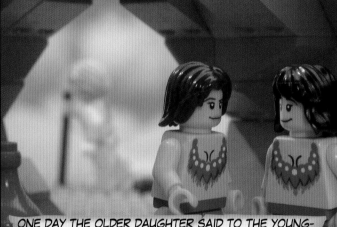

ONE DAY THE OLDER DAUGHTER SAID TO THE YOUNGER DAUGHTER, 'OUR FATHER IS OLD, AND THERE IS NO MAN ANYWHERE TO LAY WITH US IN THE NORMAL WAY OF THE WORLD. SO LET'S MAKE OUR FATHER DRUNK WITH WINE, AND WE WILL LAY WITH HIM SO THAT WE MAY PRESERVE OUR FAMILY LINE.'

THAT NIGHT THEY GOT THEIR FATHER DRUNK ON WINE, AND THE OLDER DAUGHTER LAID DOWN WITH HER FATHER.

IN THE MORNING, THE OLDER DAUGHTER SAID TO THE YOUNGER DAUGHTER, 'TONIGHT YOU WILL LAY WITH OUR FATHER SO THAT WE MAY PRESERVE OUR FAMILY LINE.'

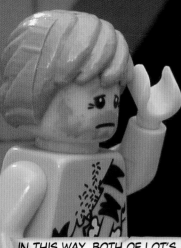

THEY MADE THEIR FATHER DRUNK WITH WINE AGAIN THAT NIGHT, AND THE YOUNGER DAUGHTER LAY WITH HIM.

IN THIS WAY, BOTH OF LOT'S DAUGHTERS BECAME PREGNANT BY THEIR FATHER.

THE OLDER DAUGHTER GAVE BIRTH TO A SON AND NAMED HIM MOAB, AND HE IS THE ANCESTOR OF THE MOABITES OF TODAY. THE YOUNGER DAUGHTER GAVE BIRTH TO A SON AND NAMED HIM BEN-AM-MI, AND HE IS THE ANCESTOR OF THE AMMONITES OF TODAY.

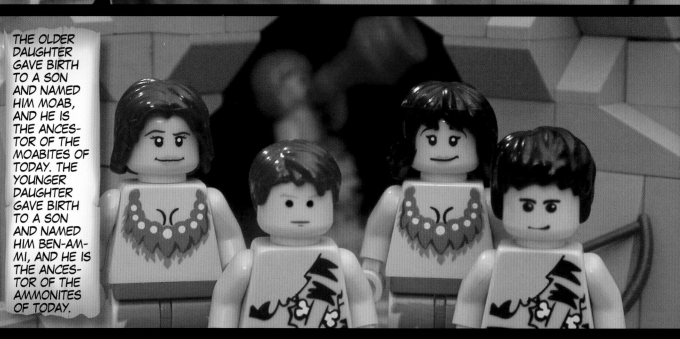

SARAH BECAME PREGNANT AND BORE ABRAHAM A SON, AND ABRAHAM NAMED HIM ISAAC. ABRAHAM WAS 100 YEARS OLD WHEN ISAAC WAS BORN.

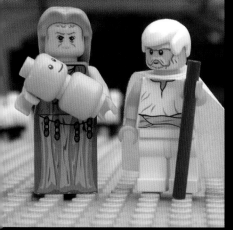

SOMETIME LATER GOD TESTED ABRAHAM. HE SAID TO HIM, 'ABRAHAM!' AND ABRAHAM REPLIED, 'HERE I AM.'

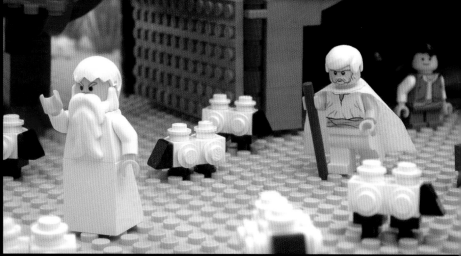

THEN GOD SAID, 'TAKE YOUR ONLY AND BELOVED SON ISAAC AND GO TO THE LAND OF MORIAH. OFFER HIM THERE AS A BURNT SACRIFICE ON ONE OF THE MOUNTAINS I WILL SHOW YOU.'

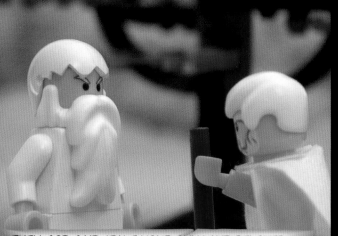

SO ABRAHAM GOT UP EARLY IN THE MORNING, AND WHEN HE HAD CUT ENOUGH WOOD FOR THE BURNT SACRIFICE, HE SADDLED HIS DONKEY AND SET OUT FOR THE PLACE GOD TOLD HIM ABOUT, TAKING WITH HIM TWO SERVANTS AND HIS SON ISAAC.

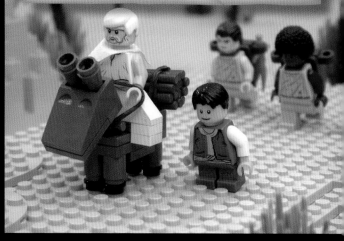

ON THE THIRD DAY, ABRAHAM SAW THE PLACE IN THE DISTANCE. HE SAID TO HIS SERVANTS, 'STAY HERE WITH THE DONKEY. THE BOY AND I WILL GO OVER THERE AND WORSHIP, THEN WE WILL COME BACK TO YOU.'

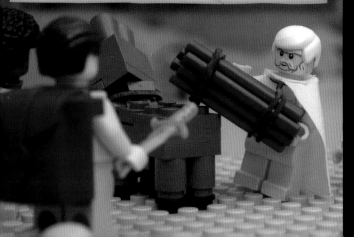

ABRAHAM LAID THE WOOD FOR THE BURNT SACRIFICE ON HIS SON ISAAC, WHILE HE CARRIED THE FIRE AND THE KNIFE, AND THE TWO OF THEM WALKED TOGETHER. ISAAC SAID TO HIS FATHER, 'FATHER, THERE IS WOOD AND FIRE FOR THE BURNT SACRIFICE, BUT WHERE IS THE LAMB?'

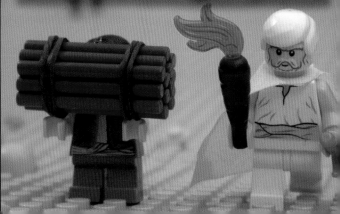

ABRAHAM REPLIED, 'GOD HIMSELF WILL PROVIDE THE LAMB FOR THE BURNT OFFERING, MY SON.' AND THE TWO OF THEM WALKED TOGETHER.

WHEN THEY REACHED THE PLACE GOD TOLD HIM ABOUT, ABRAHAM BUILT AN ALTAR, AND ON IT HE ARRANGED THE WOOD. THEN HE TIED UP HIS SON.

HE LAID HIM ON TOP OF THE WOOD ON THE ALTAR, THEN ABRAHAM REACHED OUT HIS HAND AND TOOK THE KNIFE TO KILL HIS SON.

BUT THE ANGEL OF YAHWEH CALLED TO HIM FROM THE SKY, 'ABRAHAM! ABRAHAM!' AND ABRAHAM REPLIED, 'HERE I AM.'

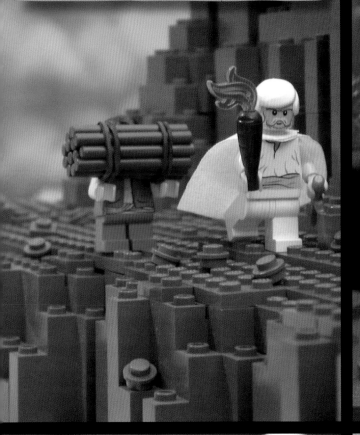

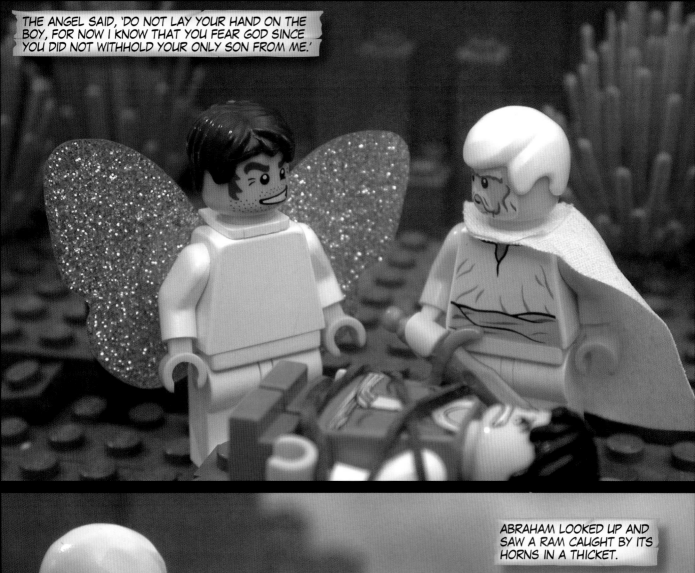

THE ANGEL SAID, 'DO NOT LAY YOUR HAND ON THE BOY, FOR NOW I KNOW THAT YOU FEAR GOD SINCE YOU DID NOT WITHHOLD YOUR ONLY SON FROM ME.'

ABRAHAM LOOKED UP AND SAW A RAM CAUGHT BY ITS HORNS IN A THICKET.

HE TOOK THE RAM AND OFFERED IT AS A BURNT SACRIFICE INSTEAD OF HIS SON.

ABRAHAM DIED AND LEFT EVERYTHING HE OWNED TO ISAAC. ISAAC PRAYED TO YAHWEH FOR HIS WIFE REBEKAH BECAUSE SHE WAS UNABLE TO BEAR CHILDREN.

YAHWEH RESPONDED TO HIS PRAYER, AND HIS WIFE BECAME PREGNANT, BUT THE CHILDREN INSIDE HER STRUGGLED WITH EACH OTHER, AND SHE SAID, 'WHY IS IT LIKE THIS?' AND YAHWEH SAID, 'TWO NATIONS ARE IN YOUR WOMB. ONE WILL BE STRONGER THAN THE OTHER. THE ELDER WILL SERVE THE YOUNGER.'

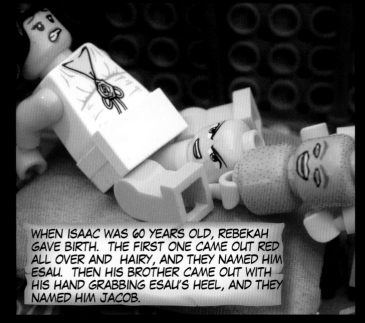

WHEN ISAAC WAS 60 YEARS OLD, REBEKAH GAVE BIRTH. THE FIRST ONE CAME OUT RED ALL OVER AND HAIRY, AND THEY NAMED HIM ESAU. THEN HIS BROTHER CAME OUT WITH HIS HAND GRABBING ESAU'S HEEL, AND THEY NAMED HIM JACOB.

THE BOYS GREW UP, AND ESAU BECAME A SKILLED HUNTER OF THE FIELDS. AND ISAAC PREFERRED ESAU BECAUSE HE HAD A TASTE FOR WILD GAME.

JACOB, ON THE OTHER HAND, WAS A QUIET MAN WHO STAYED IN THE TENTS. AND REBEKAH PREFERRED JACOB.

ONE DAY ESAU CAME HOME FROM THE FIELD FAMISHED, AND JACOB WAS COOKING SOME STEW.

ESAU SAID, 'LOOK, I AM ABOUT TO DIE! WHAT GOOD IS AN INHERITANCE TO ME?' AND JACOB REPLIED, 'FIRST SWEAR AN OATH TO ME.'

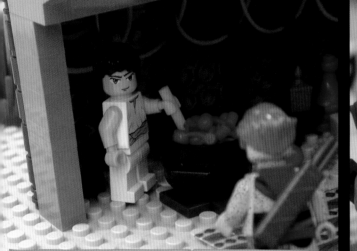

ESAU SAID TO JACOB, 'FEED ME SOME OF THAT RED STUFF, FOR I AM FAMISHED.' JACOB REPLIED, 'FIRST TRANSFER TO ME YOUR INHERITANCE.'

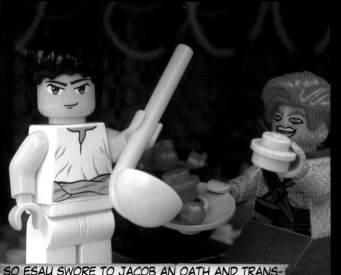

SO ESAU SWORE TO JACOB AN OATH AND TRANSFERRED HIS INHERITANCE, AND THEN JACOB GAVE ESAU SOME BREAD AND LENTIL STEW.

NOW WHEN ISAAC WAS OLD, HIS EYES WERE SO WEAK HE COULD NOT SEE. AND ONE DAY HE CALLED TO HIS ELDER SON ESAU AND SAID, 'MY SON, GO OUT IN THE FIELD AND HUNT SOME GAME FOR ME, AND PREPARE THE KIND OF TASTY DISH I LIKE SO I CAN GIVE YOU MY SPECIAL BLESSING BEFORE I DIE.'

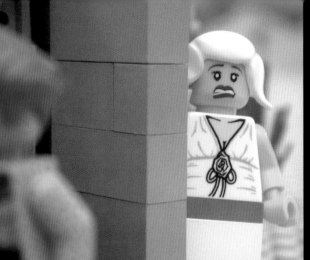

NOW REBEKAH WAS LISTENING WHILE ISAAC WAS TALKING TO HIS SON ESAU.

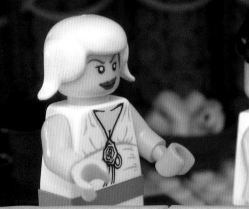

AND REBEKAH SAID TO HER SON JACOB, 'GO TO THE FLOCK AND BRING ME TWO YOUNG GOATS, SO THAT I CAN MAKE THE KIND OF TASTY DISH YOUR FATHER LIKES. THEN TAKE IT TO YOUR FATHER, SO THAT HE MAY BLESS YOU BEFORE HE DIES.'

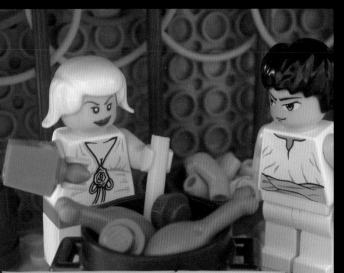

SO HE WENT TO FETCH THEM AND BROUGHT THEM TO HIS MOTHER, AND SHE MADE THE KIND OF TASTY DISH HIS FATHER LIKED.

REBEKAH DRESSED JACOB IN ESAU'S CLOTHES, COVERING HIS ARMS AND THE SMOOTH OF HIS NECK WITH GOAT SKINS. THEN SHE HANDED THE TASTY DISH SHE HAD MADE TO HER SON JACOB.

JACOB SAID TO HIS FATHER, 'FATHER! I HAVE DONE AS YOU TOLD ME, NOW SIT UP AND EAT SOME OF MY WILD GAME SO YOU CAN GIVE ME YOUR SPECIAL BLESSING.'

ISAAC SAID TO JACOB, 'COME CLOSER, SON, SO THAT I CAN FEEL YOU AND BE SURE WHETHER YOU REALLY ARE MY SON ESAU.'

JACOB WENT CLOSER TO HIS FATHER ISAAC, WHO FELT HIM AND SAID, 'THE VOICE IS JACOB'S BUT THE ARMS ARE ESAU'S!'

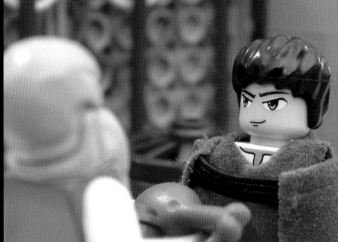

ISAAC SAID, 'ARE YOU REALLY MY SON ESAU?' AND JACOB REPLIED, 'I AM.'

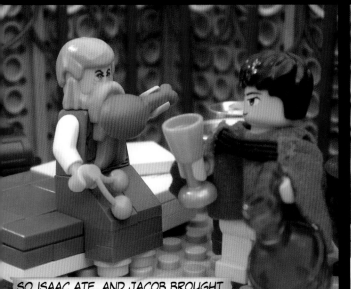

SO ISAAC ATE, AND JACOB BROUGHT HIM WINE, AND HE DRANK.

THEN HE BLESSED HIM, SAYING, 'MAY GOD GIVE YOU THE EARTH'S BOUNTY! MAY NATIONS SERVE YOU AND BOW DOWN TO YOU. RULE OVER YOUR BROTHERS. MAY THOSE WHO CURSE YOU BE CURSED AND THOSE WHO BLESS YOU BE BLESSED!'

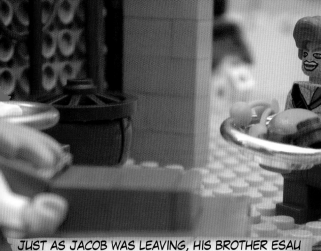

JUST AS JACOB WAS LEAVING, HIS BROTHER ESAU RETURNED FROM HUNTING. HE, TOO, MADE A TASTY DISH AND BROUGHT IT TO HIS FATHER, SAYING, 'FATHER, SIT UP AND EAT SOME OF MY WILD GAME SO YOU CAN GIVE ME YOUR SPECIAL BLESSING.'

AT THIS, ISAAC TREMBLED VIOLENTLY AND SAID, 'WHO WAS IT, THEN, THAT JUST BROUGHT ME WILD GAME? I ATE IT JUST BEFORE YOU RETURNED AND BLESSED HIM. AND NOW BLESSED HE WILL REMAIN!'

HEARING HIS FATHER'S WORDS, ESAU CRIED OUT LOUDLY AND BITTERLY AND SAID TO HIS FATHER, 'FATHER, BLESS ME, TOO! HAVE YOU NOT KEPT A BLESSING FOR ME?'

ISAAC REMAINED SILENT, AND ESAU BEGAN TO WEEP ALOUD. THEN HIS FATHER ISAAC SAID, 'INDEED, YOU WILL LIVE FAR FROM THE BOUNTY OF THE EARTH. YOU WILL LIVE BY YOUR SWORD AND BE A SERVANT TO YOUR BROTHER.'

WHEN ESAU WAS FORTY YEARS OLD, HE MARRIED JUDITH DAUGHTER OF BEERI THE HITTITE, AND BASEMETH DAUGHTER OF ELON THE HITTITE.

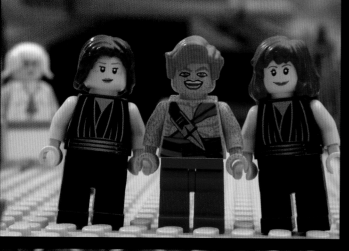

THESE WERE A BITTER DISAPPOINTMENT TO ISAAC AND REBEKAH. REBEKAH SAID TO ISAAC, 'I AM UTTERLY DISGUSTED BY HITTITE WOMEN. IF JACOB WERE TO MARRY A HITTITE WOMAN, WHY EVEN GO ON LIVING?'

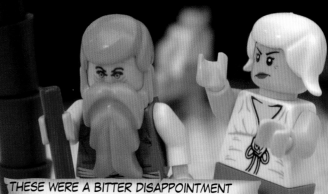

SO ISAAC SUMMONED JACOB AND COMMANDED HIM, SAYING, 'YOU MUST NOT MARRY ONE OF THE CANAANITE WOMEN! LEAVE IMMEDIATELY FOR PADDAN-ARAM AND ACQUIRE AS A WIFE ONE OF YOUR UNCLE LABAN'S DAUGHTERS.'

JACOB WAS TRAVELING TOWARD HARAN WHEN HE CAME TO A CERTAIN PLACE AND DECIDED TO STAY THE NIGHT BECAUSE THE SUN WAS GOING DOWN.

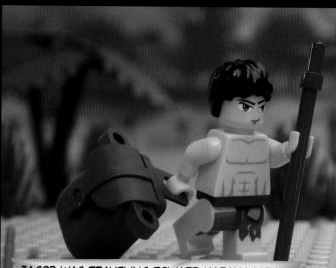

HE TOOK ONE OF THE STONES, LAID IT UNDER HIS HEAD, AND LAY DOWN TO SLEEP.

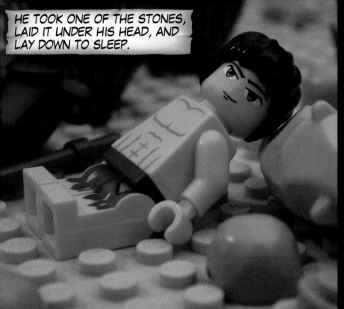

HE HAD A DREAM AND SAW A LADDER SET ON THE GROUND. ITS TOP REACHED UP INTO THE SKY, AND THE ANGELS OF GOD WERE ASCENDING AND DESCENDING IT.

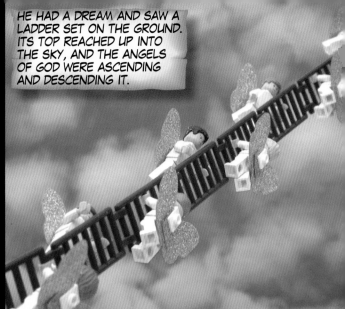

NOW LABAN HAD TWO DAUGHTERS. THE ELDER WAS LEAH, AND SHE HAD WEAK EYES. THE YOUNGER WAS RACHEL, AND SHE WAS SHAPELY AND BEAUTIFUL.

JACOB STAYED WITH LABAN FOR A MONTH, AND HE FELL IN LOVE WITH RACHEL.

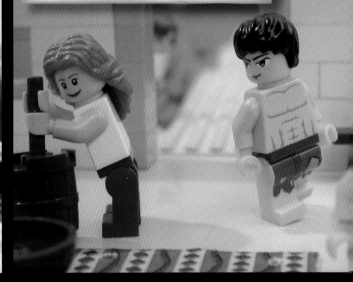

THEN LABAN SAID TO JACOB, 'SHOULD YOU WORK FOR ME FOR NOTHING JUST BECAUSE YOU'RE A RELATIVE? TELL ME WHAT YOUR WAGES SHALL BE.'

JACOB LOVED RACHEL, SO HE SAID, 'I WILL WORK FOR YOU FOR SEVEN YEARS IN RETURN FOR YOUR YOUNGER DAUGHTER RACHEL.' LABAN REPLIED, 'BETTER THAT I GIVE HER TO YOU THAN SOME OTHER MAN, SO STAY WITH ME.'

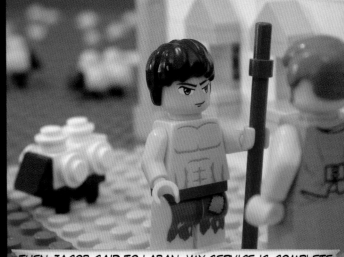

AND SO JACOB WORKED FOR SEVEN YEARS IN EXCHANGE FOR RACHEL. BUT THEY WERE LIKE A FEW DAYS TO HIM BECAUSE HE LOVED HER.

THEN JACOB SAID TO LABAN, 'MY SERVICE IS COMPLETE. NOW, GIVE ME MY WIFE SO I MAY LAY WITH HER.'

SO LABAN ASSEMBLED ALL THE PEOPLE OF THE AREA FOR A WEDDING FEAST.

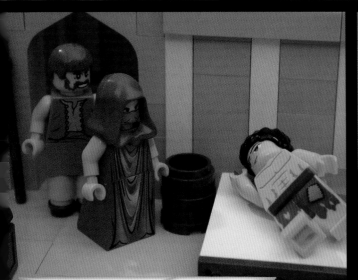

THAT EVENING, LABAN TOOK HIS DAUGHTER AND BROUGHT HER TO JACOB.

AND HE LAID WITH HER. BUT IN THE MORNING, JACOB SAW THAT IT WAS LEAH!

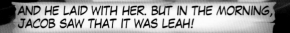

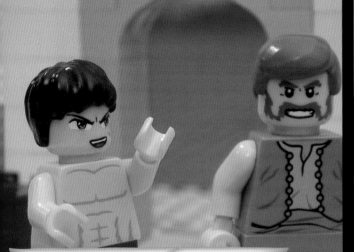

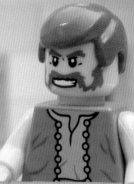

AND HE SAID TO LABAN, 'WHAT HAVE YOU DONE TO ME? DID I NOT WORK FOR YOU IN RETURN FOR RACHEL? WHY DID YOU DECEIVE ME?'

'THAT'S NOT HOW IT'S DONE AROUND HERE, MARRYING OFF THE YOUNGER BEFORE THE OLDER,' REPLIED LABAN. 'BUT COMPLETE THIS WEDDING FEAST WEEK WITH HER, AND WE WILL GIVE YOU THE OTHER GIRL AS WELL—IN EXCHANGE FOR SEVEN MORE YEARS OF WORK.'

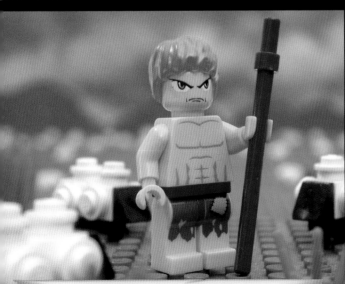

JACOB DID AS LABAN SAID, AND AFTER HE COMPLETED THE WEEK OF LEAH'S WEDDING FEAST, LABAN GAVE HIM HIS DAUGHTER RACHEL AS A WIFE.

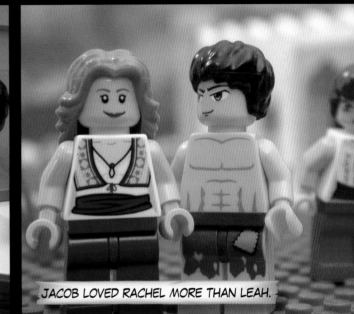

JACOB LOVED RACHEL MORE THAN LEAH.

AND HE WORKED FOR LABAN ANOTHER SEVEN YEARS.

THEN JACOB SET OUT FOR CANAAN. AT NIGHT HE SENT HIS TWO WIVES, HIS TWO SLAVE-GIRLS, AND HIS ELEVEN CHILDREN, ACROSS A SHALLOW SECTION OF THE JABBOK RIVER.

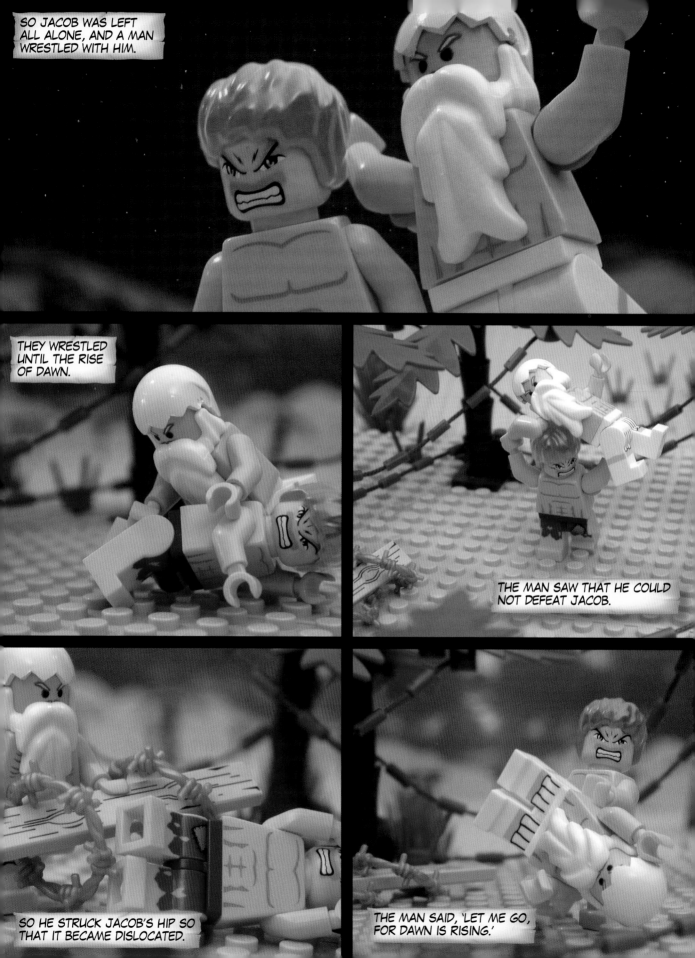

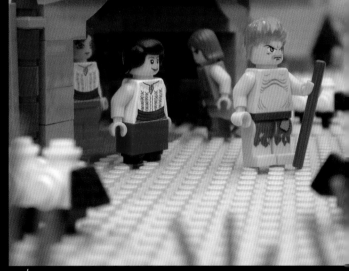
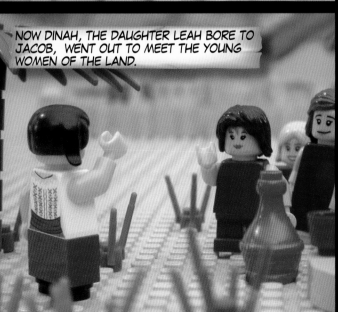
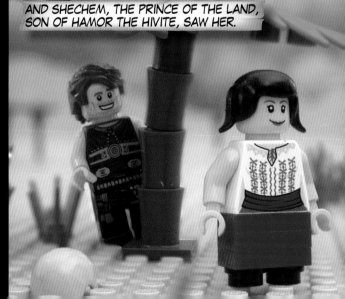

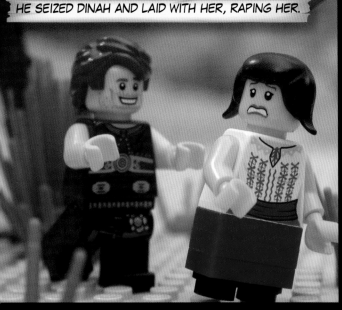

HE SEIZED DINAH AND LAID WITH HER, RAPING HER.

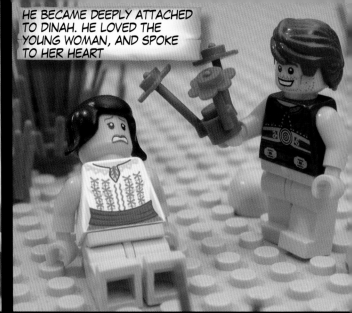

HE BECAME DEEPLY ATTACHED TO DINAH. HE LOVED THE YOUNG WOMAN, AND SPOKE TO HER HEART

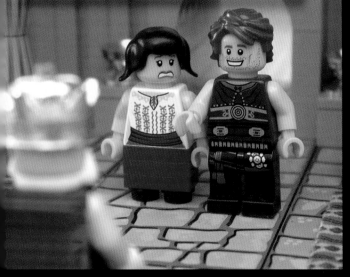

SHECHEM SAID TO HIS FATHER HAMOR, 'ACQUIRE THIS YOUNG WOMAN FOR ME AS A WIFE.'

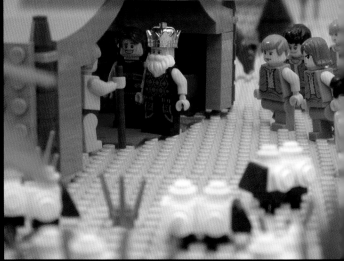

SO HAMOR WENT TO JACOB TO TALK WITH HIM. WHEN JACOB'S SONS HEARD ABOUT THIS, THEY CAME IN FROM THE FIELD.

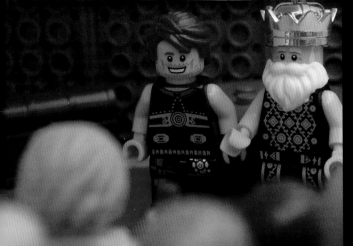

HAMOR SAID TO THEM, 'MY SON SHECHEM IS DEEPLY IN LOVE WITH YOUR DAUGHTER. PLEASE GIVE HER TO HIM AS A WIFE. INTERMARRY WITH US. GIVE YOUR DAUGHTERS TO US, AND TAKE OUR DAUGHTERS FOR YOURSELVES.'

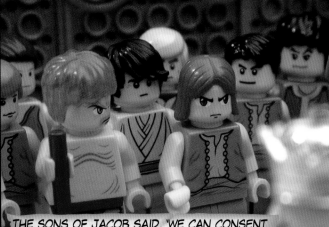

THE SONS OF JACOB SAID, 'WE CAN CONSENT ONLY ON ONE CONDITION: THAT YOU BECOME LIKE US AND HAVE EVERY ONE OF YOUR MALES CIRCUMCISED. ONLY THEN WILL WE GIVE OUR DAUGHTERS TO YOU AND TAKE YOUR DAUGHTERS TO US AND BECOME ONE PEOPLE.'

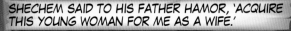

THE OFFER PLEASED HAMOR AND HIS SON SHECHEM, AND THE YOUNG MAN DID WHAT THEY ASKED WITHOUT DELAY BECAUSE HE WANTED JACOB'S DAUGHTER DINAH SO BADLY.

THEN HAMOR AND SHECHEM WENT TO THE GATE OF THEIR CITY AND SAID TO THE MEN OF THE CITY, 'THESE ARE PEACEFUL MEN. LET THEM LIVE IN THE LAND, AND WE WILL INTERMARRY WITH THEM, AND THEIR LIVESTOCK AND POSSESSIONS WILL BECOME OURS.'

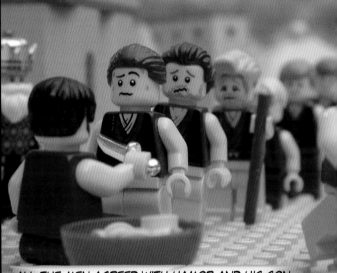

'BUT THEY WILL CONSENT TO LIVE WITH US ONLY IF EVERY MAN AMONG US BECOMES CIRCUMCISED. LET'S CONSENT TO THEIR DEMAND SO THEY WILL LIVE AMONG US.'

ALL THE MEN AGREED WITH HAMOR AND HIS SON SHECHEM, AND EVERY MALE WAS CIRCUMCISED.

THREE DAYS LATER, WHILE THE MEN WERE STILL IN PAIN, TWO OF JACOB'S SONS, SIMEON AND LEVI, EACH TOOK HIS SWORD AND CAME INTO THE UNSUSPECTING CITY.

THEY SLAUGHTERED ALL THE MALES.

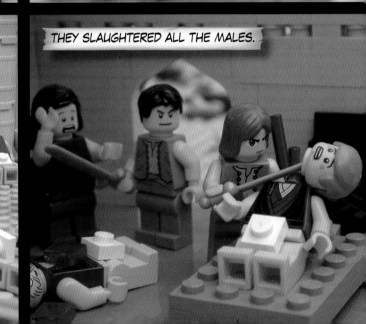

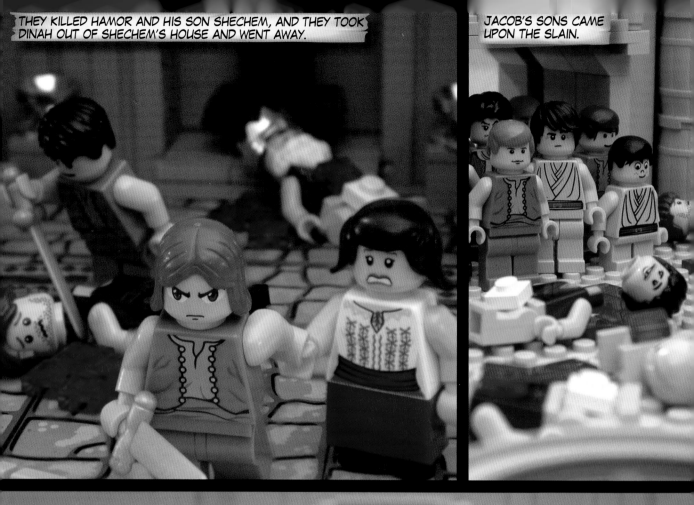

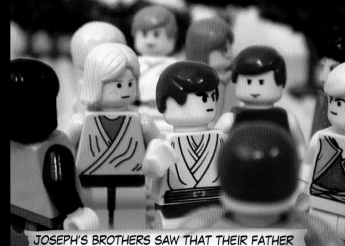

NOW ISRAEL LOVED JOSEPH MORE THAN ANY OF HIS OTHER SONS BECAUSE HE WAS THE SON OF HIS OLD AGE, AND HE MADE HIM A COAT OF MANY COLORS.

JOSEPH'S BROTHERS SAW THAT THEIR FATHER LOVED HIM MORE THAN ANY OF THEM, AND THEY HATED JOSEPH AND COULD NOT SPEAK A FRIENDLY WORD TO HIM.

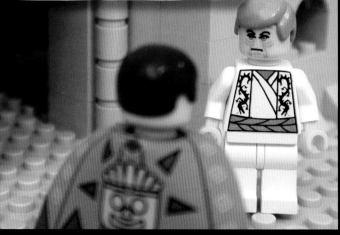

NOW ISRAEL SAID TO JOSEPH, 'YOUR BROTHERS ARE GRAZING THE FLOCK AT SHECHEM. GO AND SEE IF ALL IS WELL WITH YOUR BROTHERS AND THE FLOCK, AND THEN BRING ME WORD.'

JOSEPH'S BROTHERS SAW HIM COMING, AND THEY CONSPIRED TO KILL HIM. 'COME ON, LET'S KILL HIM AND THROW HIM INTO ONE OF THE WELLS,' THEY SAID ONE TO ANOTHER, 'AND WE WILL SAY A WILD ANIMAL HAS DEVOURED HIM.'

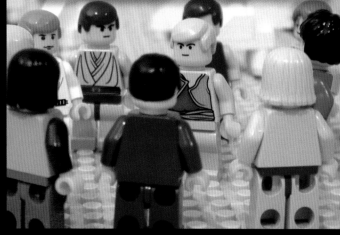

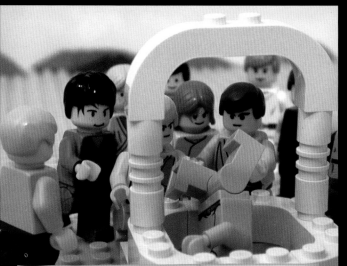

WHEN JOSEPH REACHED HIS BROTHERS, THEY STRIPPED HIM OF HIS COAT OF MANY COLORS, AND THEY TOOK HIM AND THREW HIM INTO THE WELL.

THEY TOOK JOSEPH'S COAT, SLAUGHTERED A GOAT, AND DIPPED THE COAT IN ITS BLOOD.

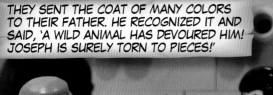

THEY SENT THE COAT OF MANY COLORS TO THEIR FATHER. HE RECOGNIZED IT AND SAID, 'A WILD ANIMAL HAS DEVOURED HIM! JOSEPH IS SURELY TORN TO PIECES!'

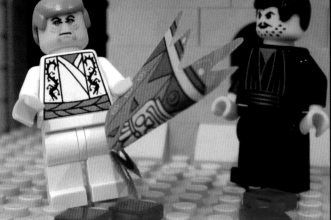

NOW SOME MIDIANITE MERCHANTS WERE PASSING BY, AND THEY PULLED JOSEPH UP OUT OF THE WELL.

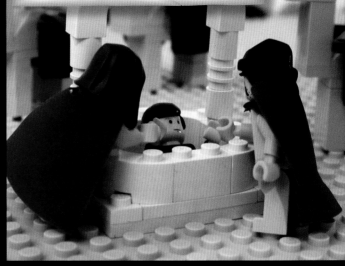

THEY SOLD JOSEPH TO THE ISHMAELITES FOR TWENTY PIECES OF SILVER, AND THE ISHMAELITES BROUGHT JOSEPH TO EGYPT.

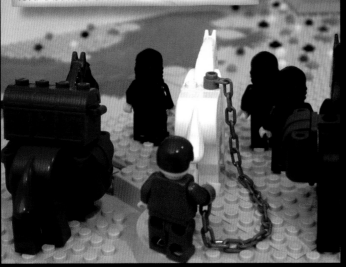

AN EGYPTIAN NAMED POTIPHAR, WHO WAS ONE OF PHARAOH'S OFFICIALS, BOUGHT JOSEPH FROM THEM.

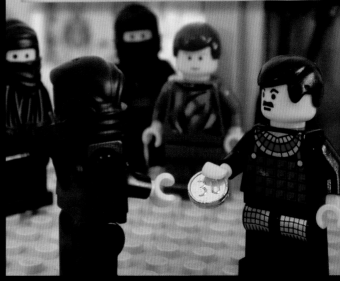

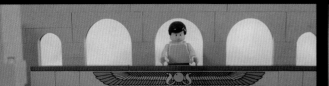

JOSEPH LIVED IN THE HOUSE OF HIS EGYPTIAN MASTER, AND WHEN HIS MASTER SAW THAT YAHWEH WAS WITH HIM AND HOW YAHWEH MADE ALL HIS UNDERTAKINGS SUCCESSFUL, HE PUT HIM IN CHARGE OF HIS HOUSEHOLD.

NOW JOSEPH WAS WELL BUILT AND HANDSOME.

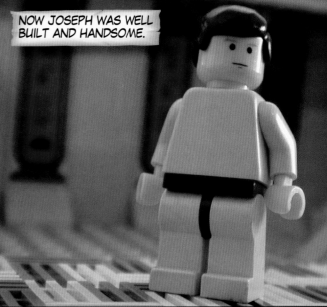

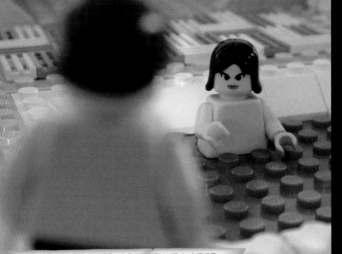

AND IT HAPPENED SOMETIME LATER THAT HIS MASTER'S WIFE LOOKED UPON JOSEPH AND SAID, 'LAY WITH ME.'

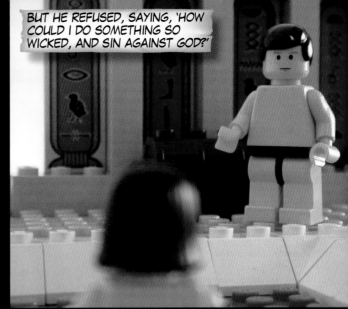

BUT HE REFUSED, SAYING, 'HOW COULD I DO SOMETHING SO WICKED, AND SIN AGAINST GOD?'

ALTHOUGH SHE SPOKE TO JOSEPH DAY AFTER DAY, HE REFUSED TO LAY WITH HER.

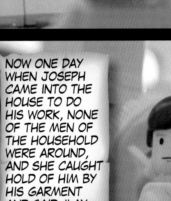

NOW ONE DAY WHEN JOSEPH CAME INTO THE HOUSE TO DO HIS WORK, NONE OF THE MEN OF THE HOUSEHOLD WERE AROUND, AND SHE CAUGHT HOLD OF HIM BY HIS GARMENT AND SAID, 'LAY WITH ME.'

SO JOSEPH LEFT THE GARMENT IN HER HAND AND FLED.

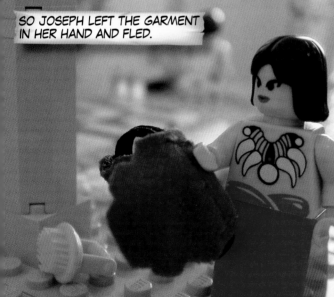

THEN SHE CALLED HER SERVANTS AND SAID TO THEM, 'LOOK AT THIS! A HEBREW MAN CAME TO LAY WITH ME BUT I SCREAMED, AND HE LEFT HIS GARMENT BESIDE ME AND RAN OUT OF THE HOUSE.'

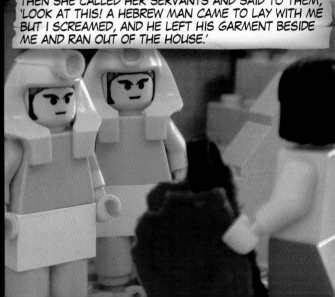

JOSEPH'S MASTER PUT HIM IN THE JAIL WHERE THE KING'S PRISONERS WERE KEPT.

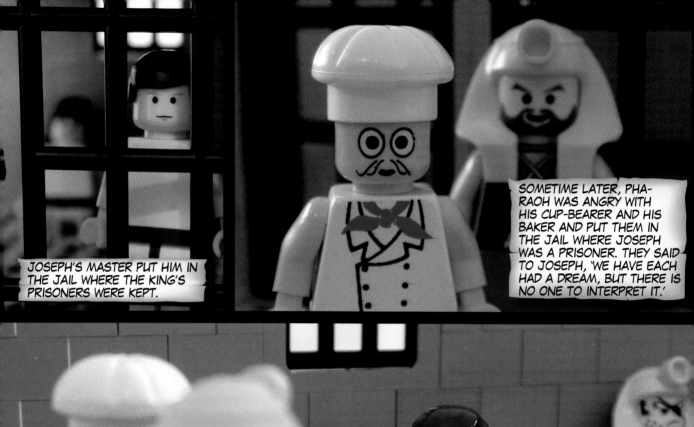

SOMETIME LATER, PHARAOH WAS ANGRY WITH HIS CUP-BEARER AND HIS BAKER AND PUT THEM IN THE JAIL WHERE JOSEPH WAS A PRISONER. THEY SAID TO JOSEPH, 'WE HAVE EACH HAD A DREAM, BUT THERE IS NO ONE TO INTERPRET IT.'

JOSEPH SAID TO THEM, 'ARE NOT INTERPRETATIONS GOD'S BUSINESS? TELL ME ABOUT THE DREAMS.'

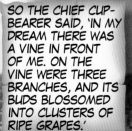

SO THE CHIEF CUP-BEARER SAID, 'IN MY DREAM THERE WAS A VINE IN FRONT OF ME. ON THE VINE WERE THREE BRANCHES, AND ITS BUDS BLOSSOMED INTO CLUSTERS OF RIPE GRAPES.'

'I HAD THE PHARAOH'S CUP IN MY HAND. I SQUEEZED THE GRAPES INTO PHARAOH'S CUP AND PUT THE CUP IN PHARAOH'S HAND.'

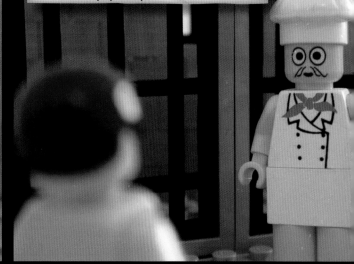

'THIS IS WHAT IT MEANS,' SAID JOSEPH. 'THE THREE BRANCHES ARE THREE DAYS. IN THREE DAYS PHARAOH WILL LIFT YOUR HEAD BY RESTORING YOU TO YOUR POSITION.'

SEEING THAT THE INTERPRETATION HAD BEEN FAVORABLE, THE CHIEF BAKER SAID TO JOSEPH, 'I, TOO, HAD A DREAM.'

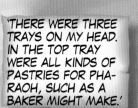

'THERE WERE THREE TRAYS ON MY HEAD. IN THE TOP TRAY WERE ALL KINDS OF PASTRIES FOR PHARAOH, SUCH AS A BAKER MIGHT MAKE.'

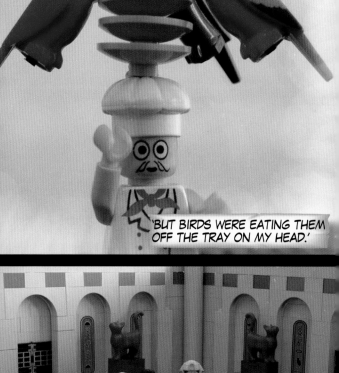

'BUT BIRDS WERE EATING THEM OFF THE TRAY ON MY HEAD.'

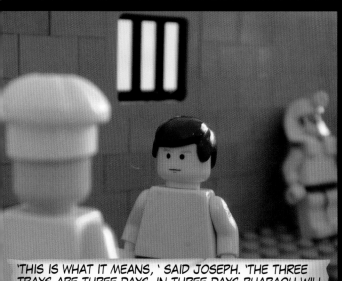

'THIS IS WHAT IT MEANS, ' SAID JOSEPH. 'THE THREE TRAYS ARE THREE DAYS. IN THREE DAYS PHARAOH WILL LIFT YOUR HEAD BY HANGING YOU ON A GALLOWS, AND THE BIRDS WILL EAT THE FLESH OFF YOUR BONES.'

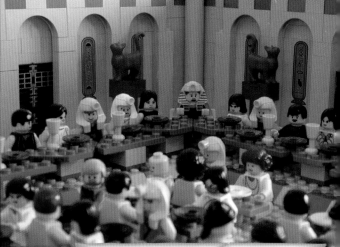

AND SO IT HAPPENED. THE THIRD DAY WAS PHARAOH'S BIRTHDAY, AND HE GAVE A BANQUET FOR ALL HIS OFFICIALS.

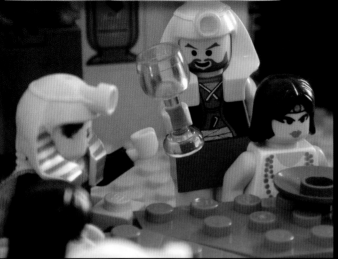

HE LIFTED THE HEADS OF BOTH HIS OFFICIALS: THE CUP-BEARER BY RESTORING HIM TO HIS CUP-BEARING POSITION.

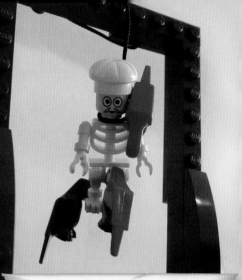

AND THE CHIEF BAKER BY HANGING HIM, AS JOSEPH HAD EXPLAINED TO THEM.

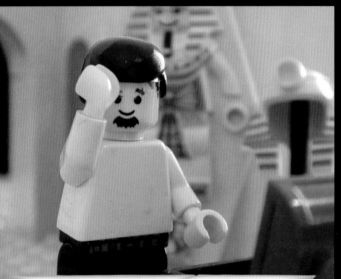

TWO YEARS LATER, PHARAOH HAD A DREAM, AND IN THE MORNING HIS MIND WAS TROUBLED.

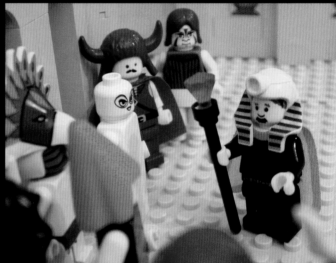

HE SUMMONED ALL THE MAGICIANS AND WISE MEN OF EGYPT, BUT THERE WAS NO ONE TO INTERPRET IT FOR PHARAOH.

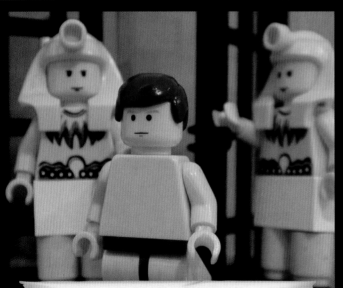

SO PHARAOH HAD JOSEPH SUMMONED, AND THEY HURRIED HIM FROM THE DUNGEON.

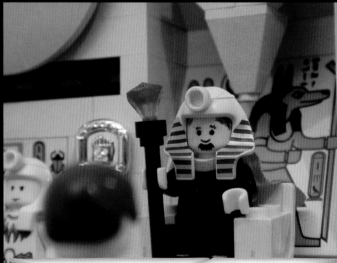

PHARAOH SAID TO JOSEPH, 'I HAVE HAD A DREAM, AND THERE IS NO ONE TO INTERPRET IT. BUT I HAVE HEARD IT SAID THAT YOU CAN INTERPRET ANY DREAM YOU HEAR.'

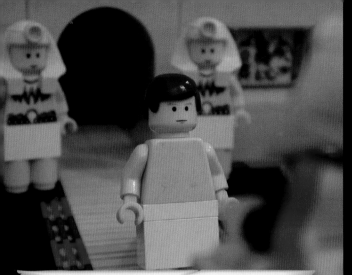

'NOT I,' SAID JOSEPH TO PHARAOH, 'BUT GOD WILL GIVE PHARAOH A FAVORABLE ANSWER.'

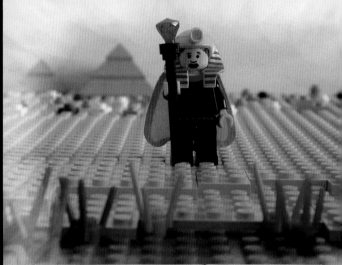

SO PHARAOH SAID TO JOSEPH, 'IN MY DREAM, BEHOLD, I WAS STANDING ON THE BANK OF THE NILE.'

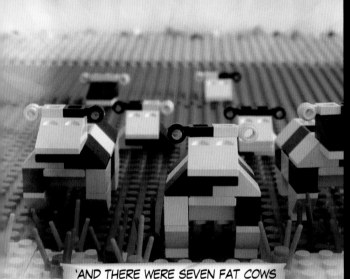

'AND THERE WERE SEVEN FAT COWS COMING UP OUT OF THE NILE.'

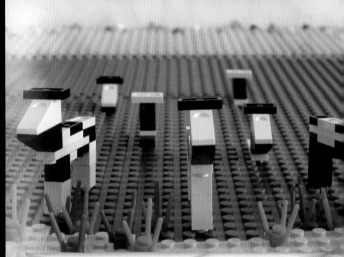

'THEN SEVEN OTHER COWS CAME UP BEHIND THEM, STARVED, UGLY, AND GAUNT. I HAVE NEVER SEEN SUCH POOR COWS IN ALL OF EGYPT!'

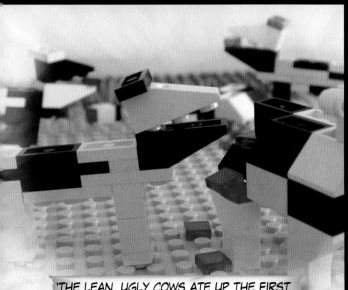

'THE LEAN, UGLY COWS ATE UP THE FIRST SEVEN FAT COWS. THEN I WOKE UP.'

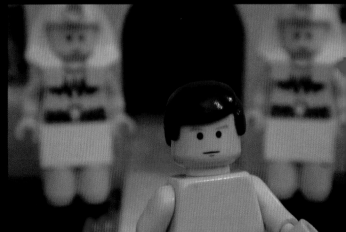

JOSEPH SAID, 'GOD HAS REVEALED TO PHARAOH WHAT HE IS ABOUT TO DO. SEVEN YEARS OF PLENTY ARE COMING, BUT SEVEN YEARS OF FAMINE WILL FOLLOW THEM, WHEN ALL THE PLENTY IN EGYPT WILL BE FORGOTTEN, BECAUSE THE FAMINE WILL BE SEVERE.'

'PHARAOH SHOULD FIND A WISE, INTELLIGENT MAN TO GOVERN EGYPT AND STORE ALL THE EXTRA FOOD PRODUCED DURING THE SEVEN YEARS OF PLENTY, SO THAT THE COUNTRY WILL NOT BE DESTROYED BY THE SEVEN YEARS OF FAMINE.'

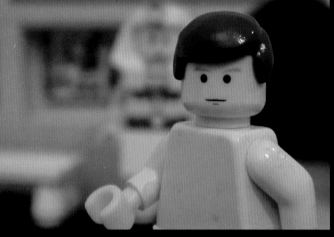

SO PHARAOH SAID, 'SINCE GOD HAS GIVEN YOU KNOWLEDGE OF ALL THIS, THERE IS NO ONE AS INTELLIGENT AND WISE AS YOU. I AM HEREBY MAKING YOU GOVERNOR OF THE WHOLE OF EGYPT.'

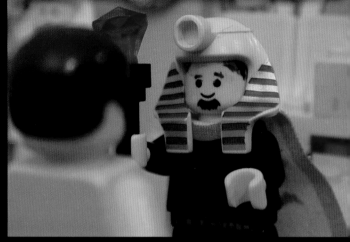

THUS JOSEPH BECAME GOVERNOR OF THE WHOLE OF EGYPT.

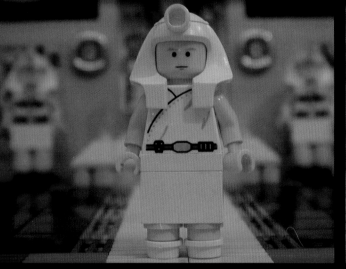

WHEN THE YEARS OF PLENTY ENDED IN EGYPT, THERE WAS FAMINE IN EVERY COUNTRY. JACOB SAID TO HIS SONS, 'WHY DO YOU KEEP STARING AT ONE ANOTHER? GO DOWN TO EGYPT AND GET SOME SUPPLIES FOR US, SO THAT WE DO NOT DIE!'

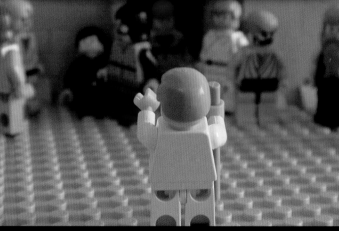

SO TEN OF JOSEPH'S BROTHERS WENT DOWN TO BUY GRAIN IN EGYPT.

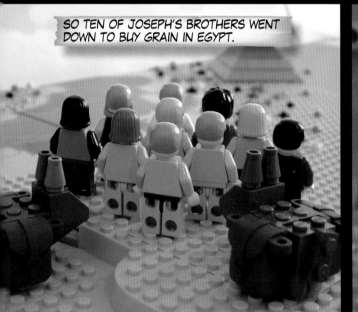

BUT JACOB DID NOT SEND JOSEPH'S BROTHER BENJAMIN WITH HIS BROTHERS, FOR HE WORRIED THAT SOMETHING MIGHT HAPPEN TO HIM.

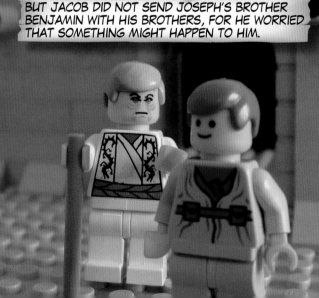

WHEN JOSEPH RECOGNIZED HIS BROTHERS, BUT THEY DID NOT RECOGNIZE HIM, HE SPOKE TO THEM HARSHLY, SAYING, 'WHERE HAVE YOU COME FROM? YOU ARE SPIES! YOU HAVE COME TO DISCOVER THE COUNTRY'S WEAK POINTS.'

'NO, MY LORD,' THEY SAID, 'YOUR SERVANTS HAVE COME TO BUY FOOD. WE ARE SONS OF THE SAME MAN IN CANAAN, BUT THE YOUNGEST IS CURRENTLY WITH OUR FATHER. WE ARE HONEST MEN, YOUR SERVANTS, NOT SPIES.'

JOSEPH SAID TO THEM, 'IF YOU ARE HONEST MEN, LET ONE OF YOUR BROTHERS BE HELD IN PRISON WHILE THE REST OF YOU TAKE SUPPLIES TO YOUR FAMILIES. YOU MUST BRING YOUR YOUNGEST BROTHER TO ME, SO THAT WHAT YOU SAID WILL BE VERIFIED, AND YOU WILL NOT HAVE TO DIE!'

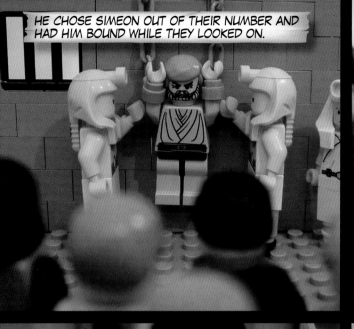

HE CHOSE SIMEON OUT OF THEIR NUMBER AND HAD HIM BOUND WHILE THEY LOOKED ON.

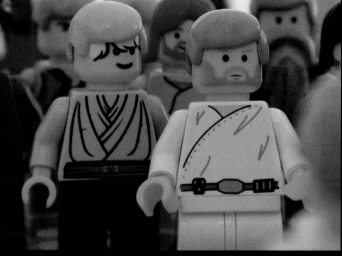

RETURNING TO THEIR FATHER IN CANAAN, THEY TOLD HIM ALL THE THINGS THAT HAPPENED TO THEM.

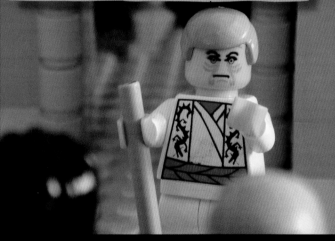

THEN JACOB SAID TO THEM, 'YOU ARE ROBBING ME OF MY CHILDREN! JOSEPH IS GONE! SIMEON IS GONE! AND NOW YOU WANT TO TAKE BENJAMIN? IF ANY HARM CAME TO HIM, YOU WOULD SEND MY GRAY HAIRS DOWN TO SHEOL IN MISERY!'

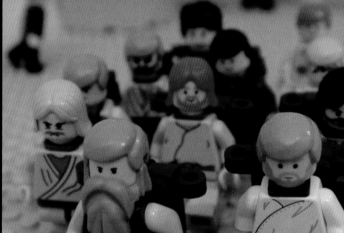

BUT THE FAMINE IN THE COUNTRY GREW WORSE. AND WHEN THEY HAD FINISHED THE SUPPLIES, THEY SET OFF, HEADING DOWN TO EGYPT TO PRESENT THEMSELVES BEFORE JOSEPH.

WHEN JOSEPH SAW BENJAMIN WITH THEM, HE SAID TO HIS HOUSEHOLD SERVANT, 'TAKE THESE MEN INTO THE HOUSE. SLAUGHTER AN ANIMAL AND PREPARE IT, FOR THESE MEN ARE TO EAT WITH ME AT NOON.'

WHEN JOSEPH ARRIVED AT THE HOUSE, HE GREETED THEM PLEASANTLY. 'IS THIS YOUR YOUNGEST BROTHER?' HE ASKED, 'THE ONE YOU TOLD ME ABOUT?'

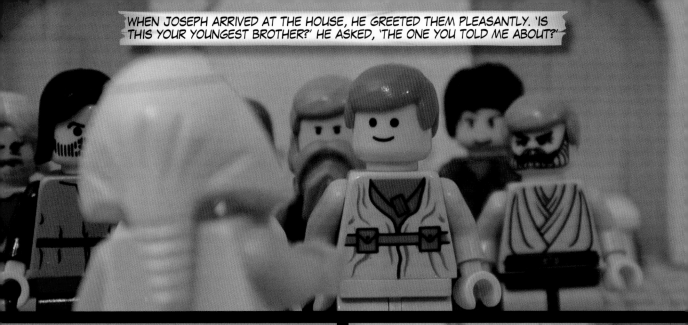

THEN JOSEPH COULD NOT CONTROL HIMSELF, AND HE SHOUTED, 'I AM JOSEPH! I AM YOUR BROTHER JOSEPH WHOM YOU SOLD INTO EGYPT. IS MY FATHER STILL ALIVE?'

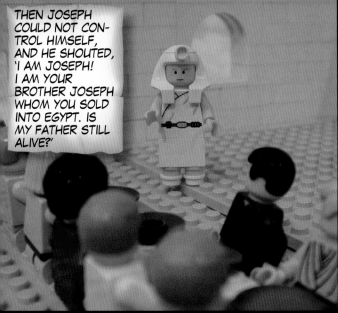

BUT HIS BROTHERS COULD NOT ANSWER HIM, BECAUSE THEY WERE SO DUMBFOUNDED.

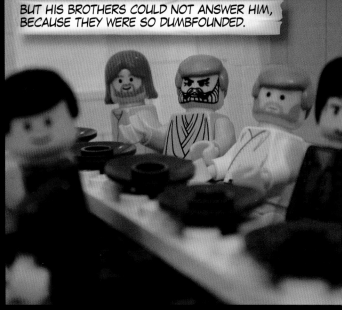

THEN HE THREW HIS ARMS AROUND THE NECK OF BENJAMIN, AND HE WEPT.

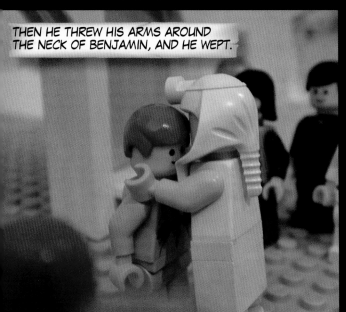

AND THE SOUND OF THIS WAS HEARD IN THE HOUSE OF PHARAOH.

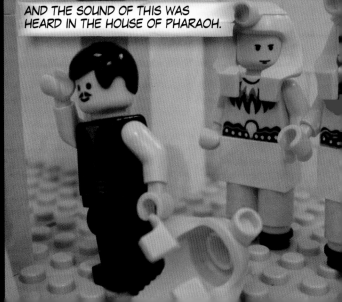

PHARAOH TOLD JOSEPH, 'SAY TO YOUR BROTHERS, "GET YOUR FATHER AND YOUR FAMILIES AND RETURN TO ME. I WILL GIVE YOU THE BEST LAND IN EGYPT, WHERE YOU WILL EAT FROM THE BOUNTY OF THE LAND."'

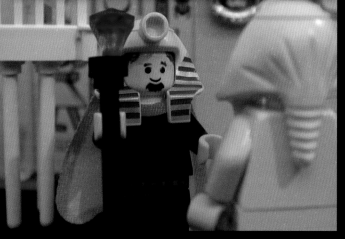

ISRAEL'S SONS DID AS THEY WERE TOLD. JOSEPH GAVE THEM PROVISIONS FOR THE JOURNEY. HE GAVE EACH ONE NEW CLOTHES, AND TO BENJAMIN HE GAVE THREE HUNDRED SHEKELS OF SILVER AND FIVE CHANGES OF CLOTHES.

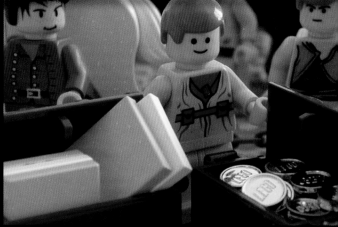

WHEN THEY REACHED THEIR FATHER IN CANAAN, THEY TOLD HIM, 'JOSEPH IS STILL ALIVE! INDEED, HE IS GOVERNOR OF ALL EGYPT!'

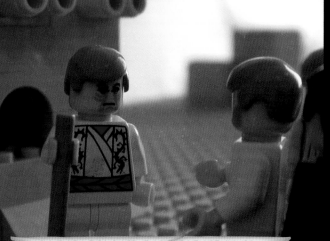

HE WAS STUNNED AND DID NOT BELIEVE THEM. BUT WHEN THEY TOLD HIM ALL JOSEPH HAD SAID TO THEM, AND WHEN HE SAW ALL THE WAGONS THAT JOSEPH HAD SENT TO FETCH HIM, THE SPIRIT OF THEIR FATHER JACOB REVIVED.

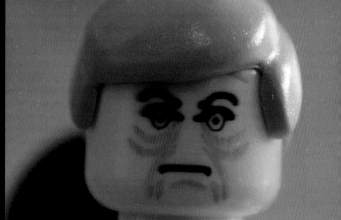

SO ISRAEL SET OUT WITH ALL HIS POSSESSIONS. HE BROUGHT HIS SONS AND GRANDSONS, HIS DAUGHTERS AND GRANDDAUGHTERS. THE MEMBERS OF JACOB'S FAMILY WHO WENT TO EGYPT WERE SEVENTY IN ALL.

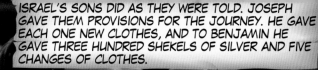

WHEN THEY ARRIVED IN GOSHEN, JOSEPH WENT TO MEET HIS FATHER ISRAEL. AS SOON AS HE APPEARED, HE THREW HIS ARMS AROUND HIS NECK AND WEPT ON HIS SHOULDER FOR A LONG TIME.

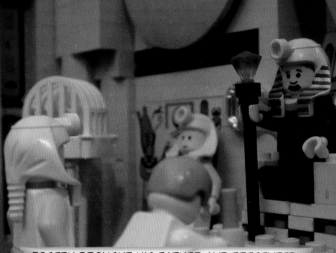

JOSEPH BROUGHT HIS FATHER AND PRESENTED HIM TO PHARAOH. PHARAOH ASKED JACOB, 'HOW MANY YEARS HAVE YOU LIVED?'

JACOB SAID TO PHARAOH, 'THE YEARS OF MY JOURNEY ON EARTH HAVE BEEN 130 YEARS. FEW AND UNHAPPY MY YEARS HAVE BEEN, FALLING SHORT OF MY ANCESTORS' YEARS IN THEIR JOURNEYS ON EARTH.'

JACOB THEN TOOK LEAVE OF PHARAOH, WITHDRAWING FROM HIS PRESENCE.

WHEN ISRAEL'S TIME TO DIE DREW NEAR HE SENT FOR HIS SON JOSEPH AND SAID TO HIM, 'IF YOU LOVE ME, PLACE YOUR HAND UNDER MY THIGH AS AN OATH THAT YOU WILL ACT WITH FAITHFUL LOYALTY TO ME: DO NOT BURY ME IN EGYPT!'

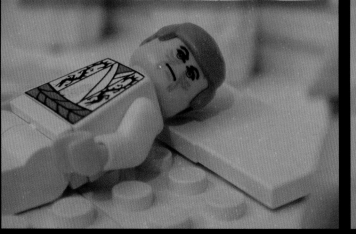

SO HE SWORE TO HIM, AND ISRAEL SANK BACK ON THE PILLOW. HE DREW HIS FEET UP INTO BED, AND BREATHING HIS LAST, JACOB WAS GATHERED TO HIS ANCESTORS. AT THIS JOSEPH THREW HIMSELF ON HIS FATHER'S FACE, COVERING IT WITH TEARS AND KISSES.

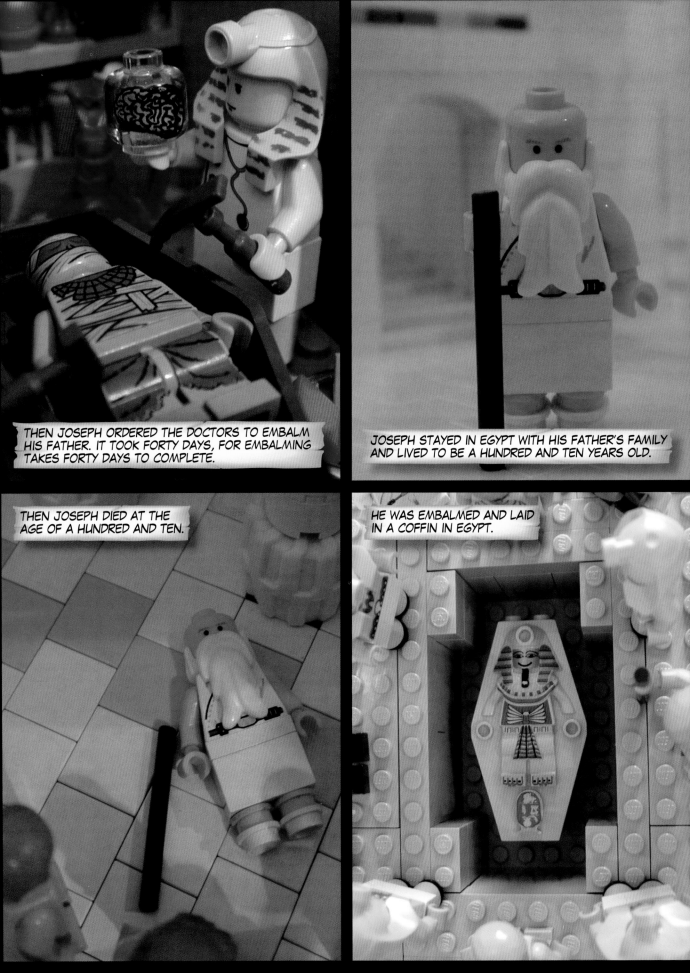

THEN JOSEPH ORDERED THE DOCTORS TO EMBALM HIS FATHER. IT TOOK FORTY DAYS, FOR EMBALMING TAKES FORTY DAYS TO COMPLETE.

JOSEPH STAYED IN EGYPT WITH HIS FATHER'S FAMILY AND LIVED TO BE A HUNDRED AND TEN YEARS OLD.

THEN JOSEPH DIED AT THE AGE OF A HUNDRED AND TEN.

HE WAS EMBALMED AND LAID IN A COFFIN IN EGYPT.

EXODUS

JOSEPH, HIS BROTHERS AND ALL THAT GENERATION DIED, BUT THE ISRAELITES WHO WENT TO EGYPT WERE FRUITFUL AND PROLIFIC. THEY BECAME SO NUMEROUS AND POWERFUL THAT EVENTUALLY THE WHOLE LAND WAS FULL OF THEM.

THERE CAME TO POWER IN EGYPT A NEW KING WHO HAD NEVER HEARD OF JOSEPH. 'LOOK,' HE SAID TO HIS PEOPLE, 'THE ISRAELITES ARE NOW MORE NUMEROUS AND POWERFUL THAN WE ARE.'

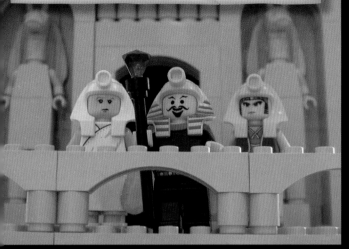

'WE MUST TAKE PRECAUTIONS TO STOP THEM FROM INCREASING ANY FURTHER, OR IF WAR SHOULD BREAK OUT, THEY MIGHT JOIN THE RANKS OF OUR ENEMIES, AND THEY MIGHT TAKE UP ARMS AGAINST US.'

ACCORDINGLY, THEY PUT TASKMASTERS OVER THE ISRAELITES TO WEAR THEM DOWN BY FORCED LABOR.

THE KING OF EGYPT THEN SPOKE TO THE HEBREW MID-WIVES, SHIPHRAH AND PUAH. 'WHEN YOU ATTEND HEBREW WOMEN IN CHILDBIRTH,' HE SAID, 'EXAMINE THE CHILD. IF IT IS A BOY, KILL HIM. IF IT IS A GIRL, LET HER LIVE.'

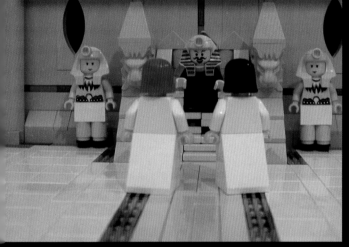

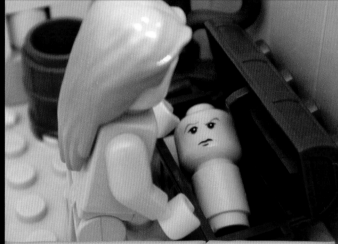

NOW THERE WAS A MAN DESCENDED FROM LEVI WHO HAD TAKEN A WOMAN OF LEVI AS HIS WIFE. SHE CONCEIVED AND GAVE BIRTH TO A SON. SEEING WHAT A FINE CHILD HE WAS, SHE KEPT HIM HIDDEN FOR THREE MONTHS.

WHEN SHE COULD HIDE HIM NO LONGER, SHE GOT A PAPYRUS BASKET FOR HIM, COATING IT WITH BITUMEN AND PITCH. AND SHE LAID IT AMONGST THE REEDS AT THE RIVER'S EDGE.

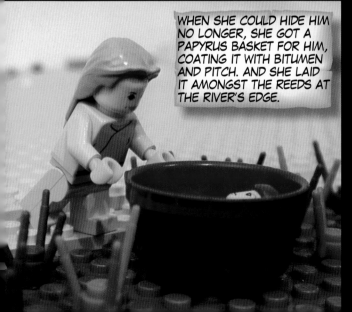

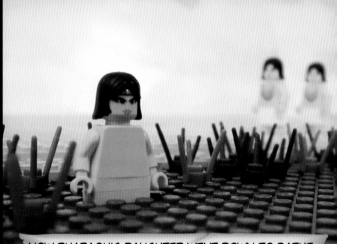

NOW PHARAOH'S DAUGHTER WENT DOWN TO BATHE IN THE RIVER WHILE HER MAIDS WALKED ALONG THE RIVERSIDE. AMONG THE REEDS SHE NOTICED THE BASKET, AND SHE SENT HER MAID TO FETCH IT.

SHE OPENED IT AND SAW THE CHILD. THE BABY WAS CRYING. FEELING SORRY FOR IT, SHE SAID, 'THIS IS ONE OF THE LITTLE HEBREWS.'

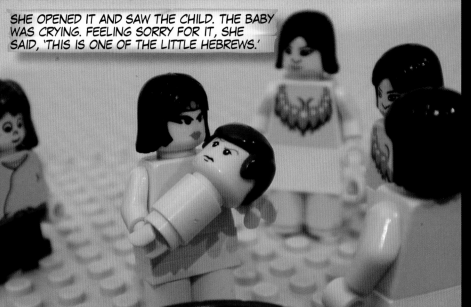

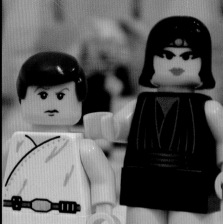

HE BECAME HER SON, AND SHE NAMED HIM MOSES, SHE SAID, 'BECAUSE I DREW HIM OUT OF THE WATER.'

ONE DAY WHEN MOSES HAD GROWN UP, HE WENT OUT TO SEE HIS OWN PEOPLE.

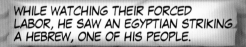

WHILE WATCHING THEIR FORCED LABOR, HE SAW AN EGYPTIAN STRIKING A HEBREW, ONE OF HIS PEOPLE.

MOSES LOOKED THIS WAY AND THAT, AND SAW THAT NO ONE WAS WATCHING.

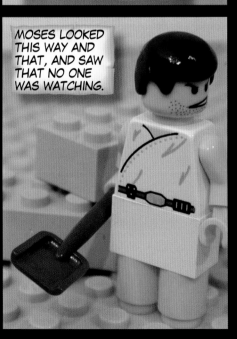

THEN HE KILLED THE EGYPTIAN.

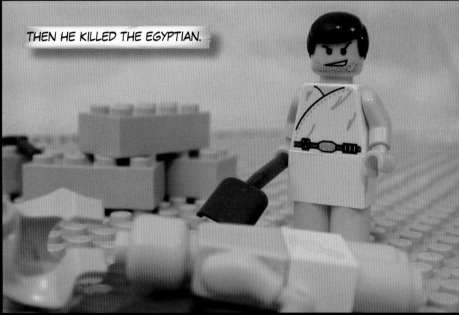

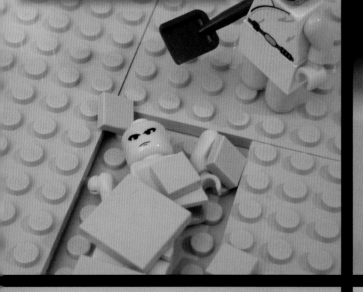

AND HE HID THE BODY IN THE SAND.

MOSES WENT OUT THE NEXT DAY AND CAME ACROSS TWO HEBREW MEN FIGHTING.

HE SAID TO THE MAN WHO WAS IN THE WRONG, 'WHY ARE YOU HITTING ONE OF YOUR OWN PEOPLE?'

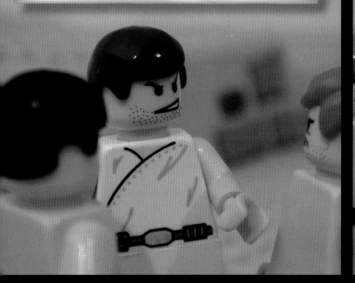

THE MAN REPLIED, 'WHO MADE YOU A RULER AND JUDGE OVER US? DO YOU PLAN TO KILL ME, AS YOU KILLED THE EGYPTIAN?'

MOSES WAS AFRAID, THINKING, 'SURELY THIS MATTER HAS BECOME KNOWN.'

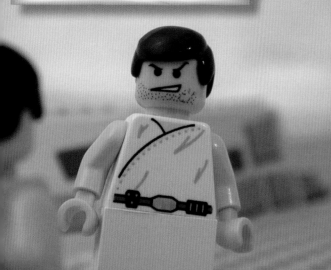

WHEN PHARAOH HEARD ABOUT THIS INCIDENT, HE SOUGHT TO HAVE MOSES KILLED. BUT MOSES FLED FROM PHARAOH.

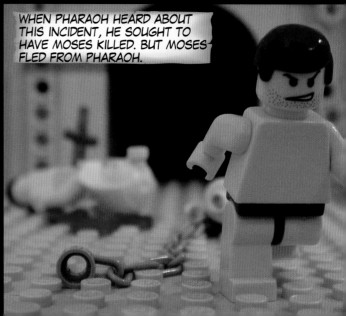

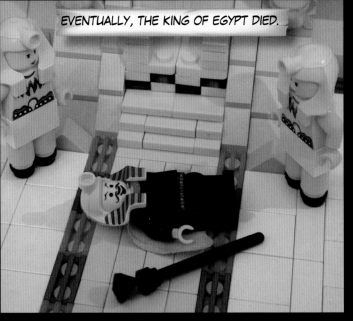

EVENTUALLY, THE KING OF EGYPT DIED.

AND THE ISRAELITES, GROANING IN THEIR SLAVERY, CRIED OUT FOR HELP.

GOD HEARD THEIR GROANING AND REMEMBERED HIS COVENANT WITH ABRAHAM, ISAAC, AND JACOB.

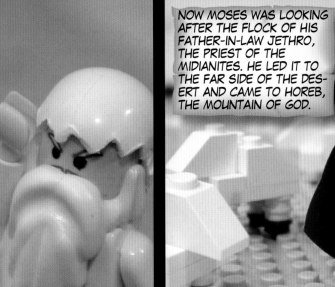

NOW MOSES WAS LOOKING AFTER THE FLOCK OF HIS FATHER-IN-LAW JETHRO, THE PRIEST OF THE MIDIANITES. HE LED IT TO THE FAR SIDE OF THE DESERT AND CAME TO HOREB, THE MOUNTAIN OF GOD.

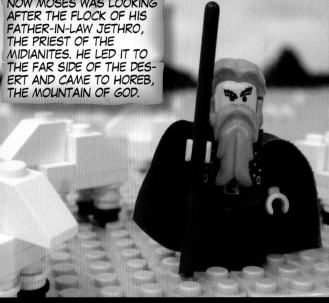

AT THIS MOSES COVERED HIS FACE, FOR HE WAS AFRAID TO LOOK AT GOD.

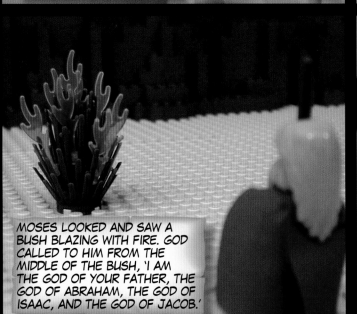

MOSES LOOKED AND SAW A BUSH BLAZING WITH FIRE. GOD CALLED TO HIM FROM THE MIDDLE OF THE BUSH, 'I AM THE GOD OF YOUR FATHER, THE GOD OF ABRAHAM, THE GOD OF ISAAC, AND THE GOD OF JACOB.'

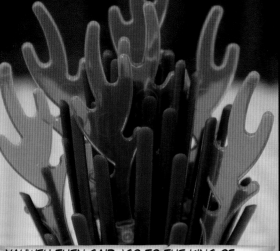

'BUT I WILL MAKE PHARAOH STUBBORN,' SAID YAHWEH. 'THEN I WILL DISPLAY MY MIGHT BY STRIKING DOWN THE EGYPTIANS WITH MANY MIRACULOUS DEEDS.'

YAHWEH THEN SAID, 'GO TO THE KING OF EGYPT AND SAY TO HIM, "LET US GO AND MAKE A THREE-DAY JOURNEY INTO THE DESERT TO OFFER SACRIFICES TO YAHWEH OUR GOD."'

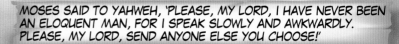

MOSES SAID TO YAHWEH, 'PLEASE, MY LORD, I HAVE NEVER BEEN AN ELOQUENT MAN, FOR I SPEAK SLOWLY AND AWKWARDLY. PLEASE, MY LORD, SEND ANYONE ELSE YOU CHOOSE!'

AT THIS, YAHWEH'S ANGER BLAZED AGAINST MOSES, AND HE SAID, 'WHAT ABOUT YOUR BROTHER AARON? I KNOW THAT HE IS A GOOD SPEAKER. HE WILL SPEAK TO THE PEOPLE FOR YOU, ACTING AS YOUR MOUTHPIECE.'

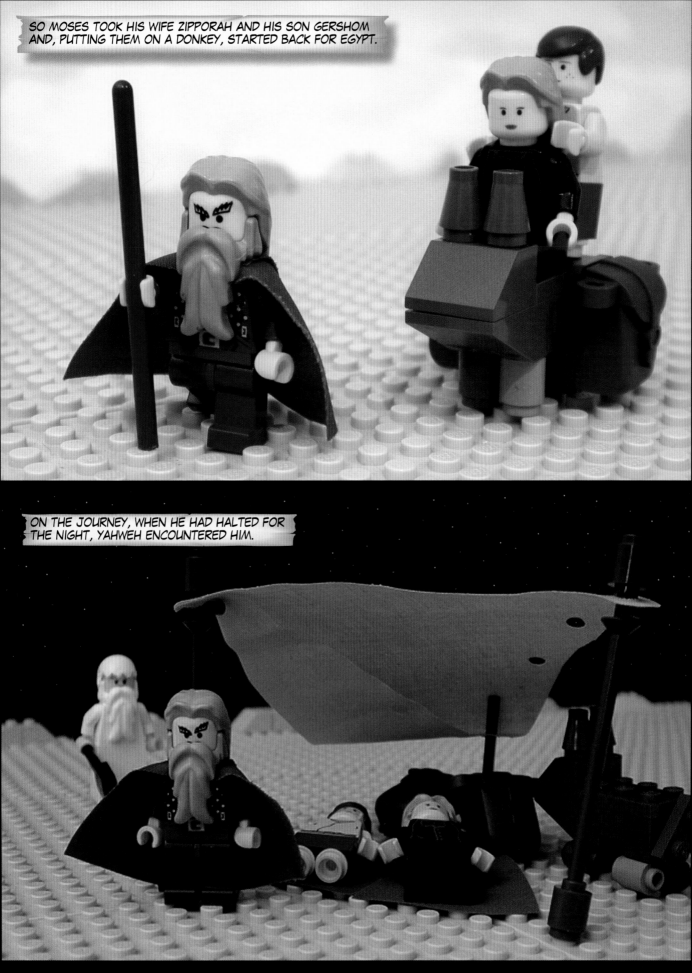

SO MOSES TOOK HIS WIFE ZIPPORAH AND HIS SON GERSHOM AND, PUTTING THEM ON A DONKEY, STARTED BACK FOR EGYPT.

ON THE JOURNEY, WHEN HE HAD HALTED FOR THE NIGHT, YAHWEH ENCOUNTERED HIM.

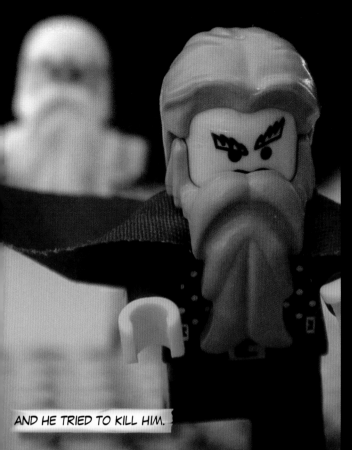

THEN ZIPPORAH, TAKING UP A FLINT KNIFE, CUT OFF HER SONS'S FORESKIN.

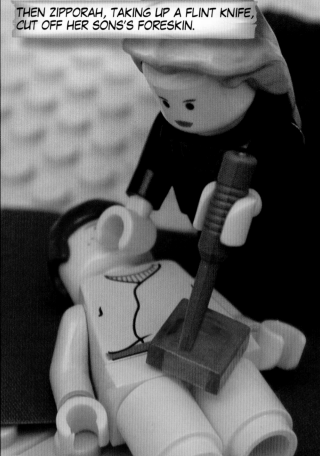

AND HE TRIED TO KILL HIM.

AND WITH IT, SHE TOUCHED MOSES'S FEET AND SAID, 'YOU ARE MY BLOOD-BRIDEGROOM!' SHE SAID 'BLOOD-BRIDEGROOM' WITH REFERENCE TO THE CIRCUMCISION. SO YAHWEH LET HIM GO.

MOSES AND AARON WENT TO PHARAOH, DOING AS YAHWEH HAD ORDERED. MOSES WAS EIGHTY YEARS OLD AND AARON WAS EIGHTY-THREE WHEN THEY SPOKE TO PHARAOH.

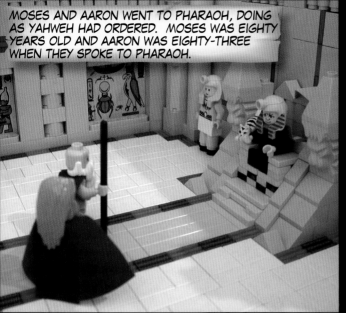

THEY SAID TO PHARAOH, 'THIS IS WHAT YAHWEH, GOD OF ISRAEL SAYS: "LET MY PEOPLE GO, SO THAT THEY CAN HOLD A FEAST IN MY HONOR IN THE DESERT."'

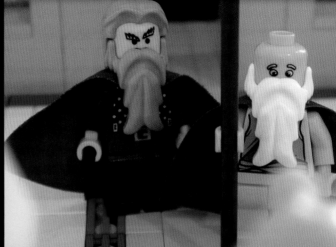

'WHO IS YAHWEH FOR ME TO OBEY WHAT HE SAYS?' PHARAOH REPLIED, 'I KNOW NOTHING OF YAHWEH AND WILL NOT LET ISRAEL GO.'

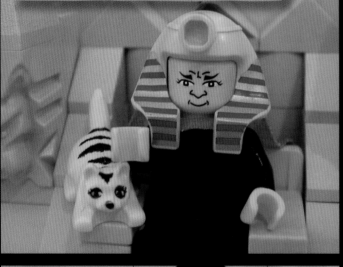

AARON THREW DOWN HIS STAFF IN FRONT OF PHARAOH, AND IT TURNED INTO A SNAKE.

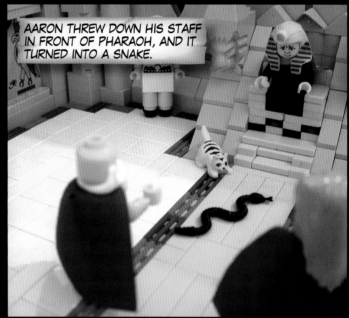

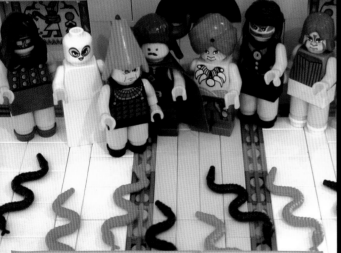

USING THEIR SPELLS, THE MAGICIANS OF EGYPT DID THE SAME. EACH THREW HIS STAFF DOWN AND THESE TURNED INTO SNAKES.

BUT AARON'S STAFF SWALLOWED UP THEIRS.

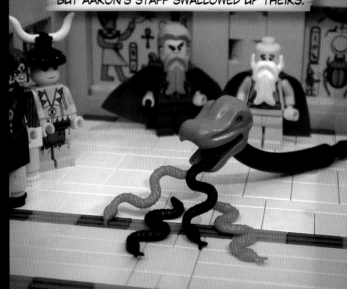

PHARAOH, HOWEVER, REMAINED OBSTINATE AND, AS YAHWEH HAD FORETOLD, REFUSED TO LISTEN TO MOSES AND AARON.

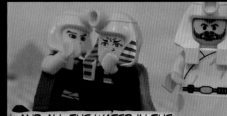

YAHWEH THEN SAID TO MOSES, 'I HAVE MADE HIM STUBBORN SO THAT YOU MAY TELL YOUR CHILDREN AND GRANDCHILDREN HOW I MADE FOOLS OF THE EGYPTIANS. GO TO PHARAOH IN THE MORNING AS HE COMES TO NILE'S EDGE.'

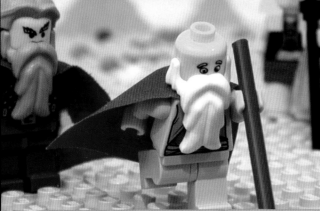

MOSES AND AARON DID AS YAHWEH ORDERED. AARON RAISED HIS STAFF AND STRUCK THE WATERS OF THE RIVER, WITH THE PHARAOH AND HIS OFFICIALS LOOKING ON.

AND ALL THE WATER IN THE RIVER TURNED TO BLOOD. THE RIVER STANK AND THE EGYPTIANS COULD NO LONGER DRINK THE WATER.

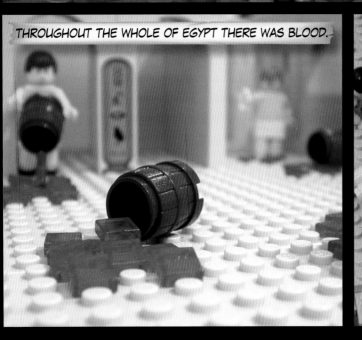

THROUGHOUT THE WHOLE OF EGYPT THERE WAS BLOOD.

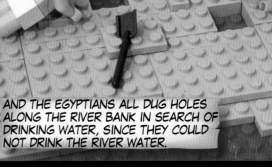

AND THE EGYPTIANS ALL DUG HOLES ALONG THE RIVER BANK IN SEARCH OF DRINKING WATER, SINCE THEY COULD NOT DRINK THE RIVER WATER.

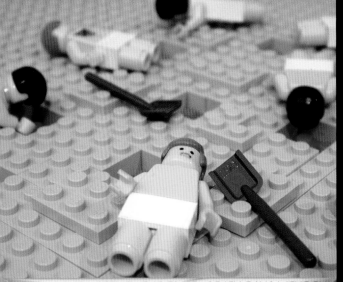

AFTER YAHWEH STRUCK THE RIVER, SEVEN DAYS WENT BY.

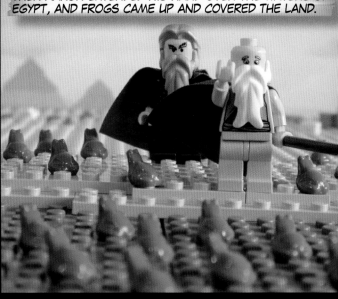

THEN AARON EXTENDED HIS HAND OVER THE WATERS OF EGYPT, AND FROGS CAME UP AND COVERED THE LAND.

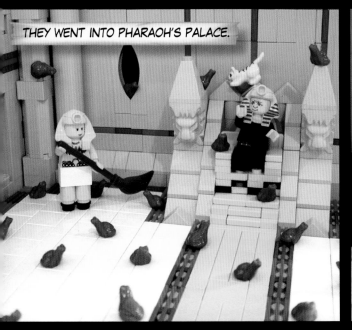

THEY WENT INTO PHARAOH'S PALACE.

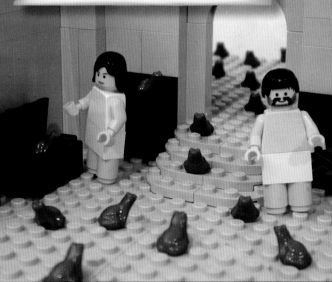

THEY WENT INTO THE HOUSES OF HIS PEOPLE.

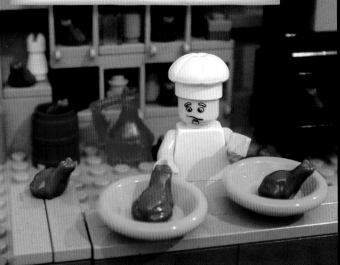

AND THEY WENT INTO THEIR OVENS AND THEIR KNEADING BOWLS.

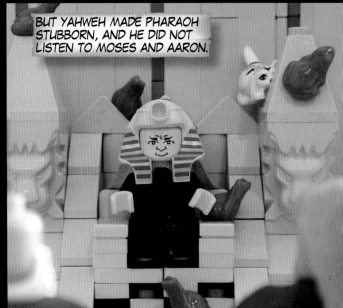

BUT YAHWEH MADE PHARAOH STUBBORN, AND HE DID NOT LISTEN TO MOSES AND AARON.

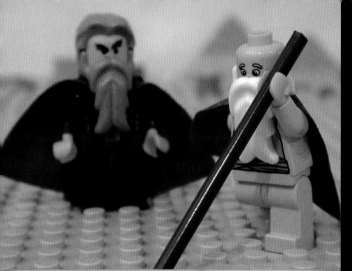

SO AARON STRETCHED OUT HIS HAND WITH HIS STAFF, AND STRUCK THE DUST OF THE EARTH.

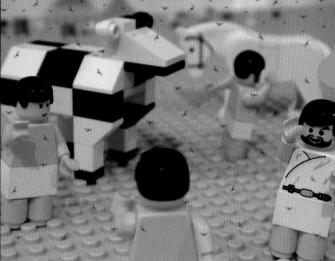

AND ALL THE DUST OF THE EARTH TURNED INTO MOSQUITOES THROUGHOUT THE LAND OF EGYPT. THERE WERE MOSQUITOES ON THE PEOPLE AND ON THE ANIMALS.

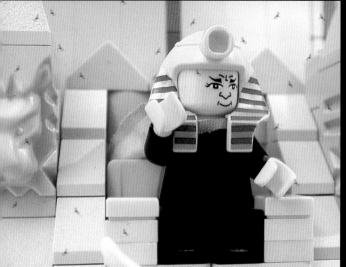

BUT PHARAOH REMAINED STUBBORN, AS YAHWEH HAD FORETOLD, AND DID NOT LISTEN TO THEM.

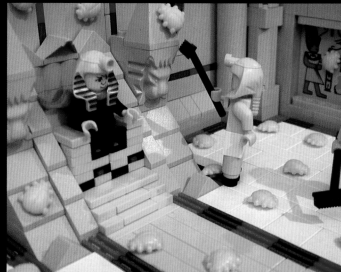

THEN YAHWEH SENT SWARMS OF BEETLES AGAINST THE EGYPTIANS. THEY WENT INTO PHARAOH'S PALACE.

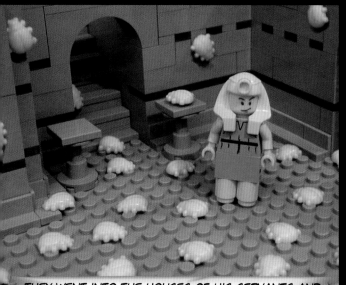

THEY WENT INTO THE HOUSES OF HIS SERVANTS AND HIS OFFICIALS.

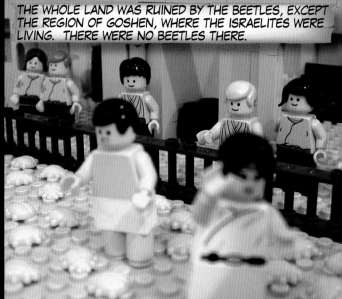

THE WHOLE LAND WAS RUINED BY THE BEETLES, EXCEPT THE REGION OF GOSHEN, WHERE THE ISRAELITES WERE LIVING. THERE WERE NO BEETLES THERE.

BUT PHARAOH BECAME OBSTINATE THIS TIME, TOO, AND DID NOT LET THE PEOPLE GO.

THE NEXT DAY, YAHWEH STRUCK THE EGYPTIANS' LIVESTOCK IN THE FIELDS WITH A TERRIBLE PLAGUE. ALL THE LIVESTOCK DIED: THE HORSES, THE DONKEYS, THE CAMELS, THE OXEN, THE SHEEP, AND THE GOATS.

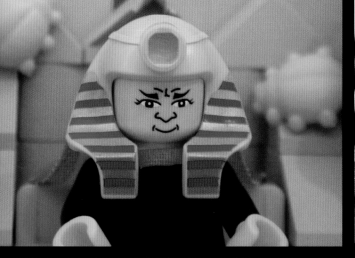

BUT PHARAOH REMAINED STUBBORN AND DID NOT LET THE PEOPLE GO.

YAHWEH THEN SAID TO MOSES AND AARON, 'TAKE HANDFULS OF ASHES FROM THE FURNACE, AND HAVE MOSES THROW IT IN THE AIR IN SIGHT OF PHARAOH. IT WILL BECOME A FINE DUST OVER THE WHOLE OF EGYPT AND CAUSE FESTERING BOILS ON PEOPLE AND ANIMALS.'

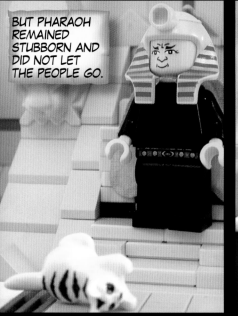

SO THEY TOOK ASHES FROM THE FURNACE AND STOOD IN FRONT OF PHARAOH, AND MOSES THREW IT IN THE AIR.

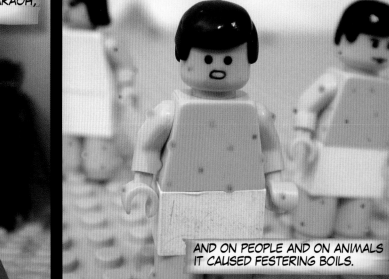

AND ON PEOPLE AND ON ANIMALS IT CAUSED FESTERING BOILS.

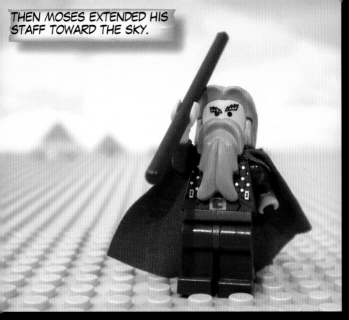

THEN MOSES EXTENDED HIS STAFF TOWARD THE SKY.

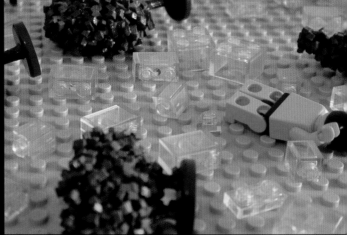

AND YAHWEH SENT HAIL THAT STRUCK DOWN ANYTHING THAT WAS IN THE FIELDS, BOTH PEOPLE AND ANIMALS. IT DESTROYED EVERYTHING THAT GREW IN THE FIELDS, AND BROKE ALL THE TREES.

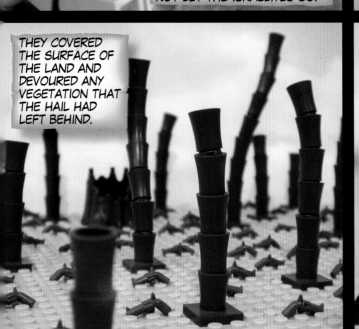

BUT WHEN PHARAOH SAW THAT THE HAIL HAD STOPPED, HE AND HIS OFFICIALS BECAME STUBBORN AGAIN, AS YAHWEH HAD FORETOLD, AND HE DID NOT LET THE ISRAELITES GO.

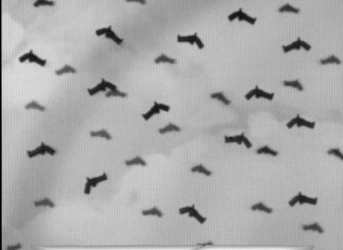

YAHWEH THEN MADE AN EAST WIND BLOW ALL THAT DAY AND NIGHT, AND BY MORNING IT HAD BROUGHT THE LOCUSTS.

THEY COVERED THE SURFACE OF THE LAND AND DEVOURED ANY VEGETATION THAT THE HAIL HAD LEFT BEHIND.

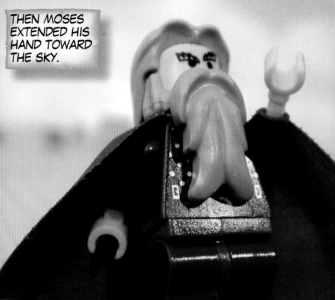

THEN MOSES EXTENDED HIS HAND TOWARD THE SKY.

AND THERE WAS THICK DARKNESS OVER ALL OF EGYPT FOR THREE DAYS. NO ONE COULD SEE ONE ANOTHER OR MOVE ABOUT FOR THREE DAYS.

YAHWEH THEN SAID TO MOSES, 'I SHALL BRING ONE MORE PLAGUE ON PHARAOH AND EGYPT. AFTER THAT, HE WILL LET YOU LEAVE THIS PLACE.'

'TELL THE WHOLE COMMUNITY OF ISRAEL: "EACH MAN MUST TAKE A ONE-YEAR-OLD MALE SHEEP OR A GOAT WITHOUT ANY BLEMISHES. YOU SHALL SLAUGHTER IT AT TWILIGHT."'

'THEN PUT SOME OF THE BLOOD ON THE SIDES AND TOP OF THE DOORFRAME OF THE HOUSES WHERE IT WILL BE EATEN.'

'I SHALL GO THROUGHOUT EGYPT THAT NIGHT AND KILL THE FIRSTBORN OF ALL THE PEOPLE AND ANIMALS, BUT WHEN I SEE THE BLOOD, I SHALL PASS OVER YOU, SO YOU WILL NOT BE DESTROYED.'

AND SO AT MIDNIGHT, GOD KILLED ALL THE FIRSTBORN IN THE LAND OF EGYPT.

FROM THE FIRSTBORN OF PHARAOH...

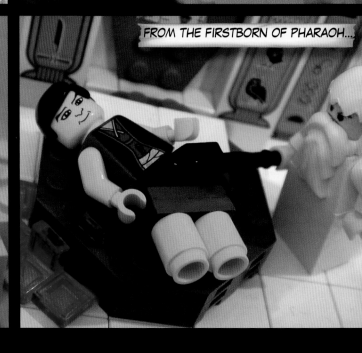
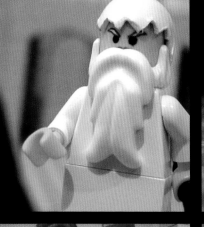

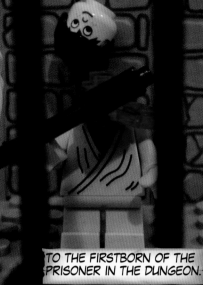

TO THE FIRSTBORN OF THE PRISONER IN THE DUNGEON.

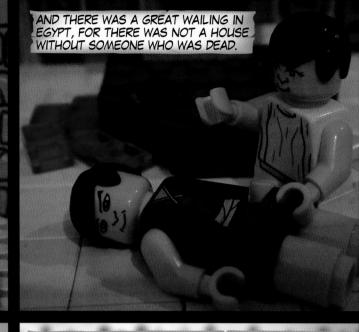

AND THERE WAS A GREAT WAILING IN EGYPT, FOR THERE WAS NOT A HOUSE WITHOUT SOMEONE WHO WAS DEAD.

PHARAOH SUMMONED MOSES AND AARON AND SAID, 'RISE! GET OUT FROM AMONG MY PEOPLE, YOU AND THE ISRAELITES! GO AND WORSHIP THE GOD OF ISRAEL AS YOU HAVE ASKED!'

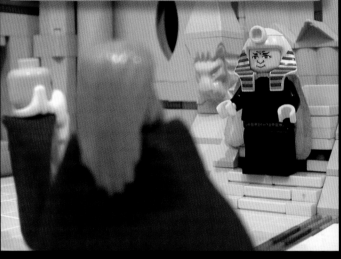

SO THE ISRAELITES TRAVELED OUT OF EGYPT ON FOOT, ABOUT 600,000 MEN STRONG, PLUS THEIR FAMILIES. THE LENGTH OF TIME THAT THE ISRAELITES HAD LIVED IN EGYPT WAS 430 YEARS.

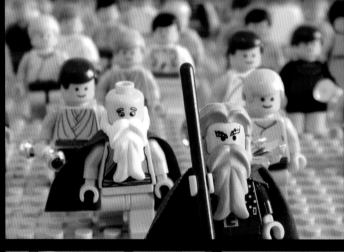

GOD SPOKE TO MOSES AND SAID, 'I SHALL MAKE PHARAOH STUBBORN AND HE WILL PURSUE THE ISRAELITES. I SHALL GAIN GLORY FOR MYSELF AT THE EXPENSE OF PHARAOH AND HIS ARMY.'

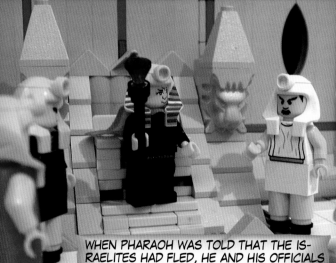

WHEN PHARAOH WAS TOLD THAT THE IS-RAELITES HAD FLED, HE AND HIS OFFICIALS CHANGED THEIR MINDS, SAYING, 'WHAT HAVE WE DONE, RELEASING ISRAEL FROM THEIR SERVICE TO US?'

SO PHARAOH PREPARED HIS ARMY, TAKING SIX HUNDRED OF HIS BEST CHARIOTS, PLUS ALL THE OTHER CHARIOTS IN EGYPT, WITH OFFICERS IN EACH ONE.

YAHWEH MADE PHARAOH STUBBORN, AND HE PURSUED THE ISRAELITES AND CAUGHT UP WITH THEM.

THEN MOSES EXTENDED HIS HAND OUT OVER THE SEA.

AS PHARAOH APPROACHED, THE ISRAELITES LOOKED UP AND SAW THE EGYPTIANS IN PURSUIT OF THEM. THE ISRAELITES WERE TERRIFIED AND CRIED OUT TO YAHWEH.

AND YAHWEH CAUSED THE SEA TO BE DRIVEN BACK WITH A STRONG EASTERLY WIND, MAKING THE SEA INTO DRY LAND. AND SO THE WATERS WERE DIVIDED.

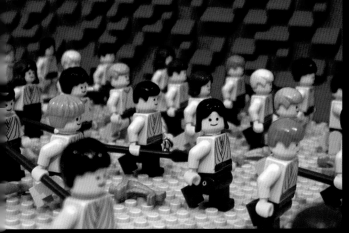

THE ISRAELITES WALKED ON DRY LAND THROUGH THE MIDDLE OF THE SEA WITH WALLS OF WATER TO THEIR RIGHT AND TO THEIR LEFT.

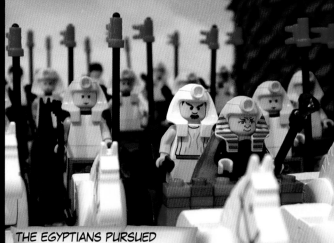

THE EGYPTIANS PURSUED THEM. ALL PHARAOH'S HORSES, CHARIOTS, AND HORSEMEN WENT INTO THE MIDDLE OF THE SEA AFTER THEM.

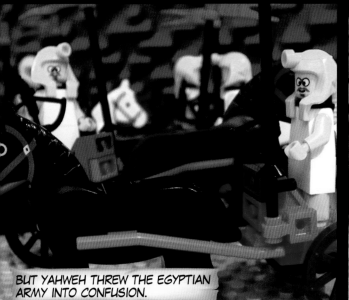

BUT YAHWEH THREW THE EGYPTIAN ARMY INTO CONFUSION.

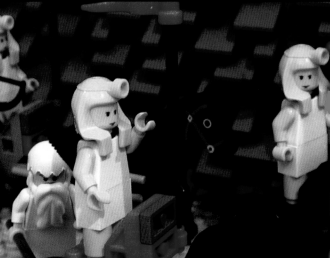

AND HE JAMMED THEIR WHEELS SO THAT THE EGYPTIANS SHOUTED, 'LET US FLEE, FOR YAHWEH IS FIGHTING FOR THEM!'

THEN YAHWEH SAID TO MOSES, 'EXTEND YOUR HAND OUT OVER THE SEA SO THAT THE WATERS WILL FLOW BACK ON THE EGYPTIANS.'

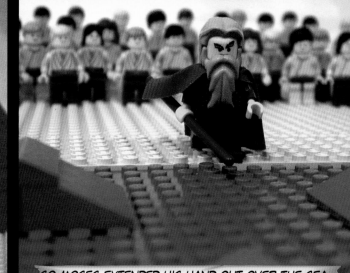

SO MOSES EXTENDED HIS HAND OUT OVER THE SEA, AND THE SEA RETURNED TO ITS PLACE.

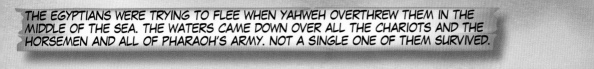

THE EGYPTIANS WERE TRYING TO FLEE WHEN YAHWEH OVERTHREW THEM IN THE MIDDLE OF THE SEA. THE WATERS CAME DOWN OVER ALL THE CHARIOTS AND THE HORSEMEN AND ALL OF PHARAOH'S ARMY. NOT A SINGLE ONE OF THEM SURVIVED.

THE ISRAELITES SAW THE DEAD EGYPTIANS ON THE SEA SHORE.

WHEN ISRAEL SAW THE GREAT POWER THAT YAHWEH HAD BROUGHT AGAINST THE EGYPTIANS, THE PEOPLE FEARED YAHWEH AND PUT THEIR FAITH IN MOSES, HIS SERVANT.

THE WHOLE COMMUNITY OF ISRAELITES ENTERED THE DESERT OF SIN ON THE FIFTEENTH DAY OF THE SECOND MONTH AFTER THEY HAD LEFT EGYPT.

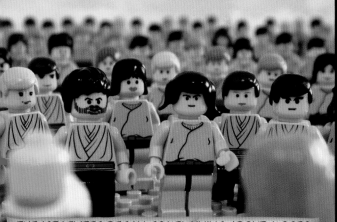

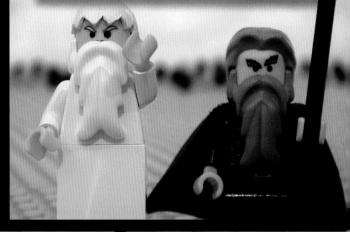

YAHWEH THEN SAID TO MOSES, 'LOOK, I SHALL RAIN DOWN BREAD FOR YOU FROM THE SKY. EACH DAY THE PEOPLE MUST GO OUT AND COLLECT THEIR RATION FOR THE DAY. ON THE SIXTH DAY, HOWEVER, THIS MUST BE TWICE AS MUCH AS THEY COLLECT ON ORDINARY DAYS.'

THE ISRAELITES BEGAN COMPLAINING ABOUT MOSES AND AARON, SAYING, 'IF ONLY WE COULD HAVE DIED IN EGYPT, WHERE WE USED TO SIT AROUND THE MEAT POTS AND ATE TO OUR HEART'S CONTENT! BUT NOW YOU HAVE LEAD US INTO THIS DESERT TO STARVE US ALL TO DEATH!'

THE NEXT MORNING THERE WAS A LAYER OF DEW ALL AROUND THE CAMP. WHEN THE LAYER OF DEW LIFTED, THERE ON THE SURFACE OF THE DESERT WAS SOMETHING FINE AND GRANULAR. AS SOON AS THE ISRAELITES SAW THIS, THEY SAID TO ONE ANOTHER, 'WHAT IS THAT?' NOT KNOWING WHAT IT WAS.

THE HOUSE OF ISRAEL NAMED IT 'MANNA'. IT WAS LIKE CORIANDER SEED. IT WAS WHITE, AND ITS TASTE WAS LIKE THAT OF WAFERS MADE WITH HONEY.

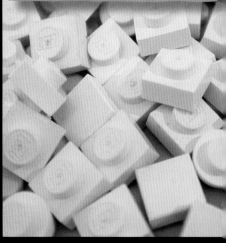

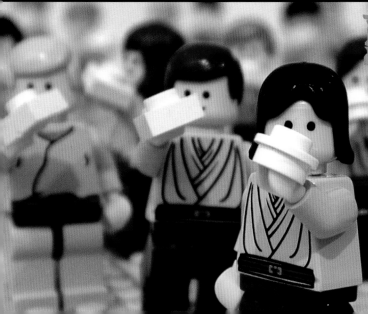

THE ISRAELITES ATE MANNA FOR FORTY YEARS, UP TO THE TIME THEY REACHED INHABITED LAND AT THE FRONTIERS OF CANAAN.

NOW ON THE SIXTH DAY THEY COLLECTED TWICE THE AMOUNT OF FOOD. AND MOSES SAID, 'FOR SIX DAYS YOU WILL COLLECT, BUT ON THE SEVENTH DAY, THE SABBATH, THERE WILL BE NONE.'

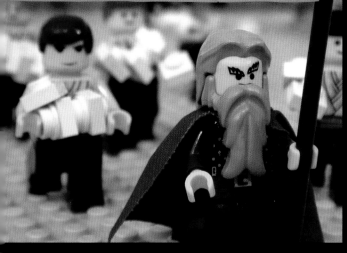

ON THE SEVENTH DAY SOME OF THE PEOPLE WENT OUT TO COLLECT IT, BUT FOUND NONE.

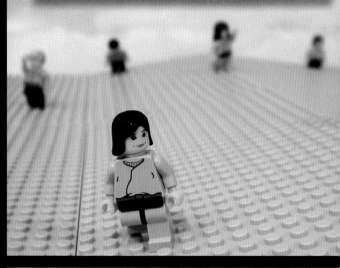

YAHWEH THEN SAID TO MOSES, 'HOW MUCH LONGER WILL YOU REFUSE TO OBEY MY COMMANDMENTS AND LAWS?'

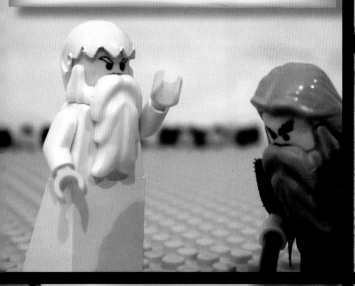

THE WHOLE COMMUNITY OF ISRAELITES THEN LEFT THE DESERT OF SIN AND ESTABLISHED CAMP AT REPHIDIM WHERE THERE WAS NO WATER FOR THE PEOPLE TO DRINK.

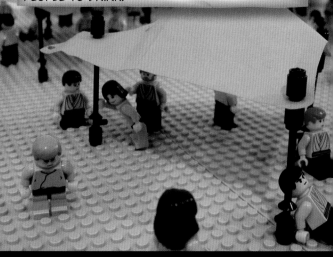

THIRSTING FOR WATER, THE PEOPLE COMPLAINED TO MOSES, SAYING, 'WHY DID YOU BRING US OUT OF EGYPT ONLY TO MAKE US, OUR CHILDREN, AND OUR LIVE-STOCK, DIE OF THIRST?'

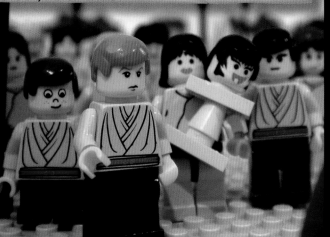

YAHWEH THEN SAID TO MOSES, 'GO ON AHEAD OF THE PEOPLE. TAKE THE STAFF WITH WHICH YOU STRUCK THE RIVER. STRIKE THE ROCK, AND WATER WILL COME OUT FOR THE PEOPLE TO DRINK.'

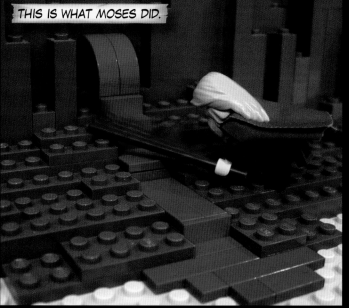

THIS IS WHAT MOSES DID.

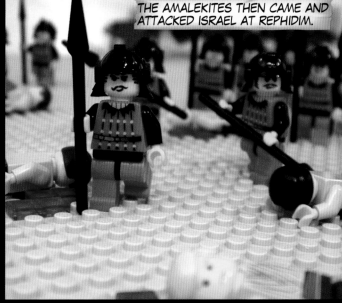

THE AMALEKITES THEN CAME AND ATTACKED ISRAEL AT REPHIDIM.

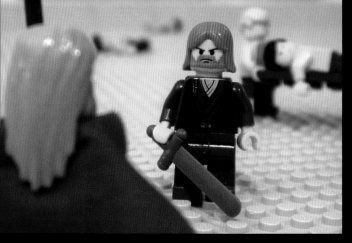

MOSES SAID TO JOSHUA, 'PICK SOME MEN AND TOMORROW MORNING GO OUT AND ATTACK THE AMALEKITES. I SHALL TAKE MY STAND ON THE HILL-TOP WITH THE STAFF OF GOD IN MY HAND.'

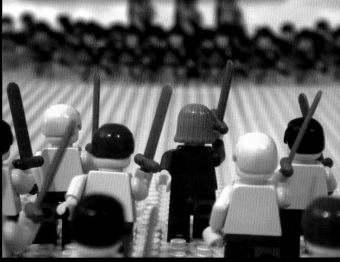

JOSHUA DID AS MOSES TOLD HIM AND WENT OUT TO ATTACK THE AMALEKITES.

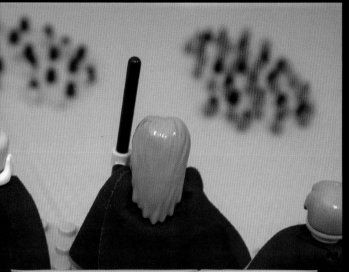

MEANWHILE, MOSES, AARON, AND HUR WENT UP TO THE TOP OF THE HILL.

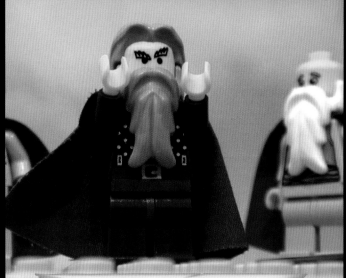

AS LONG AS MOSES KEPT HIS ARMS RAISED...

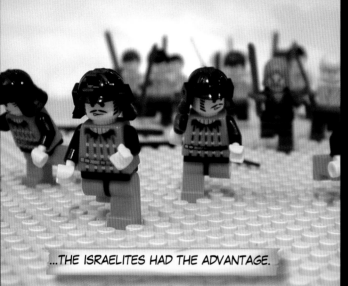

...THE ISRAELITES HAD THE ADVANTAGE.

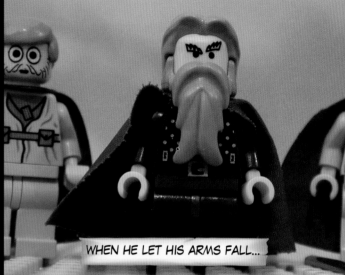

WHEN HE LET HIS ARMS FALL...

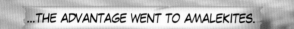

...THE ADVANTAGE WENT TO AMALEKITES.

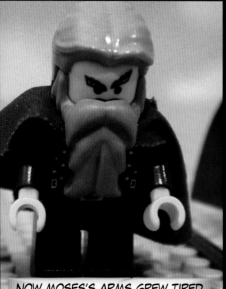

NOW MOSES'S ARMS GREW TIRED.

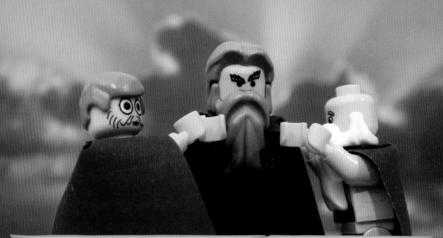

SO THEY TOOK A STONE AND PUT IT UNDER HIM, AND HE SAT WITH AARON AND HUR SUPPORTING HIS ARMS ON EACH SIDE. THUS, HIS ARMS REMAINED STEADY UNTIL SUNSET.

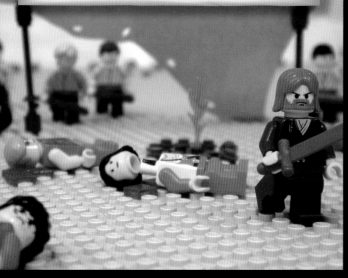

AND JOSHUA DEFEATED THE AMALEKITES, AND PUT THEIR PEOPLE TO THE SWORD.

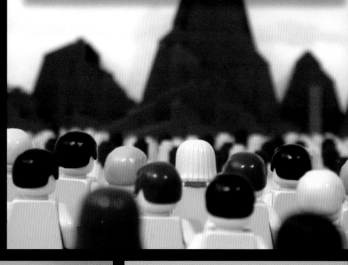

THREE MONTHS AFTER LEAVING EGYPT, THE ISRAELITES CAME TO THE DESERT OF SINAI. THERE THEY PITCHED CAMP, FACING THE MOUNTAIN.

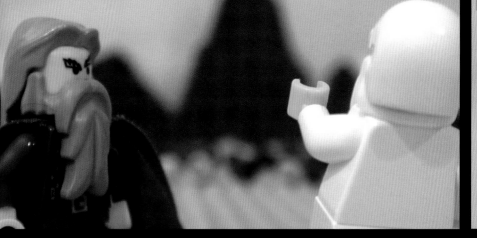

YAHWEH THEN SAID TO MOSES, 'I SHALL COME TO YOU IN A THICK CLOUD SO THAT THE PEOPLE WILL HEAR WHEN I SPEAK TO YOU. YAHWEH WILL DESCEND IN SIGHT OF ALL THE PEOPLE ON MOUNT SINAI.'

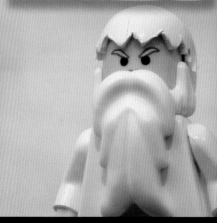

'MARK OUT THE LIMITS OF THE MOUNTAIN. ANYONE WHO TOUCHES THE MOUNTAIN MUST BE PUT TO DEATH. BUT NO ONE MUST TOUCH HIM. HE MUST BE STONED OR SHOT WITH AN ARROW.'

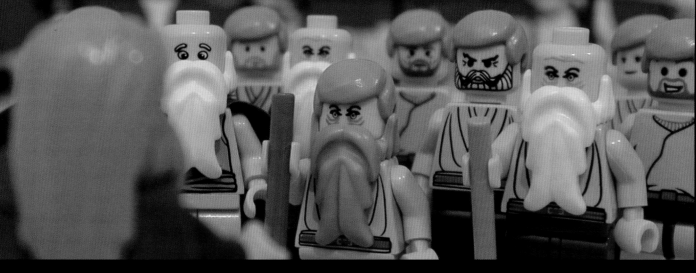

SO MOSES WENT AND SUMMONED THE PEOPLE'S ELDERS AND ACQUAINTED THEM WITH EVERYTHING YAHWEH HAD BIDDEN HIM. HE SAID TO THE PEOPLE, 'BE READY FOR THE DAY AFTER TOMORROW. DO NOT GO NEAR A WOMAN.'

IN THE MORNING TWO DAYS LATER, THERE WAS THUNDER, LIGHTNING, AND A LOUD BLAST FROM A HORN. MOSES LED THE PEOPLE TO MEET GOD, TAKING THEIR PLACE AT THE BOTTOM OF THE MOUNTAIN.

THE HORN GREW LOUDER AND LOUDER, AND YAHWEH DESCENDED ON MOUNT SINAI. THEN HE CALLED MOSES TO THE TOP OF THE MOUNTAIN, AND MOSES WENT UP.

YAHWEH THEN SAID TO MOSES, 'GO BACK DOWN AND WARN THE PEOPLE NOT TO FORCE THEIR WAY THROUGH TO LOOK AT YAHWEH, OR MANY OF THEM WILL PERISH. YAHWEH MAY SEND DESTRUCTION AGAINST THEM!'

SEEING THE LIGHTNING FLASH-
ING, THE TRUMPET BLASTING,
AND THE MOUNTAIN SMOKING,
THE PEOPLE WERE TERRIFIED.
MOSES SAID TO THE PEOPLE,
'DO NOT BE AFRAID! GOD HAS
COME TO TEST YOU, SO THAT
YOUR FEAR OF HIM MAY KEEP
YOU FROM SINNING.'

THEN GOD SPOKE ALL THESE WORDS: 'I
AM THE GOD OF ISRAEL. YOU SHALL HAVE
NO OTHER GODS BEFORE ME. ANYONE
WHO SACRIFICES TO ANY OTHER GODS
MUST BE UTTERLY DESTROYED.'

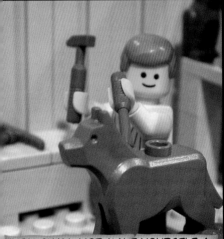

'YOU SHALL NOT MAKE YOURSELF A
CARVED IMAGE OR ANY LIKENESS
OF ANYTHING IN THE HEAVENS
ABOVE, OR ON EARTH BENEATH, OR
IN THE WATERS BELOW THE EARTH.'

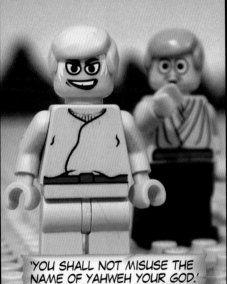

'YOU SHALL NOT MISUSE THE
NAME OF YAHWEH YOUR GOD.'

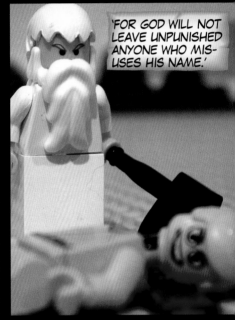

'FOR GOD WILL NOT
LEAVE UNPUNISHED
ANYONE WHO MIS-
USES HIS NAME.'

'REMEMBER THE SABBATH
DAY AND KEEP IT HOLY. YOU
SHALL DO NO WORK THAT
DAY, NOT YOUR CHILDREN,
OR YOUR SLAVES, OR YOUR
ANIMALS.'

'ANYONE WHO
WORKS ON THE
SABBATH DAY MUST
BE PUT TO DEATH.'

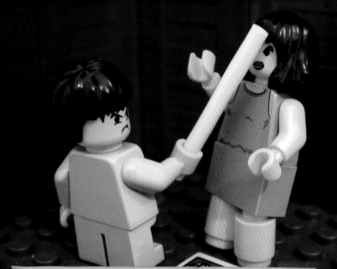

'HONOR YOUR FATHER AND YOUR MOTHER. ANYONE WHO STRIKES THEIR FATHER OR MOTHER...'

'...MUST BE PUT TO DEATH. ANYONE WHO CURSES THEIR FATHER OR MOTHER MUST BE PUT TO DEATH.'

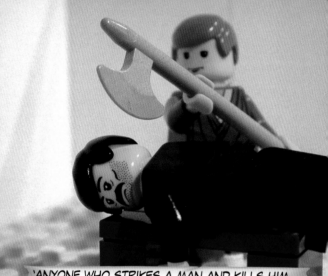

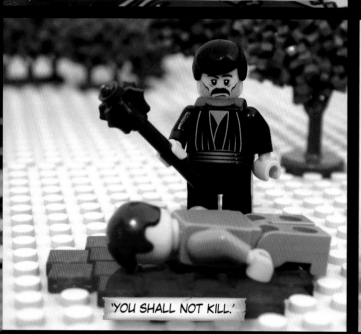

'YOU SHALL NOT KILL.'

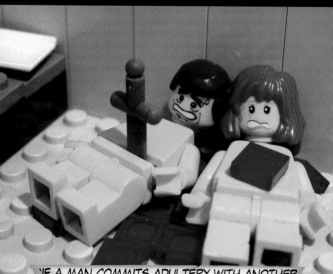

'ANYONE WHO STRIKES A MAN AND KILLS HIM MUST BE PUT TO DEATH.'

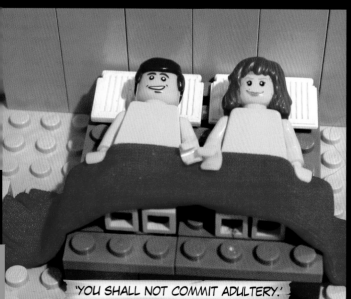

'YOU SHALL NOT COMMIT ADULTERY.'

'IF A MAN COMMITS ADULTERY WITH ANOTHER MAN'S WIFE, BOTH THE MAN AND THE WOMAN MUST BE PUT TO DEATH.'

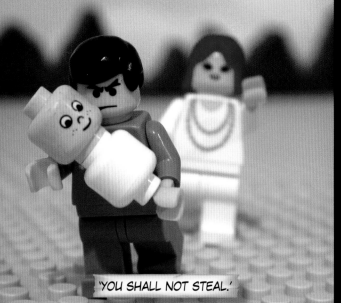

'YOU SHALL NOT STEAL.'

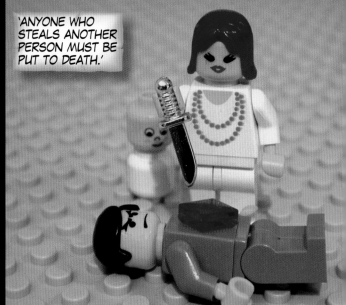

'ANYONE WHO STEALS ANOTHER PERSON MUST BE PUT TO DEATH.'

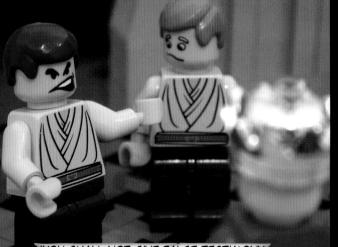

'YOU SHALL NOT GIVE FALSE TESTIMONY AGAINST YOUR NEIGHBOR.'

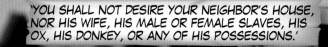

'YOU SHALL NOT DESIRE YOUR NEIGHBOR'S HOUSE, NOR HIS WIFE, HIS MALE OR FEMALE SLAVES, HIS OX, HIS DONKEY, OR ANY OF HIS POSSESSIONS.'

THEN MOSES WENT ON UP THE MOUNTAIN. MOSES STAYED ON THE MOUNTAIN FOR FORTY DAYS AND FORTY NIGHTS.

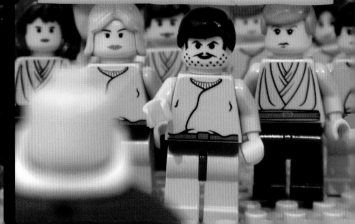

WHEN THE PEOPLE SAW THAT MOSES WAS TAKING A LONG TIME TO COME DOWN FROM THE MOUNTAIN, THEY GATHERED AROUND AARON AND SAID, 'COME, MAKE US A GOD TO LEAD US. FOR WE DO NOT KNOW WHAT HAS BECOME OF MOSES, THE MAN WHO BROUGHT US OUT OF EGYPT.'

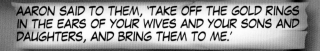

AARON SAID TO THEM, 'TAKE OFF THE GOLD RINGS IN THE EARS OF YOUR WIVES AND YOUR SONS AND DAUGHTERS, AND BRING THEM TO ME.'

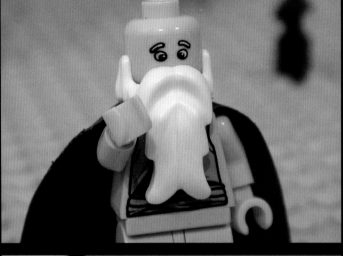

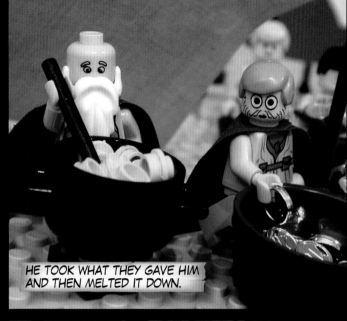

HE TOOK WHAT THEY GAVE HIM AND THEN MELTED IT DOWN.

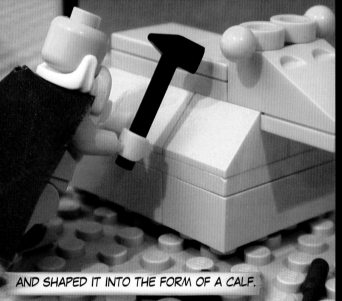

AND SHAPED IT INTO THE FORM OF A CALF.

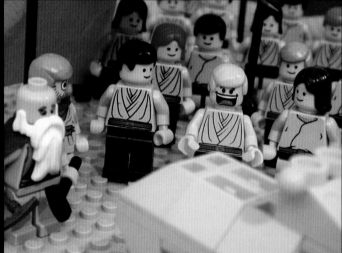

THEN THE PEOPLE SAID, 'ISRAEL, THIS IS YOUR GOD WHO BROUGHT YOU UP OUT OF EGYPT.'

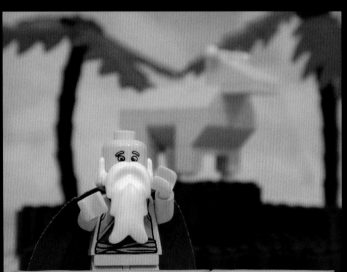

SEEING THIS, AARON BUILT AN ALTAR BEFORE THE CALF AND ANNOUNCED, 'TOMORROW WILL BE A FEAST TO GOD OF ISRAEL!'

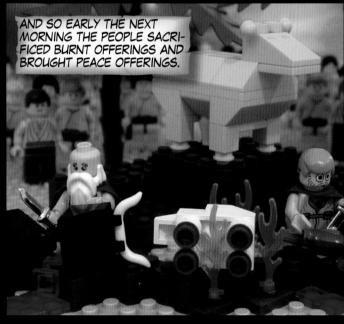

AND SO EARLY THE NEXT MORNING THE PEOPLE SACRIFICED BURNT OFFERINGS AND BROUGHT PEACE OFFERINGS.

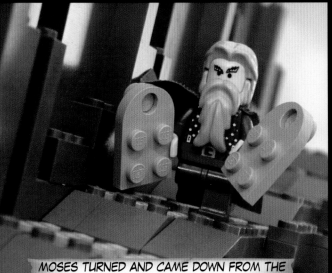

THE PEOPLE SAT DOWN TO EAT AND TO DRINK, AND THEN GOT UP TO PLAY.

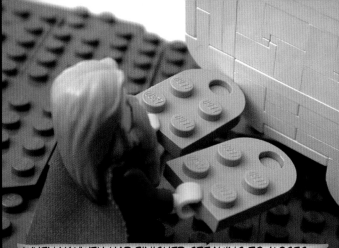

WHEN YAHWEH HAD FINISHED SPEAKING TO MOSES ON MOUNT SINAI, HE GAVE HIM THE TWO STONE TABLETS OF THE TESTIMONY INSCRIBED ON BOTH SIDES, FRONT AND BACK, WRITTEN BY THE FINGER OF GOD.

MOSES TURNED AND CAME DOWN FROM THE MOUNTAIN WITH THE TWO TABLETS OF THE TESTIMONY IN HIS HANDS.

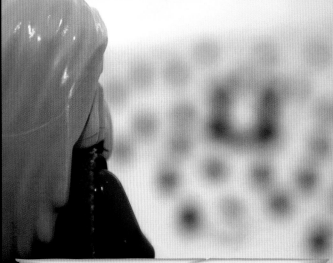

WHEN HE APPROACHED THE CAMP, HE SAW THE CALF AND THE PEOPLE DANCING.

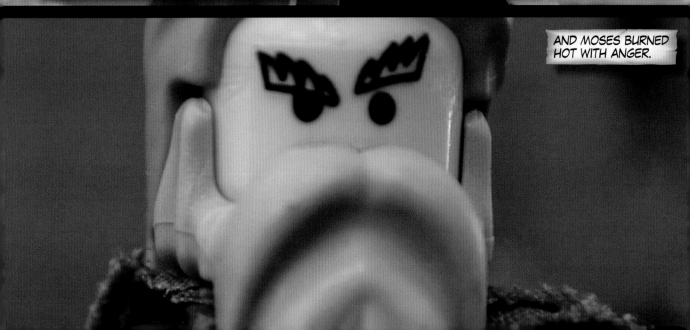

AND MOSES BURNED HOT WITH ANGER.

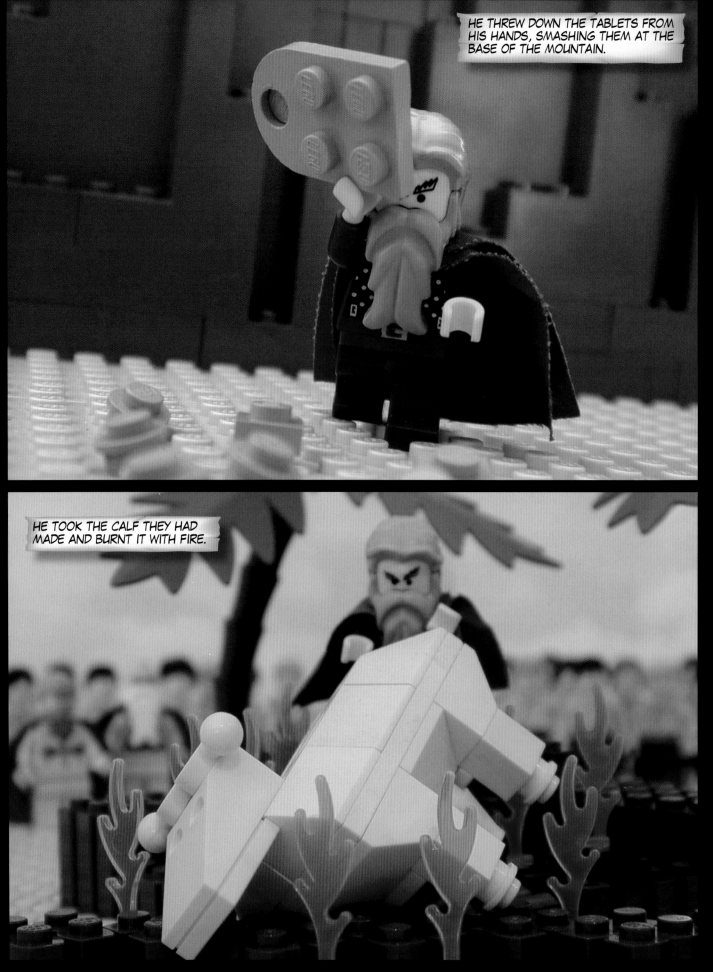

AND HE GROUND IT INTO POWDER.

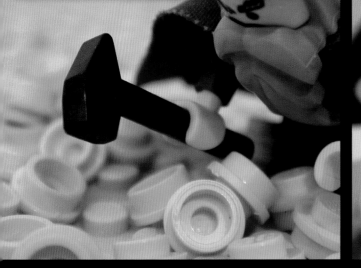

THEN HE SCATTERED THE POWDER ON THE WATER AND MADE THE ISRAELITES DRINK IT.

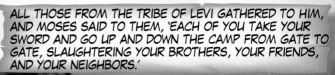

WHEN MOSES SAW THAT THE PEOPLE WERE OUT OF CONTROL, HE STOOD AT THE ENTRANCE OF THE CAMP AND SAID, 'WHOEVER IS FOR YAHWEH, COME TO ME!'

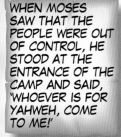

ALL THOSE FROM THE TRIBE OF LEVI GATHERED TO HIM, AND MOSES SAID TO THEM, 'EACH OF YOU TAKE YOUR SWORD AND GO UP AND DOWN THE CAMP FROM GATE TO GATE, SLAUGHTERING YOUR BROTHERS, YOUR FRIENDS, AND YOUR NEIGHBORS.'

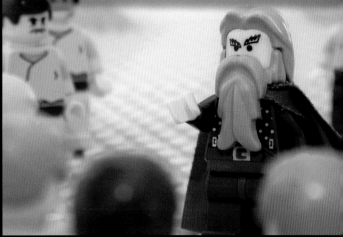

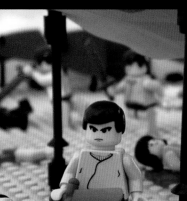

THE LEVITES DID AS MOSES ORDERED.

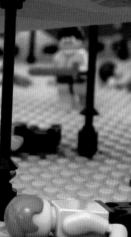

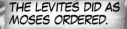

AND ABOUT THREE THOUSAND OF THE PEOPLE WERE KILLED THAT DAY.

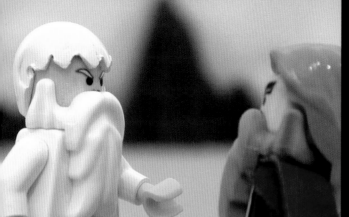

YAHWEH USED TO TALK TO MOSES FACE TO FACE, AS A MAN TALKS TO A FRIEND. YAHWEH SAID TO MOSES, 'CUT TWO TABLETS OF STONE LIKE THE FIRST ONES, AND I WILL WRITE THE WORDS THAT WERE ON THE FIRST TABLETS, WHICH YOU BROKE.'

SO HE CUT TWO TABLETS OF STONE LIKE THE FIRST.

AND WITH THE TWO TABLETS OF STONE IN HIS HANDS, MOSES WENT UP MOUNT SINAI IN THE EARLY MORNING AS YAHWEH HAD ORDERED.

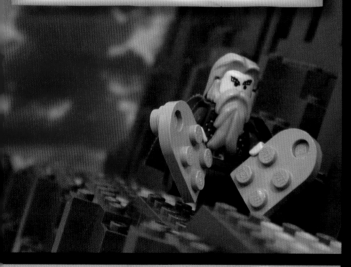

HE STAYED WITH YAHWEH FOR FORTY DAYS AND FORTY NIGHTS, EATING AND DRINKING NOTHING, AND ON THE TABLETS HE WROTE THE WORDS OF THE COVENANT, THE TEN WORDS.

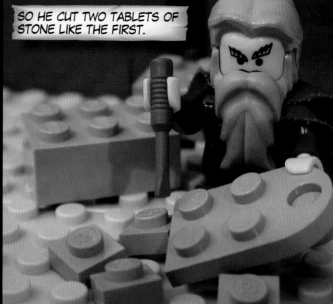

YAHWEH SPOKE TO MOSES AND SAID, 'MAKE ME A SANCTUARY SO I CAN DWELL AMONG THE PEOPLE. YOU MUST MAKE IT ALL ACCORDING TO THE DESIGNS FOR THE DWELLING WHICH I SHALL NOW SHOW YOU.'

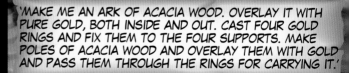

'MAKE ME AN ARK OF ACACIA WOOD. OVERLAY IT WITH PURE GOLD, BOTH INSIDE AND OUT. CAST FOUR GOLD RINGS AND FIX THEM TO THE FOUR SUPPORTS. MAKE POLES OF ACACIA WOOD AND OVERLAY THEM WITH GOLD AND PASS THEM THROUGH THE RINGS FOR CARRYING IT.'

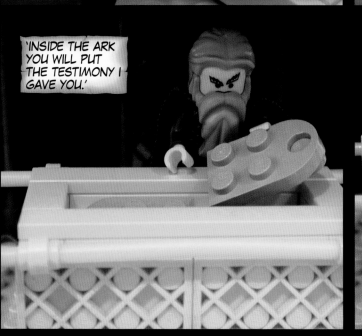

'MAKE A COVER OF PURE GOLD, AND MAKE TWO WINGED CREATURES OUT OF HAMMERED GOLD, AND PUT THEM AT EITHER END OF THE COVER.'

'THE WINGED CREATURES MUST HAVE THEIR WINGS SPREAD UPWARDS AND BE FACING EACH OTHER. THERE ABOVE THE COVER, BETWEEN THE TWO WINGED CREATURES, I WILL COME TO MEET YOU, AND I SHALL GIVE YOU ALL MY COMMANDS FOR THE ISRAELITES.'

'INSIDE THE ARK YOU WILL PUT THE TESTIMONY I GAVE YOU.'

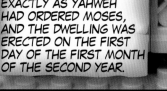

ALL THE WORK FOR THE DWELLING WAS DONE EXACTLY AS YAHWEH HAD ORDERED MOSES, AND THE DWELLING WAS ERECTED ON THE FIRST DAY OF THE FIRST MONTH OF THE SECOND YEAR.

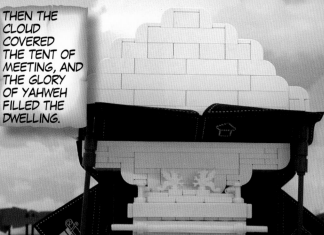

THEN THE CLOUD COVERED THE TENT OF MEETING, AND THE GLORY OF YAHWEH FILLED THE DWELLING.

THROUGHOUT THEIR JOURNEYS, WHENEVER THE CLOUD ROSE FROM THE DWELLING, THE ISRAELITES WOULD MOVE ONWARD. BUT IF THE CLOUD DID NOT RISE, THEY WOULD NOT MOVE ON UNTIL THE DAY IT ROSE UP.

AND AT NIGHT THERE WAS FIRE INSIDE THE CLOUD FOR THE WHOLE HOUSE OF
ISRAEL TO SEE THROUGHOUT THEIR TRAVELS.

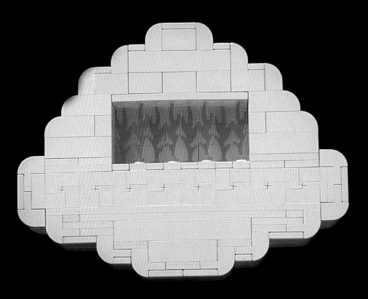

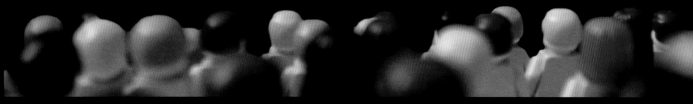

LEVITICUS

YAHWEH SAID TO MOSES, 'TAKE AARON, HIS SONS, A BULL, TWO RAMS, AND A BASKET OF UNLEAVENED BREAD, AND CALL THE WHOLE COMMUNITY TOGETHER.'

SO MOSES MADE AARON AND HIS SONS COME FORWARD, AND HE WASHED THEM WITH WATER.

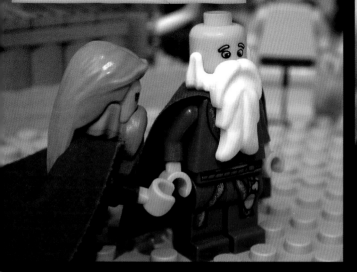

HE DRESSED AARON IN THE TUNIC AND CLOTHED HIM IN THE ROBE WITH THE SKILLFULLY WOVEN BAND AROUND HIM.

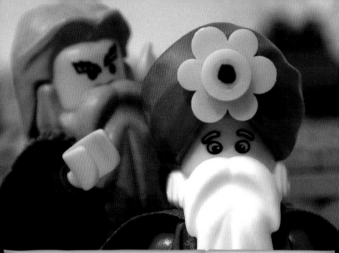

HE PUT THE TURBAN ON HIS HEAD, AND ON THE FRONT OF THE TURBAN, THE GOLDEN FLOWER, THE HOLY CROWN, AS YAHWEH HAD ORDERED HIM.

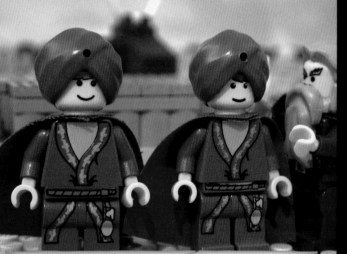

MOSES THEN HAD AARON'S SONS COME FORWARD. HE DRESSED THEM IN TUNICS, WAISTBANDS, AND HEADDRESSES, AS YAHWEH HAD ORDERED HIM.

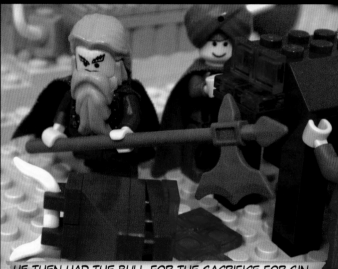

HE THEN HAD THE BULL FOR THE SACRIFICE FOR SIN BROUGHT FORWARD. AARON AND HIS SONS LAID THEIR HANDS ON IT, AND MOSES SLAUGHTERED IT.

HE POURED ITS BLOOD ALL AROUND THE ALTAR.

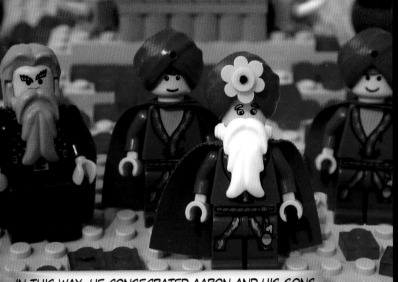

IN THIS WAY, HE CONSECRATED AARON AND HIS SONS.

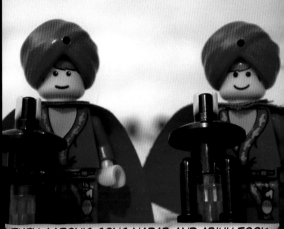

THEN AARON'S SONS NADAB AND ABIHU TOOK THEIR CENSERS, PUT FIRE IN THEM, AND ADDED INCENSE TO THE FIRE. THEY THEN PRESENTED THE STRANGE FIRE BEFORE YAHWEH.

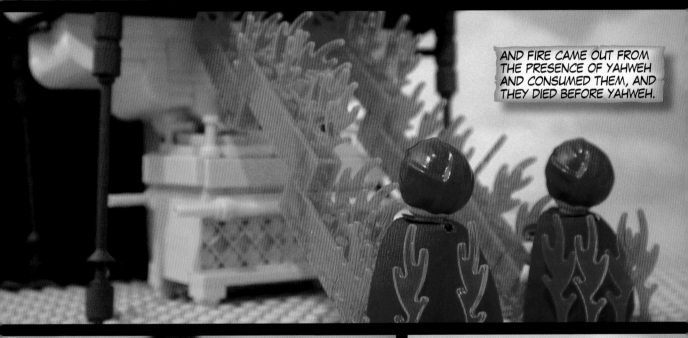

AND FIRE CAME OUT FROM THE PRESENCE OF YAHWEH AND CONSUMED THEM, AND THEY DIED BEFORE YAHWEH.

AARON'S NEPHEWS MISHAEL AND ELZAPHAN CAME AND CARRIED THEM AWAY, STILL IN THEIR TUNICS, TO A PLACE OUTSIDE THE CAMP.

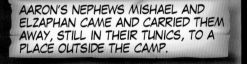

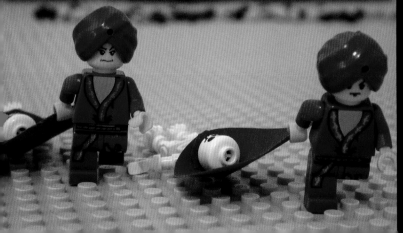

MOSES SAID TO AARON, 'DO NOT SHOW THE SIGNS OF MOURNING OR YOU WILL DIE, AND YAHWEH'S WRATH WILL COME UPON THE WHOLE COMMUNITY.'

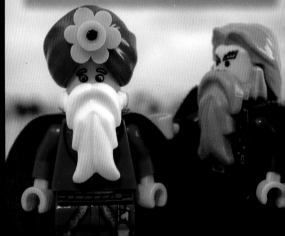

NUMBERS

THEY SET OUT FROM YAHWEH'S MOUNTAIN AND TRAVELED FOR THREE DAYS. THE ARK OF THE COVENANT OF YAHWEH PRECEDED THEM, SEARCHING FOR A PLACE FOR THEM TO REST.

AND THE PEOPLE BEGAN COMPLAINING ABOUT THEIR HARDSHIPS.

YAHWEH HEARD THIS, AND HIS ANGER BLAZED AGAINST THEM.

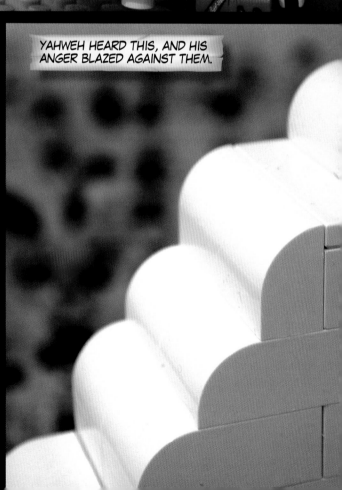

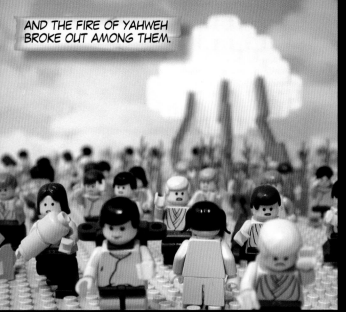

AND THE FIRE OF YAHWEH BROKE OUT AMONG THEM.

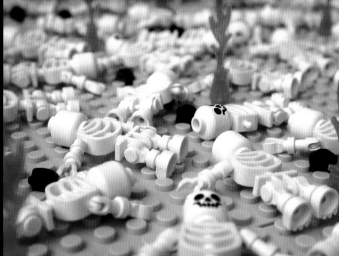

IT DEVOURED ONE END OF THE CAMP.

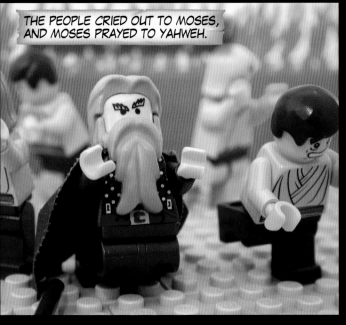

THE PEOPLE CRIED OUT TO MOSES, AND MOSES PRAYED TO YAHWEH.

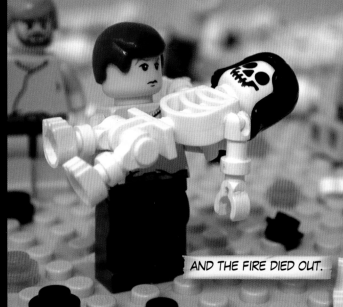

AND THE FIRE DIED OUT.

THE RABBLE AMONG THEM BEGAN TO CRAVE FOOD, AND THE ISRAELITES BEGAN TO WEEP AND SAID, 'WHO WILL GIVE US SOME MEAT? THINK OF THE FISH WE USED TO EAT FREELY IN EGYPT. THE CUCUMBERS, THE MELONS, THE LEEKS, THE ONIONS, AND THE GARLIC!'

YAHWEH SAID TO MOSES, 'TELL THE PEOPLE, "SINCE YOU HAVE WEPT IN YAHWEH'S HEARING, VERY WELL, YAHWEH WILL GIVE YOU MEAT TO EAT UNTIL IT COMES OUT OF YOUR NOSTRILS AND SICKENS YOU."'

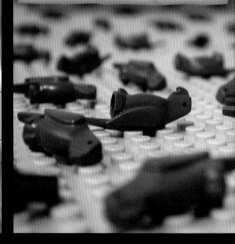

A WIND SENT BY YAHWEH STARTED BLOWING, BRINGING QUAIL WHICH IT MADE FALL NEAR THE CAMP. THEY LAY FOR A DISTANCE OF A DAY'S JOURNEY IN EACH DIRECTION.

THE PEOPLE WERE UP ALL THAT DAY AND NIGHT AND ALL THE NEXT DAY COLLECTING QUAIL.

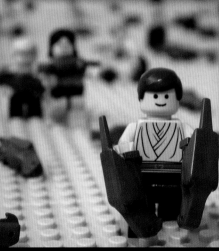

THE MEAT WAS STILL BETWEEN THEIR TEETH, NOT YET CHEWED, WHEN YAHWEH'S ANGER WAS BLAZED AGAINST THE PEOPLE.

AND YAHWEH STRUCK THEM WITH A TERRIBLE PLAGUE.

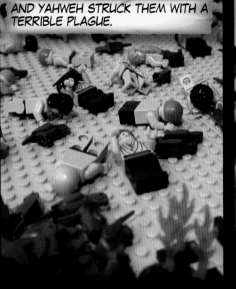

THEY CALLED THIS PLACE KIBROTH-HA-TAAVAHM BECAUSE THERE THEY BURIED THE PEOPLE WHO HAD HUNGERED.

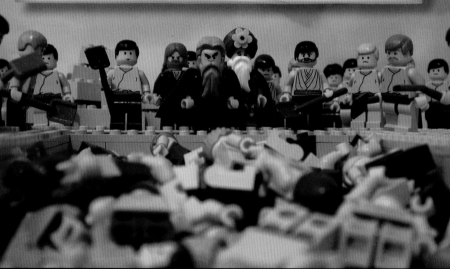

MIRIAM AND AARON BEGAN TO CRITICIZE MOSES CONCERNING THE CUSHITE WOMAN HE HAD MARRIED.

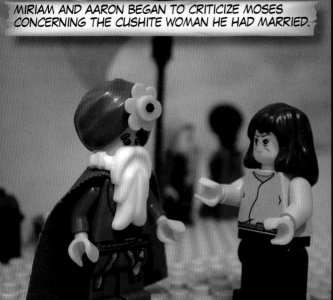

FOR MOSES HAD INDEED MARRIED A CUSHITE WOMAN.

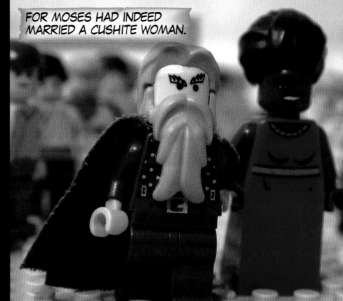

YAHWEH HEARD THIS AND SUDDENLY SAID, 'MOSES IS ENTRUSTED WITH MY WHOLE HOUSEHOLD. TO HIM I SPEAK FACE TO FACE, PLAINLY AND NOT IN RIDDLES. HOW CAN YOU NOT BE AFRAID TO CRITICIZE MOSES?'

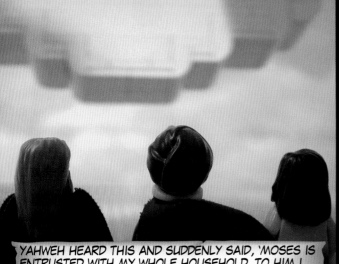

YAHWEH'S ANGER BLAZED, AND HE LEFT THEM. WHEN THE CLOUD DEPARTED, IT WAS SEEN THAT MIRIAM'S SKIN HAD TURNED LEPROUS, AS WHITE AS SNOW.

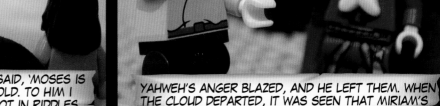

AARON SAW THAT SHE WAS LEPROUS AND SAID TO MOSES, 'PLEASE DO NOT PUNISH US! DO NOT LET MIRIAM BE LIKE A CHILD BORN DEAD WHO COMES OUT OF THE WOMB WITH HALF ITS FLESH EATEN AWAY!'

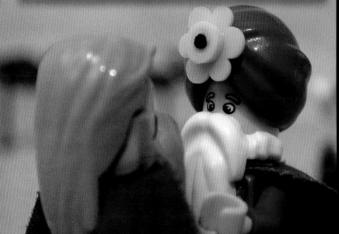

MIRIAM WAS SHUT OUT OF THE CAMP FOR SEVEN DAYS.

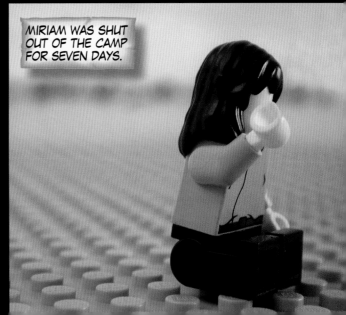

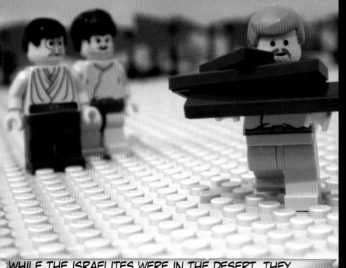

YAHWEH SAID TO MOSES, 'THIS MAN MUST CERTAINLY BE PUT TO DEATH. THE WHOLE COMMUNITY MUST STONE HIM WITH STONES OUTSIDE THE CAMP.'

WHILE THE ISRAELITES WERE IN THE DESERT, THEY CAUGHT A MAN GATHERING WOOD ON THE SABBATH DAY.

SO THE WHOLE COMMUNITY TOOK HIM OUTSIDE THE CAMP.

AND THEY STONED HIM WITH STONES UNTIL HE WAS DEAD, AS YAHWEH HAD ORDERED.

THE ISRAELITES SET OUT FROM MOUNT HOR ALONG THE ROUTE TO THE RED SEA IN ORDER TO GO AROUND EDOM.

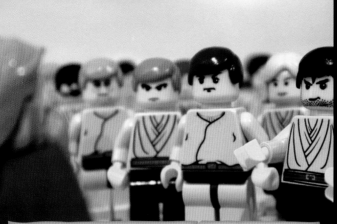

ON THE WAY, THE PEOPLE GREW IMPATIENT, AND THEY SPOKE AGAINST GOD AND AGAINST MOSES, SAYING, 'WHY DID YOU BRING US OUT OF EGYPT TO DIE IN THE DESERT? THERE IS NO BREAD OR WATER HERE, AND WE ARE SICK OF THIS WORTHLESS FOOD.'

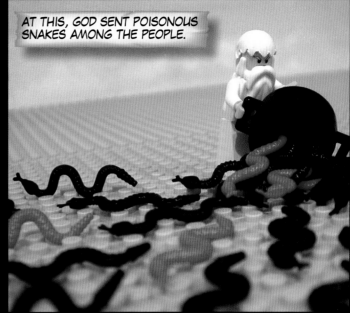

AT THIS, GOD SENT POISONOUS SNAKES AMONG THE PEOPLE.

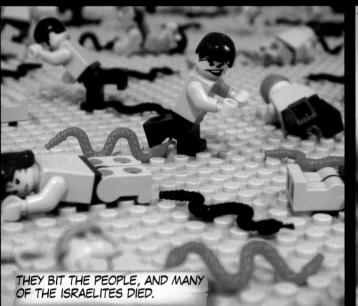

THEY BIT THE PEOPLE, AND MANY OF THE ISRAELITES DIED.

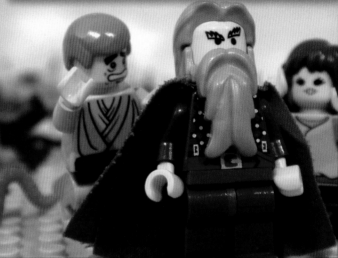

THE PEOPLE CAME AND SAID TO MOSES, 'WE HAVE SINNED BY SPEAKING AGAINST YAHWEH AND AGAINST YOU. PRAY FOR US TO YAHWEH TO SAVE US FROM THESE SNAKES!'

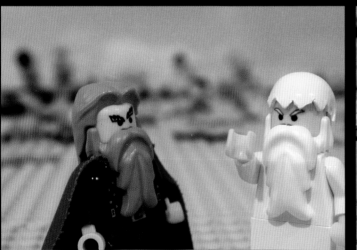

MOSES PRAYED FOR THE PEOPLE, AND YAHWEH REPLIED, 'MAKE A BRONZE SNAKE AND SET IT ON A POLE. ANYONE WHO IS BITTEN BY A SNAKE AND LOOKS AT THE BRONZE SNAKE WILL SURVIVE.'

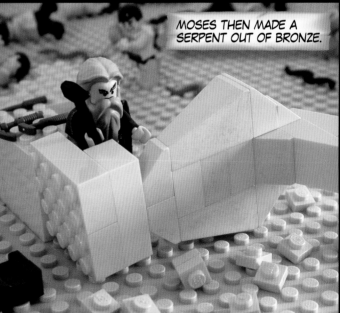

MOSES THEN MADE A SERPENT OUT OF BRONZE.

AND HE RAISED IT UP ON A POLE. ANYONE WHO WAS BITTEN BY A SNAKE AND LOOKED AT THE BRONZE SERPENT SURVIVED.

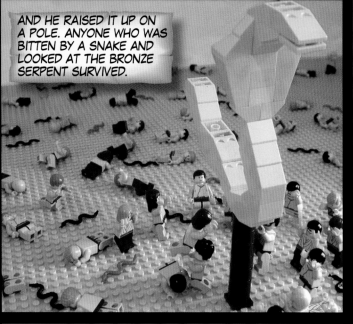

FROM THE DESERT, MOSES SENT ENVOYS TO KING SIHON OF HESHBON WITH A PEACEFUL OFFER: 'LET US PASS THROUGH YOUR COUNTRY. WE WILL ONLY MARCH THROUGH UNTIL WE CROSS THE JORDAN AND INTO THE LAND THAT YAHWEH OUR GOD IS GIVING US.'

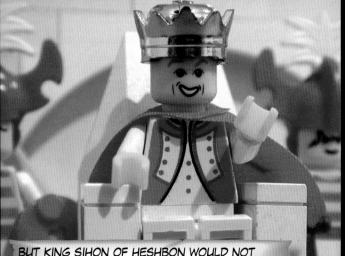

BUT KING SIHON OF HESHBON WOULD NOT ALLOW THE ISRAELITES TO PASS, FOR YAHWEH HAD MADE HIM OBSTINATE AND STUBBORN.

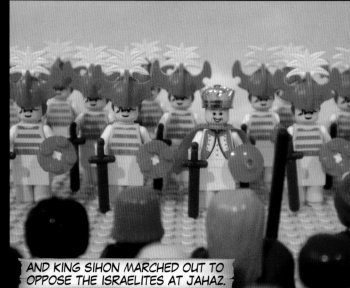

AND KING SIHON MARCHED OUT TO OPPOSE THE ISRAELITES AT JAHAZ.

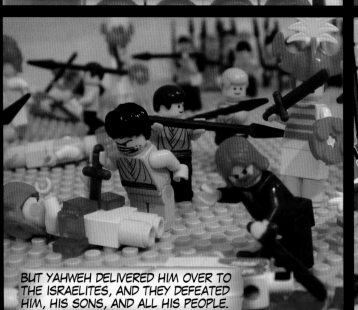

BUT YAHWEH DELIVERED HIM OVER TO THE ISRAELITES, AND THEY DEFEATED HIM, HIS SONS, AND ALL HIS PEOPLE.

THEY CAPTURED ALL HIS TOWNS AND LAID THEM UNDER THE CURSE OF DESTRUCTION. AMONGST THE MEN, WOMEN, AND CHILDREN, THERE WERE NO SURVIVORS.

THE ISRAELITES THEN TURNED AND MARCHED ON BASHAN. KING OG OF BASHAN AND ALL HIS ARMY CAME OUT TO MEET THEM AT EDREI AND GIVE BATTLE.

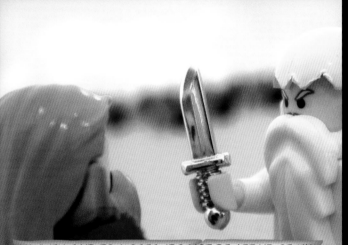

YAHWEH SAID TO MOSES, 'DO NOT BE AFRAID OF HIM, FOR I HAVE PUT HIM, ALL HIS PEOPLE, AND HIS LAND AT YOUR MERCY. TREAT HIM AS YOU TREATED KING SIHON OF THE AMORITES.'

SO THE ISRAELITES STRUCK DOWN KING OG OF BASHAN.

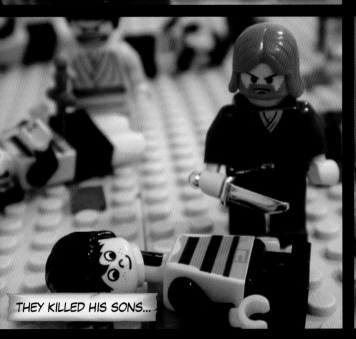

THEY KILLED HIS SONS....

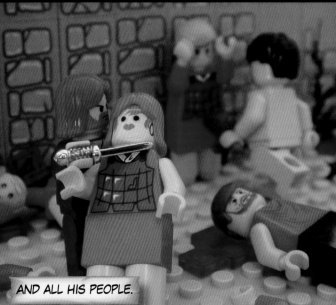

AND ALL HIS PEOPLE.

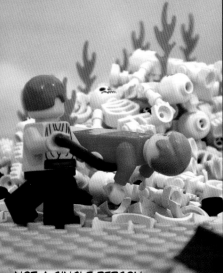

NOT A SINGLE PERSON WAS LEFT ALIVE.

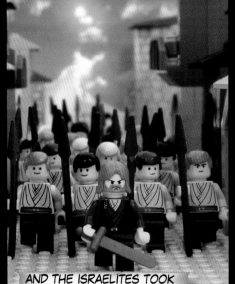

AND THE ISRAELITES TOOK POSSESSION OF THEIR LAND.

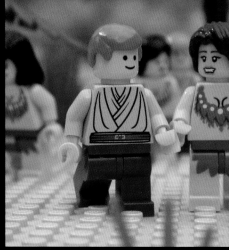

WHILE THE ISRAELITES WERE STAYING AT SHITTIM, THE MEN BEGAN LAYING WITH THE MOABITE WOMEN.

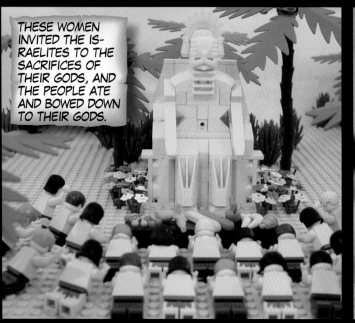

THESE WOMEN INVITED THE ISRAELITES TO THE SACRIFICES OF THEIR GODS, AND THE PEOPLE ATE AND BOWED DOWN TO THEIR GODS.

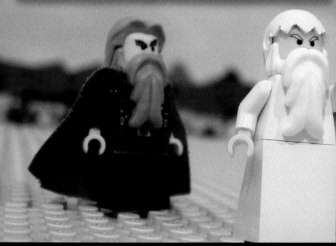

YAHWEH'S ANGER BLAZED AGAINST THEM. HE SAID TO MOSES, 'TAKE ALL THE LEADERS OF THE ISRAELITES AND IMPALE THEM FACING THE SUN SO YAHWEH'S ANGER WILL BE DIVERTED FROM THE ISRAELITES.'

MOSES SAID TO THE JUDGES OF ISRAEL, 'EACH OF YOU MUST PUT TO DEATH THOSE OF HIS PEOPLE WHO HAVE COMMITTED THEMSELVES TO THE BAAL OF PEOR.'

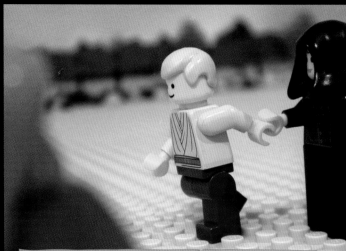

JUST THEN, ONE OF THE ISRAELITES CAME ALONG WITH A MIDIANITE WOMAN, RIGHT UNDER THE VERY EYES OF MOSES AND THE WHOLE COMMUNITY OF ISRAELITES AS THEY WERE WEEPING.

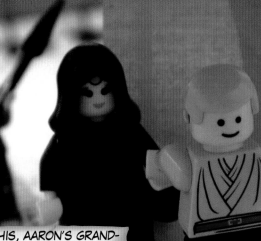

SEEING THIS, AARON'S GRAND-SON, PHINEAS THE PRIEST, GRABBED A SPEAR AND FOL-LOWED THE ISRAELITE INTO HIS TENT AND KILLED THEM BOTH.

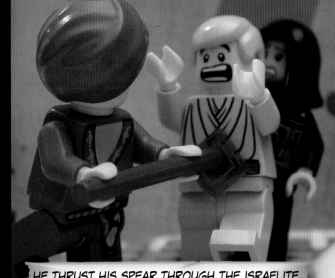

HE THRUST HIS SPEAR THROUGH THE ISRAELITE MAN AND INTO THE WOMAN'S STOMACH.

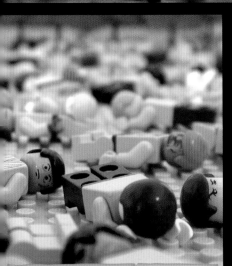

THUS THE PLAGUE WHICH HAD BEEN STRIKING THE ISRAELITES WAS STOPPED. THE PLAGUE HAD KILLED 24,000 ISRAELITES.

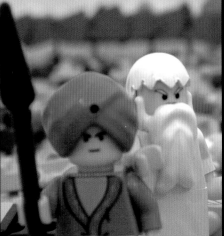

YAHWEH THEN SAID, 'PHINEAS THE PRIEST HAS TURNED MY WRATH FROM THE ISRAELITES. BECAUSE OF HIM I DID NOT DESTROY THE ISRAEL-ITES COMPLETELY.'

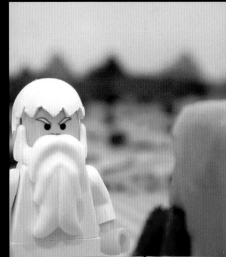

YAHWEH THEN SAID TO MOSES, 'TAKE VENGEANCE ON THE MIDIANITES AND KILL THEM. AFTER THAT YOU WILL BE GATHERED TO YOUR PEOPLE.'

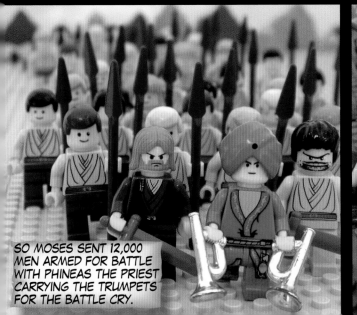

SO MOSES SENT 12,000 MEN ARMED FOR BATTLE WITH PHINEAS THE PRIEST CARRYING THE TRUMPETS FOR THE BATTLE CRY.

THEY ATTACKED THE MIDIANITES AS YAHWEH HAD ORDERED. AND THE ISRAELITES KILLED EVERY ONE OF THEIR MALES.

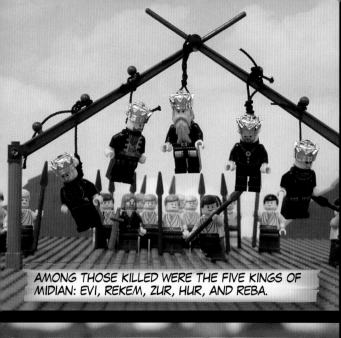

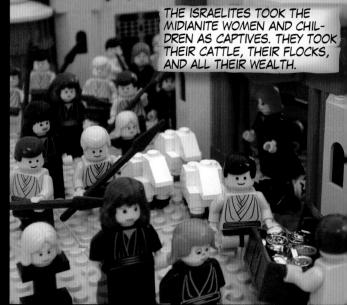

THE ISRAELITES TOOK THE MIDIANITE WOMEN AND CHILDREN AS CAPTIVES. THEY TOOK THEIR CATTLE, THEIR FLOCKS, AND ALL THEIR WEALTH.

AMONG THOSE KILLED WERE THE FIVE KINGS OF MIDIAN: EVI, REKEM, ZUR, HUR, AND REBA.

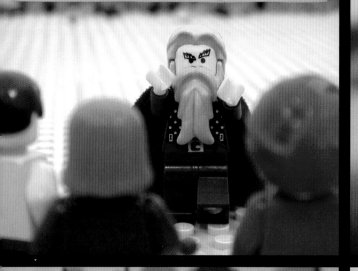

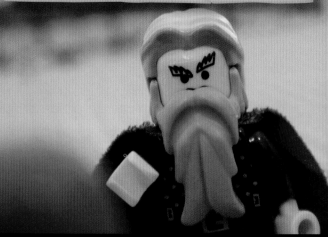

BUT MOSES WAS FURIOUS AT ARMY COMMANDERS WHO HAD RETURNED FROM THE BATTLE, SAYING, 'WHY HAVE YOU SPARED THE LIVES OF ALL THE WOMEN?'

'KILL ALL THE MALE CHILDREN! AND KILL ALL THE WOMEN WHO HAVE LAID WITH A MAN!' SAID MOSES. 'BUT SPARE THE LIVES OF THE YOUNG GIRLS WHO HAVE NEVER LAID WITH A MAN. KEEP THEM FOR YOURSELVES.'

THE WOMEN WHO HAD NEVER LAID WITH A MAN NUMBERED 32,000. HALF WERE ASSIGNED TO THOSE WHO HAD FOUGHT IN THE WAR.

YAHWEH'S PORTION WAS THIRTY-TWO. MOSES GAVE ELEAZAR THE PRIEST THE PORTION SET ASIDE FOR YAHWEH, AS YAHWEH HAD ORDERED MOSES.

DEUTERONOMY

MOSES CALLED ALL THE ISRAELITES TOGETHER AND SAID TO THEM, 'LISTEN, ISRAEL. WHEN YAHWEH YOUR GOD BRINGS YOU INTO THE LAND WHICH YOU ARE GOING TO POSSESS, MANY NATIONS MUST BE CLEARED AWAY.'

'YOU MUST PUT THEM ALL UNDER THE CURSE OF DESTRUCTION. YOU MUST NOT SPARE THE LIFE OF ANY LIVING THING. DESTROY ALL THE PEOPLE YAHWEH YOUR GOD PUTS AT YOUR MERCY. SHOW THEM NO PITY.'

MOSES SPOKE TO ALL ISRAEL AS FOLLOWS, 'TODAY I AM ONE HUNDRED AND TWENTY YEARS OLD AND CAN NO LONGER ACT AS LEADER. YAHWEH HAS TOLD ME, "YOU SHALL NOT CROSS THIS JORDAN."'

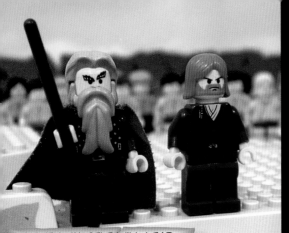

'YAHWEH HIMSELF WILL LEAD YOU ACROSS. HE HIMSELF WILL DESTROY AND DISPOSSESS THESE NATIONS. JOSHUA, TOO, WILL LEAD YOU ACROSS.'

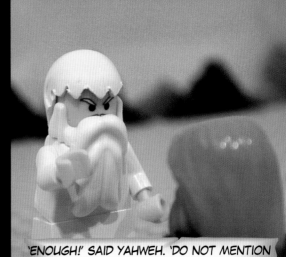

THEN YAHWEH SAID TO MOSES, 'CLIMB THIS MOUNTAIN, MOUNT NEBO, AND VIEW THE LAND OF CANAAN THAT I AM GIVING TO THE ISRAELITES. THEN DIE ON THE MOUNTAIN YOU HAVE CLIMBED.'

MOSES THEN PLEADED WITH YAHWEH, SAYING, 'MY LORD YAHWEH, MAY I NOT GO ACROSS AND SEE THE GOOD LAND ON THE OTHER SIDE OF THE JORDAN, THAT FINE HILL COUNTRY AND THE LEBANON?'

'ENOUGH!' SAID YAHWEH. 'DO NOT MENTION THE SUBJECT AGAIN. CLIMB TO THE TOP OF MOUNT PISGAH. LOOK WELL, FOR YOU SHALL NEVER GO ACROSS THE JORDAN.'

SO MOSES WENT UP MOUNT NEBO, AND YAHWEH SAID, 'THIS IS THE LAND I PROMISED ON OATH TO GIVE TO ABRAHAM, ISAAC, AND JACOB. I HAVE ALLOWED YOU TO SEE IT, BUT YOU WILL NOT CROSS INTO IT.'

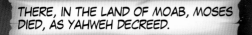

THERE, IN THE LAND OF MOAB, MOSES DIED, AS YAHWEH DECREED.

YAHWEH BURIED HIM IN THE LAND OF MOAB, IN THE VALLEY OPPOSITE BETH-PEOR. BUT TO THIS DAY, NO ONE HAS FOUND HIS GRAVE.

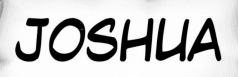

JOSHUA

WHEN MOSES WAS DEAD, YAHWEH SPOKE TO JOSHUA, SAYING, 'GO NOW AND CROSS THE JORDAN RIVER. YOU WILL LEAD THE PEOPLE TO TAKE POSSESSION OF THE LAND I SWORE TO THEIR ANCESTORS I WOULD GIVE THEM.'

SO JOSHUA SENT OUT TWO SPIES FROM SHITTIM, INSTRUCTING THEM, 'GO AND VIEW THE LAND, ESPECIALLY JERICHO.'

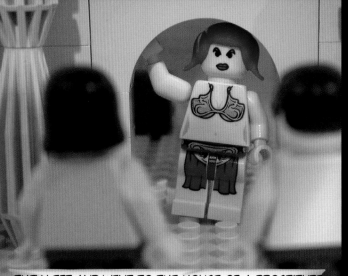

THEY LEFT AND WENT TO THE HOUSE OF A PROSTITUTE NAMED RAHAB, AND THEY SPENT THE NIGHT THERE.

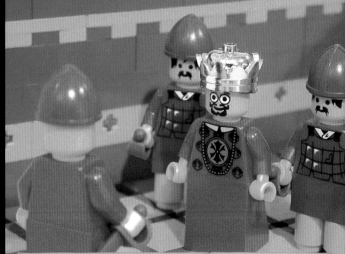

THE KING OF JERICHO WAS TOLD, 'SOME ISRAELITE MEN HAVE COME HERE TONIGHT TO SPY ON THE LAND.'

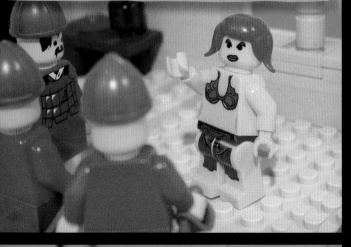

SO THE KING OF JERICHO SENT A MESSAGE TO RAHAB, BUT THE WOMAN HAD HIDDEN THE MEN. SHE SAID, 'YES, THE MEN CAME TO ME, BUT WHEN IT WAS TIME TO CLOSE THE CITY GATE AT NIGHT, THEY LEFT. HURRY AFTER THEM, AND YOU MAY CATCH THEM!'

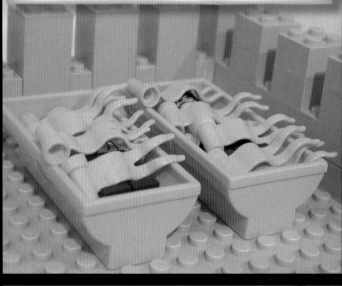

SHE HAD TAKEN THEM UP TO THE ROOF AND HIDDEN THEM UNDER THE STALKS OF FLAX SHE HAD LAID THERE.

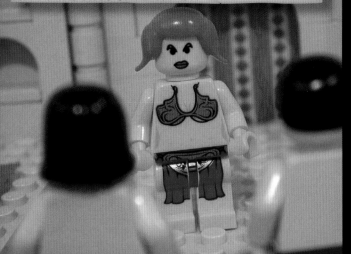

RAHAB SAID TO THEM, 'OUR PEOPLE ARE ABSOLUTELY TERRIFIED OF YOU. PLEASE SWEAR TO ME BY YAHWEH THAT, SINCE I HAVE BEEN KIND TO YOU, YOU WILL SPARE THE LIVES OF MY FAMILY.'

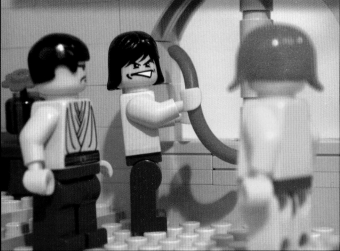

THE MEN SAID TO HER, 'WHEN WE INVADE THE LAND, GATHER YOUR FAMILY INSIDE YOUR HOUSE, AND TIE THIS SCARLET CORD IN THE WINDOW. IF ANYONE GOES OUTSIDE YOUR HOUSE, HIS BLOOD WILL BE ON HIS OWN HEAD.'

THEN RAHAB LET THEM DOWN FROM THE WINDOW ON A ROPE. HER HOUSE WAS BUILT AS PART OF THE CITY WALL.

WHEN THE PEOPLE LEFT THEIR TENTS TO CROSS THE JORDAN, THE PRIESTS CARRIED THE ARK OF THE COVENANT AHEAD OF THEM.

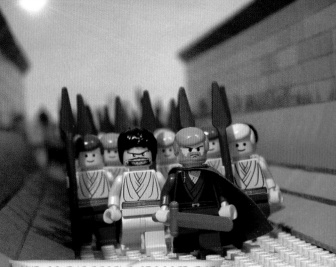

AS SOON AS THE FEET OF THE PRIESTS CARRYING THE ARK OF THE COVENANT TOUCHED THE WATER, THE WATER COMING DOWNSTREAM TOWARD THEM STOPPED.

AND SO THE PEOPLE CROSSED THE JORDAN OPPOSITE JERICHO.

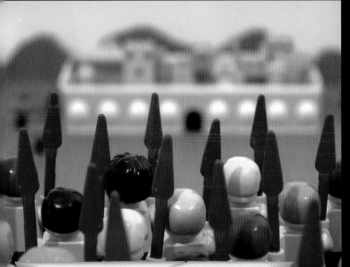

JERICHO SHUT ITSELF TIGHTLY BECAUSE OF THE ISRAELITES, WITH NO ONE ALLOWED IN OR OUT.

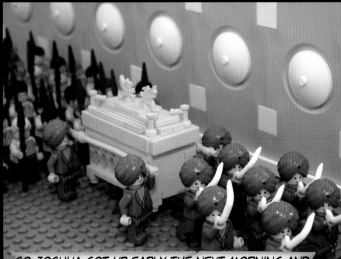

SO JOSHUA GOT UP EARLY THE NEXT MORNING AND HAD THE ARK GO AROUND THE CITY WITH SEVEN PRIESTS BLOWING THEIR TRUMPETS AND SOLDIERS MARCHING IN FRONT AND IN BACK OF THE ARK.

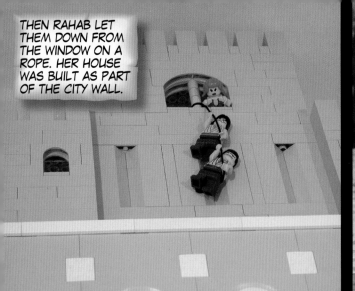

THEY DID THIS FOR SIX DAYS.

ON THE SEVENTH DAY, THEY CIRCLED THE CITY SEVEN TIMES.

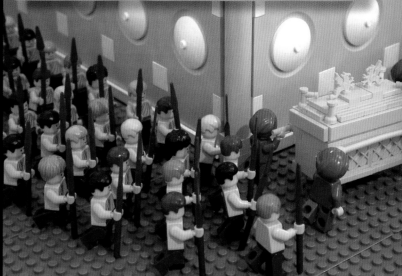

THE TRUMPETS SOUNDED, AND THE ARMY GAVE A MIGHTY WAR CRY.

THEN JOSHUA TOLD THE ARMY, 'THE CITY AND EVERYONE IN IT MUST BE OFFERED TO YAHWEH UNDER THE CURSE OF DESTRUCTION. ONLY SPARE RAHAB, THE PROSTITUTE, AND THOSE IN HER HOUSE.'

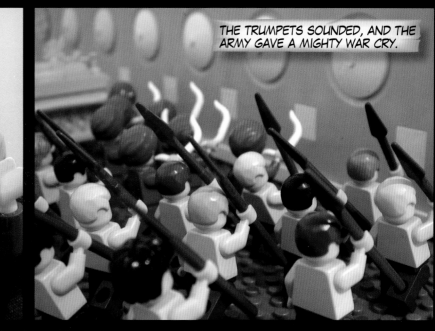

AND THE WALLS COLLAPSED.

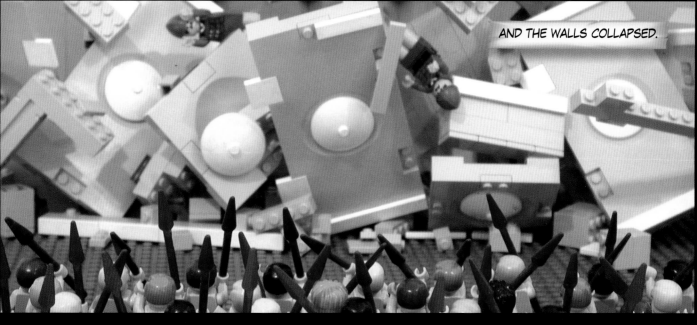

THE MEN CHARGED STRAIGHT INTO THE CITY TO DESTROY EVERY LIVING THING IN IT.

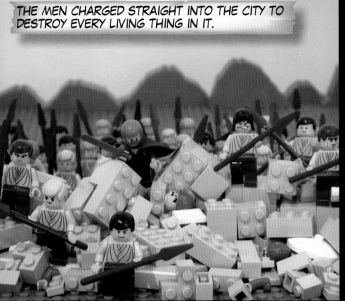

THE MEN AND WOMEN...

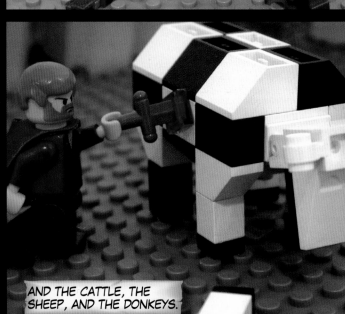

THE YOUNG AND OLD...

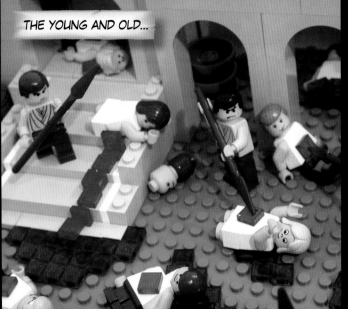

AND THE CATTLE, THE SHEEP, AND THE DONKEYS.

THE TWO SPIES WENT AND BROUGHT RAHAB AND HER FAMILY TO A PLACE OUTSIDE THE ISRAELITE CAMP.

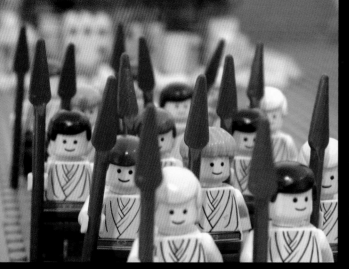

THEN THE ISRAELITES BURNED THE WHOLE CITY AND EVERYTHING IN IT.

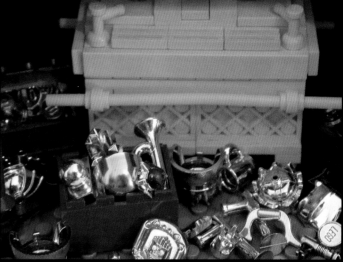

AND THEY PUT THE ITEMS OF SILVER, GOLD, BRONZE, AND IRON INTO YAHWEH'S TREASURY.

BUT THE ISRAELITES WERE UNFAITHFUL TO THE CURSE OF DESTRUCTION. ACHAN OF JUDAH TOOK SOMETHING THAT FELL UNDER THE CURSE OF DESTRUCTION.

AND YAHWEH WAS FURIOUS WITH THE ISRAELITES. EARLY THE NEXT MORNING, YAHWEH SINGLED OUT ACHAN OF JUDAH.

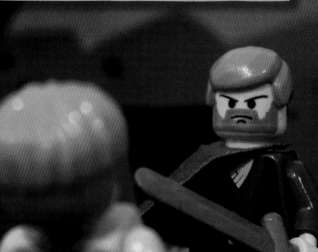

JOSHUA SAID TO ACHAN, 'MY SON, TELL ME WHAT YOU HAVE DONE, AND HIDE NOTHING FROM ME.'

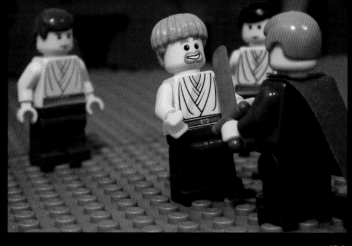

ACHAN SAID, 'AMONGST THE LOOT I SAW A BEAUTIFUL BABYLONIAN ROBE, TWO HUNDRED SHEKELS OF SILVER AND A GOLD BAR. THEY ARE HIDDEN IN THE GROUND IN MY TENT.'

THEN JOSHUA TOOK ACHAN, HIS SONS, HIS DAUGHTERS, HIS CATTLE, HIS DONKEYS, HIS SHEEP, AND HIS GOATS, AND BROUGHT THEM TO THE VALLEY OF ACHOR.

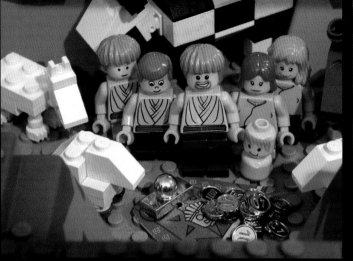

JOSHUA SAID, 'WHY HAVE YOU BROUGHT TROUBLE ON US? NOW YAHWEH WILL BRING TROUBLE ON YOU TODAY!'

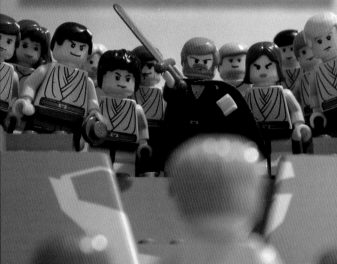

THEN THE ISRAELITES STONED THEM WITH STONES.

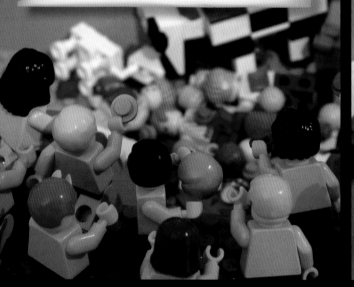

AND THEY BURNED THEM WITH FIRE. AND YAHWEH'S ANGER SUBSIDED.

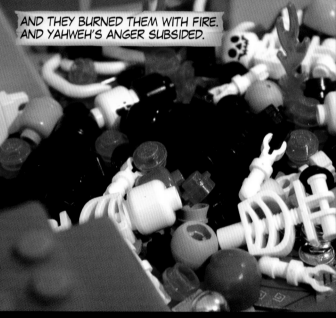

YAHWEH SAID TO JOSHUA, 'TAKE THE WHOLE ARMY TO ATTACK AI. DO TO AI WHAT YOU DID TO JERICHO, EXCEPT THIS TIME, TAKE THEIR LOOT AND THEIR CATTLE FOR YOURSELVES.'

EARLY THE NEXT MORNING, JOSHUA AND THE ARMY MARCHED NEAR TO THE FRONT OF THE CITY.

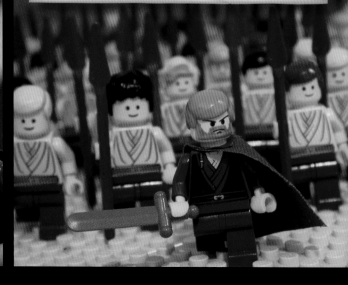

WHEN THE KING OF AI SAW THIS, HE AND ALL THE MEN OF THE CITY HURRIED OUT TO MEET ISRAEL IN BATTLE.

JOSHUA AND ALL ISRAEL ALLOWED THEMSELVES BE DRIVEN BACK, AND THEY FLED TOWARD THE DESERT. THEY CHASED JOSHUA AND WERE LURED AWAY FROM THE CITY.

NOT A SINGLE MAN WAS LEFT IN AI, LEAVING THE CITY UNDEFENDED.

THE MEN IN AMBUSH THEN ROSE UP AND TOOK THE CITY, AND IMMEDIATELY SET IT ON FIRE.

WHEN THE MEN OF AI TURNED AROUND, THEY SAW THE SMOKE FROM THE CITY RISING INTO THE SKY AND WERE TOO SHOCKED TO RUN IN ANY DIRECTION.

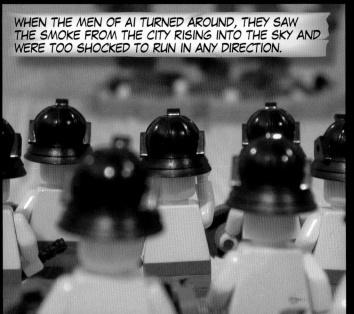

THEN JOSHUA AND THE ISRAELITES TURNED AND ATTACKED THE MEN OF AI.

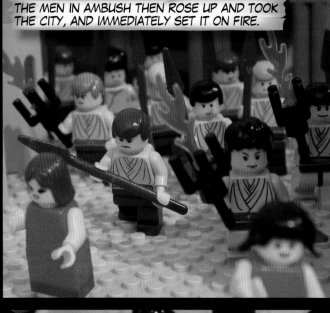

THE ISRAELITES STRUCK THEM DOWN UNTIL THERE WAS NO ONE LEFT ALIVE AND NONE WHO ESCAPED.

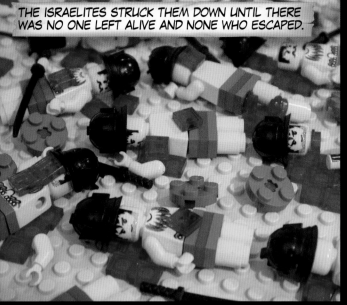

BUT THEY CAPTURED THE KING OF AI ALIVE AND BROUGHT HIM TO JOSHUA.

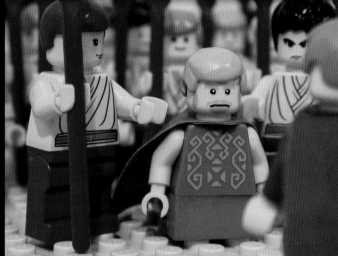

JOSHUA HUNG THE KING OF AI ON A TREE AND LEFT HIM THERE UNTIL EVENING.

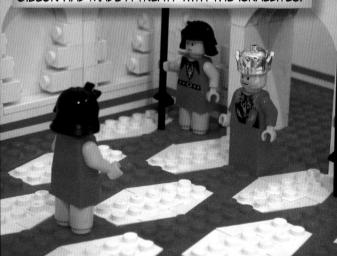

THE NUMBER OF PEOPLE WHO WERE KILLED THAT DAY, MEN AND WOMEN, WAS 12,000, THE ENTIRE POPULATION OF AI.

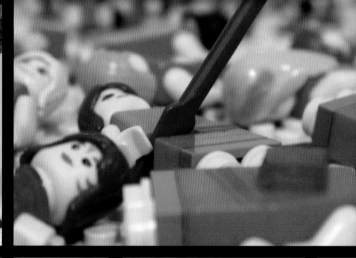

THE KING OF JERUSALEM HEARD HOW JOSHUA HAD UTTERLY DESTROYED JERICHO AND AI AND HOW GIBEON HAD MADE A TREATY WITH THE ISRAELITES.

SO HE SENT THIS MESSAGE TO THE KINGS OF HE-BRON, JARMUTH, LACHISH, AND EGLON: 'COME TO MY AID SO WE CAN ATTACK JOSHUA AND THE ISRAELITES.'

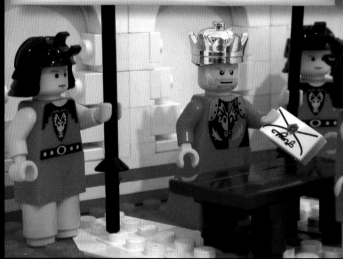

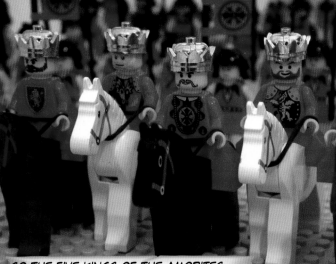

SO THE FIVE KINGS OF THE AMORITES
JOINED FORCES AND SET OUT TO ATTACK.

AND JOSHUA MARCHED UP FROM
GILGAL WITH HIS ENTIRE ARMY,
ALL HIS BRAVEST WARRIORS.

AND YAHWEH SAID TO JOSHUA,
'DO NOT BE AFRAID OF THESE
PEOPLE. I AM PUTTING THEM AT
YOUR MERCY. NOT ONE OF THEM
WILL PUT UP ANY RESISTANCE.'

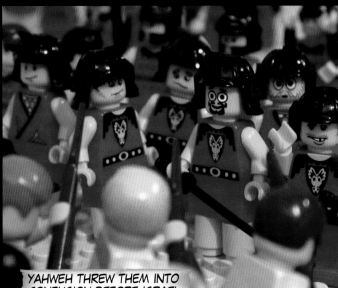

YAHWEH THREW THEM INTO
CONFUSION BEFORE ISRAEL.

AND ISRAEL THOROUGHLY
DEFEATED THEM AT GIBEON.

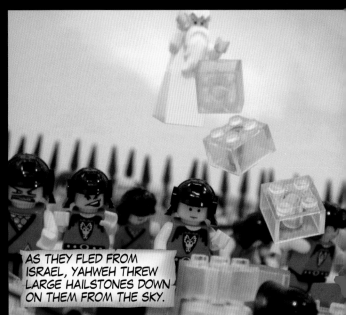

AS THEY FLED FROM
ISRAEL, YAHWEH THREW
LARGE HAILSTONES DOWN
ON THEM FROM THE SKY.

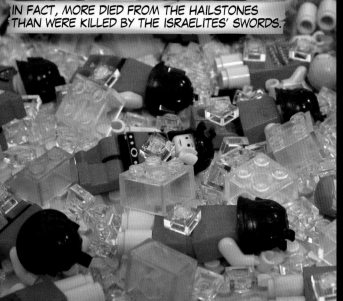

IN FACT, MORE DIED FROM THE HAILSTONES THAN WERE KILLED BY THE ISRAELITES' SWORDS.

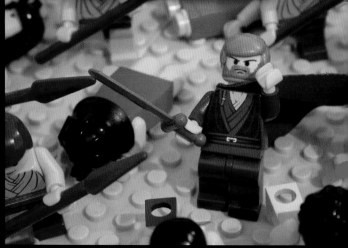

THEN, IN THE PRESENCE OF THE PEOPLE, JOSHUA SAID TO YAHWEH, 'O SUN, STAND STILL OVER GIBEON!'

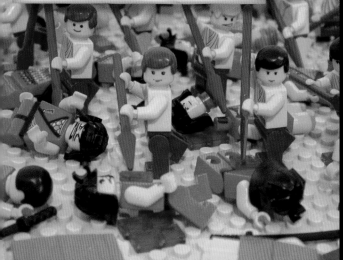

AND SO THE SUN STOOD STILL WHILE THE NATION TOOK VENGEANCE ON ITS ENEMIES.

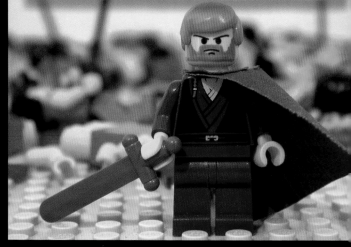

THE SUN STOOD STILL IN THE MIDDLE OF THE SKY AND DELAYED GOING DOWN ABOUT A FULL DAY. THERE HAS NEVER BEEN A DAY LIKE IT BEFORE OR SINCE, A DAY WHEN YAHWEH OBEYED THE VOICE OF A MAN.

THE FIVE AMORITE KINGS HAD FLED AND WERE HIDING IN THE CAVE AT MAKKEDAH.

SO THEY BROUGHT THE FIVE KINGS OUT OF THE CAVE - THE KINGS OF JERUSALEM, HEBRON, JARMUTH, LACHISH AND EGLON.

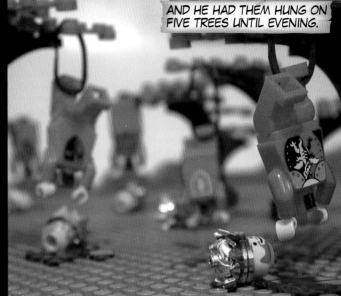

JOSHUA THEN STRUCK AND KILLED ALL THE KINGS.

AND HE HAD THEM HUNG ON FIVE TREES UNTIL EVENING.

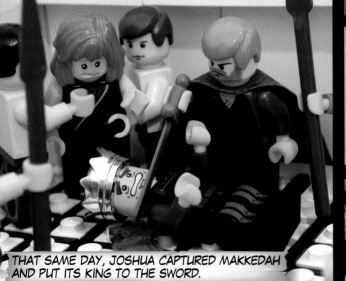

THAT SAME DAY, JOSHUA CAPTURED MAKKEDAH AND PUT ITS KING TO THE SWORD.

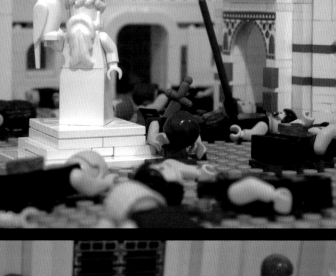

HE ANNIHILATED EVERYONE WHO LIVED THERE AND LEFT NO SURVIVORS.

THEN JOSHUA AND ALL ISRAEL MARCHED FROM MAKKEDAH TO LIBNAH AND ATTACKED IT.

ISRAEL PUT THE SWORD TO ALL WHO LIVED THERE AND THEY LEFT NO SURVIVORS.

THEY DID TO ITS KING WHAT THEY HAD DONE TO THE KING OF JERICHO.

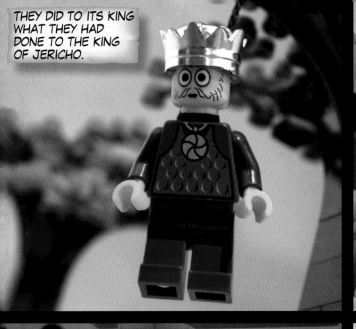

THEN JOSHUA AND ALL ISRAEL MARCHED FROM LIBNAH TO LACHISH AND ATTACKED IT.

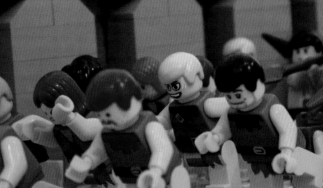

THEY PUT THE SWORD TO ALL WHO LIVED THERE, JUST AS THEY HAD DONE TO LIBNAH.

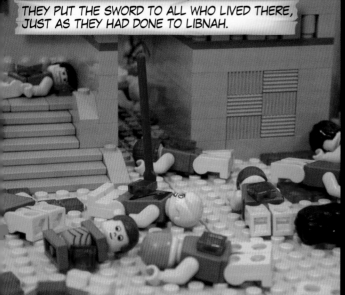

MEANWHILE, KING HORAM OF GEZER CAME UP TO HELP LACHISH.

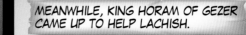
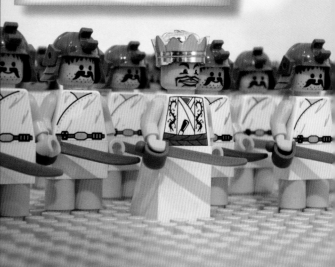

BUT JOSHUA STRUCK DOWN HIM AND HIS ARMY UNTIL THERE WAS NO ONE LEFT ALIVE.

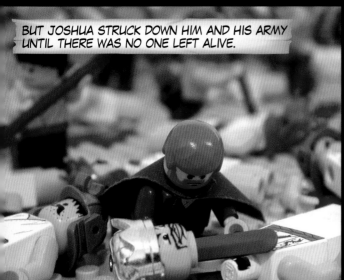

THEN JOSHUA AND ALL ISRAEL MARCHED FROM LACHISH TO EGLON AND ATTACKED IT.

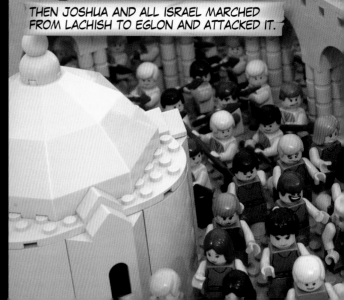

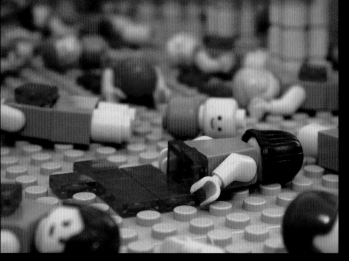

THEY CAPTURED IT AND PUT THE SWORD TO ALL WHO LIVED THERE, UTTERLY DESTROYING EVERYONE IN IT, JUST AS THEY HAD DONE TO LACHISH.

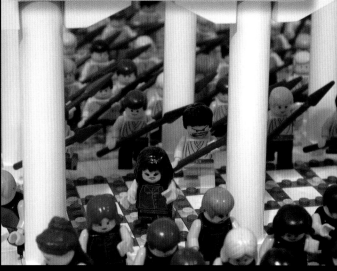

THEN JOSHUA AND ALL ISRAEL MARCHED UP FROM EGLON TO HEBRON AND ATTACKED IT.

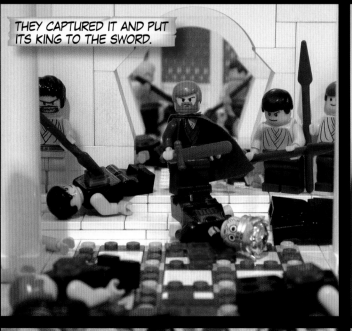

THEY CAPTURED IT AND PUT ITS KING TO THE SWORD.

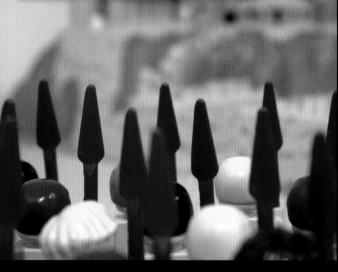

THEN JOSHUA AND ALL ISRAEL TURNED TO DEBIR AND ATTACKED IT.

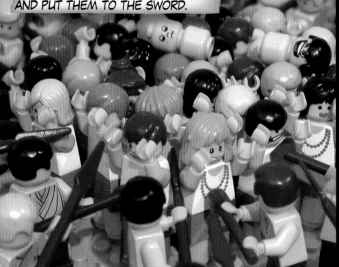

THEY CAPTURED DEBIR AND ITS KING AND ALL ITS SURROUNDING TOWNS AND PUT THEM TO THE SWORD.

THEY UTTERLY DESTROYED EVERYONE WHO LIVED THERE AND LEFT NO ONE ALIVE.

THEY DID TO DEBIR AND ITS KING WHAT THEY HAD DONE TO HEBRON AND TO LIBNAH AND THEIR KINGS.

THUS, JOSHUA STRUCK THE WHOLE COUNTRY. HE LEFT NOT ONE SURVIVOR, AS YAHWEH, GOD OF ISRAEL, HAD COMMANDED.

JOSHUA THEN TURNED AROUND AND CAPTURED HAZOR, PUTTING ITS KING TO THE SWORD.

IN ACCORDANCE WITH THE CURSE OF DESTRUCTION, EVERYONE WHO LIVED THERE WAS PUT TO THE SWORD, NOT SPARING ANYTHING THAT BREATHED.

AND HE BURNED HAZOR TO THE GROUND. HAZOR HAD BEEN THE CAPITAL OF ALL THESE KINGDOMS.

THE ISRAELITES DID NOT BURN ALL THE CITIES BUILT ON MOUNDS, JUST HAZOR. BUT THEY PLUNDERED ALL THE LOOT OF THESE CITIES AND TOOK THEIR CATTLE.

AND THEY UTTERLY DESTROYED ALL THE HUMAN BEINGS, NOT SPARING A SINGLE SOUL.

THIS WAS HOW YAHWEH GAVE ISRAEL ALL THE LAND HE HAD SWORN TO GIVE THEIR ANCESTORS, AND THEY TOOK POSSESSION OF IT AND SETTLED IN IT.

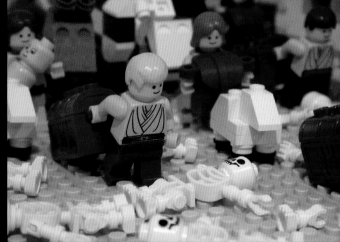

YAHWEH PROVIDED TRANQUILITY ON ALL THEIR FRONTIERS, JUST AS HE HAD SWORN TO THEIR ANCESTORS. OF ALL THE PROMISES THAT YAHWEH HAD MADE TO THE FAMILY OF ISRAEL, NOT ONE FAILED: ALL WERE FULFILLED.

A LONG TIME PASSED, AND JOSHUA WAS VERY OLD. HE SUMMONED ALL ISRAEL AND SAID, 'JUST AS YAHWEH HAS FULFILLED EVERY PROMISE MADE TO YOU, YAHWEH WILL ALSO FULFILL EVERY THREAT MADE AGAINST YOU, UNTIL HE DESTROYS YOU FROM THIS GOOD LAND WHICH HE HAS GIVEN YOU.'

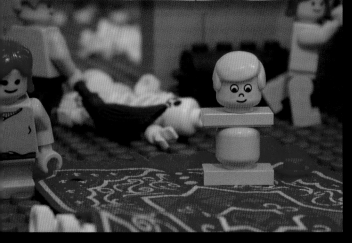

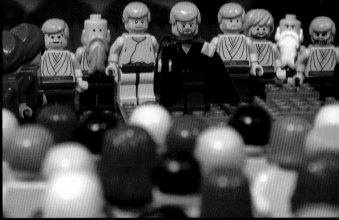

'YAHWEH IS A JEALOUS GOD AND WILL NOT FORGIVE YOUR TRANSGRESSIONS OR YOUR SINS. IF YOU WORSHIP A FOREIGN GOD, HE WILL BRING DISASTER ON YOU AND DESTROY YOU.'

AFTER THIS, JOSHUA DIED AT THE AGE OF ONE HUNDRED AND TEN.

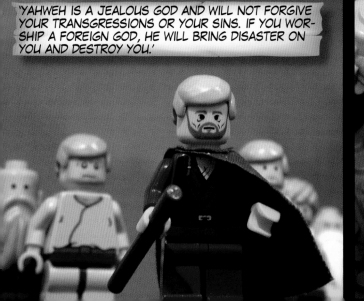

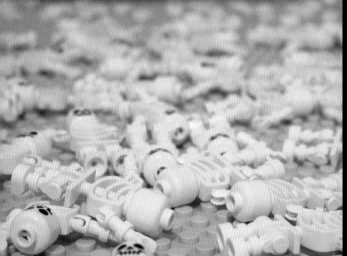

JUDGES

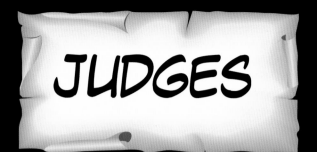

AFTER JOSHUA DIED, THE ISRAELITES ASKED YAHWEH, 'WHO IS TO LEAD THE INVASION AGAINST THE CANAANITES?'

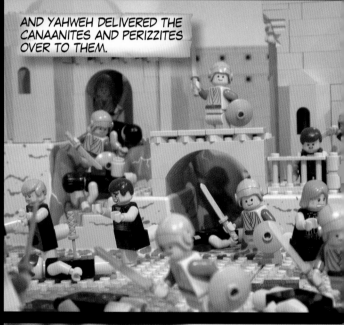

YAHWEH SAID, 'THE TRIBE OF JUDAH IS TO ATTACK FIRST. I WILL DELIVER THE LAND INTO THEIR HANDS.'

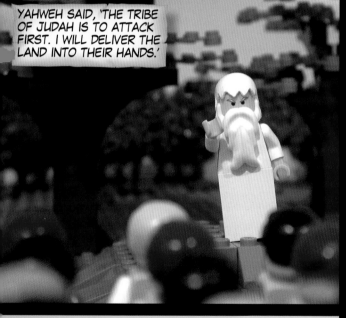

AND YAHWEH DELIVERED THE CANAANITES AND PERIZZITES OVER TO THEM.

AT BEZEK, THEY FOUND ADONI-BEZEK AND FOUGHT AGAINST HIM.

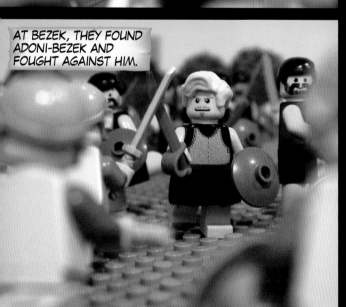

THEY DEFEATED THE CANAANITES AND PERIZZITES.

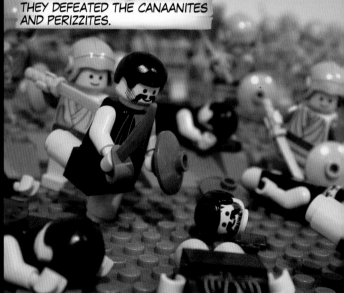

THEY KILLED 10,000 MEN AT BEZEK.

ADONI-BEZEK RAN AWAY, BUT THEY CHASED HIM DOWN AND CAPTURED HIM.

THEN THEY CUT OFF HIS THUMBS AND HIS BIG TOES.

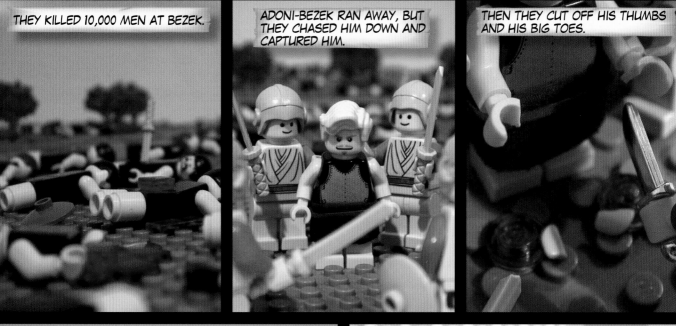

THEN THE MEN OF JUDAH ATTACKED JERUSALEM.

THEY CAPTURED IT AND KILLED EVERYONE WHO LIVED THERE.

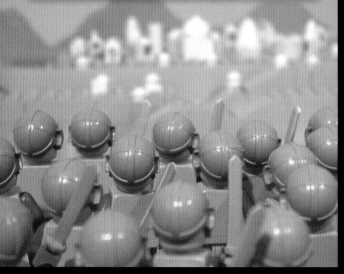

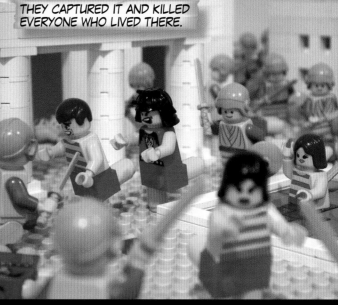

AND THEY BURNED IT TO THE GROUND.

THE MEN OF JUDAH AND THE MEN OF SIMEON THEN ATTACKED THE CANAANITES WHO LIVED IN ZEPHATH.

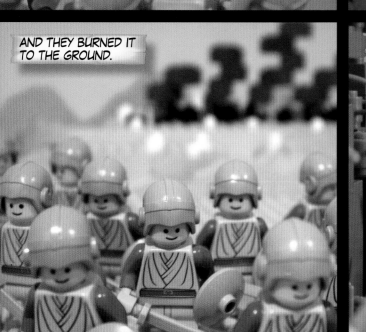

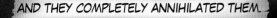

AND THEY COMPLETELY ANNIHILATED THEM.

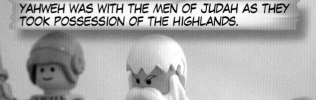

YAHWEH WAS WITH THE MEN OF JUDAH AS THEY TOOK POSSESSION OF THE HIGHLANDS.

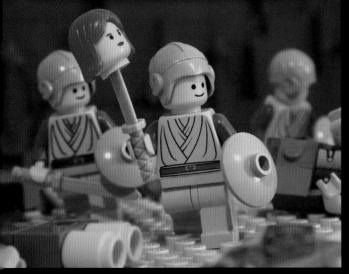

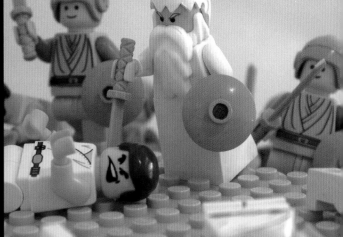

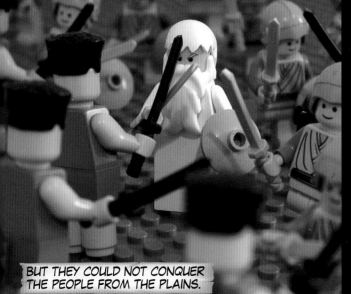

BUT THEY COULD NOT CONQUER THE PEOPLE FROM THE PLAINS.

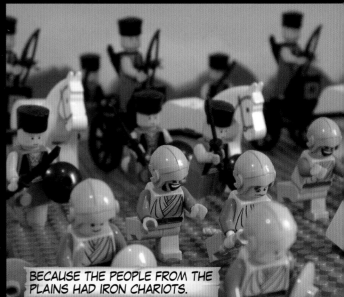

BECAUSE THE PEOPLE FROM THE PLAINS HAD IRON CHARIOTS.

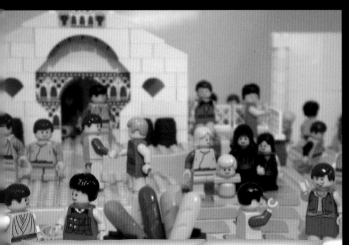

AFTER JOSHUA'S GENERATION DIED, A NEW GENERATION AROSE THAT DID NOT KNOW YAHWEH OR WHAT HE HAD DONE FOR ISRAEL. AND THE ISRAELITES DWELT AMONGST THE CANAANITES, HITTITES, AMORITES, PERIZZITES, HIVITES, AND JEBUSITES.

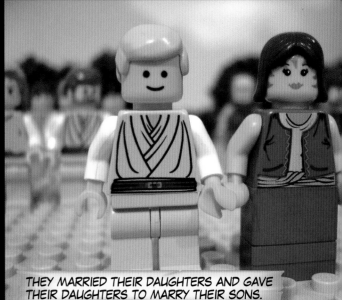

THEY MARRIED THEIR DAUGHTERS AND GAVE THEIR DAUGHTERS TO MARRY THEIR SONS.

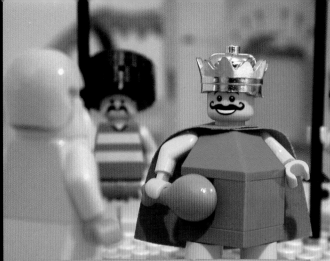

THEY FORGOT YAHWEH AND WORSHIPED THEIR GODS, THE BAALS AND ASHERAS.

AND YAHWEH'S ANGER BLAZED AGAINST ISRAEL. YAHWEH GAVE KING EGLON OF MOAB POWER OVER ISRAEL. KING EGLON WAS A VERY FAT MAN.

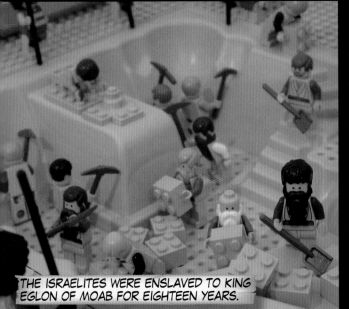

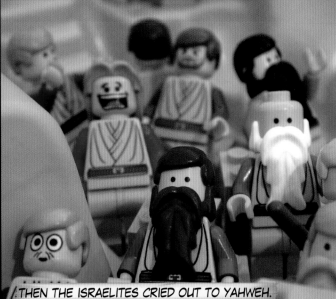

THE ISRAELITES WERE ENSLAVED TO KING EGLON OF MOAB FOR EIGHTEEN YEARS.

THEN THE ISRAELITES CRIED OUT TO YAHWEH.

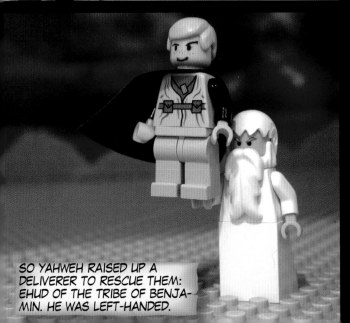

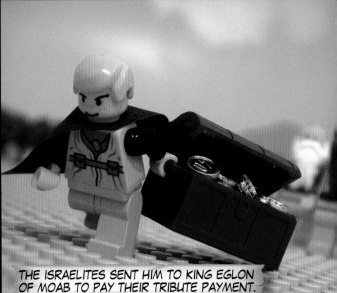

SO YAHWEH RAISED UP A DELIVERER TO RESCUE THEM: EHUD OF THE TRIBE OF BENJAMIN. HE WAS LEFT-HANDED.

THE ISRAELITES SENT HIM TO KING EGLON OF MOAB TO PAY THEIR TRIBUTE PAYMENT.

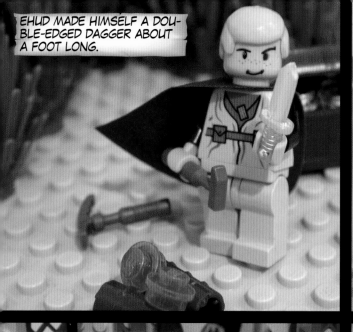

EHUD MADE HIMSELF A DOU-
BLE-EDGED DAGGER ABOUT
A FOOT LONG.

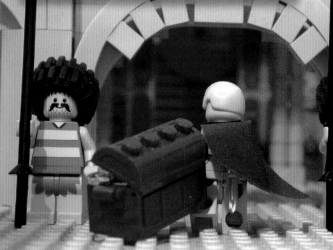

HE STRAPPED THE DAGGER UNDER HIS CLOAK
ON HIS RIGHT THIGH AND BROUGHT THE TRIBUTE
PAYMENT TO KING EGLON OF MOAB.

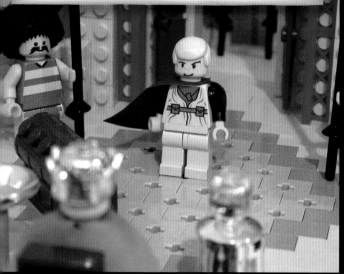

AFTER PRESENTING THE TRIBUTE, EHUD SAID TO KING
EGLON, 'I HAVE A SECRET MESSAGE FOR YOU, O KING.'

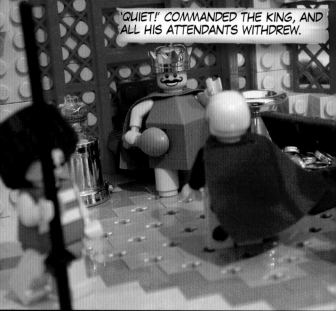

'QUIET!' COMMANDED THE KING, AND
ALL HIS ATTENDANTS WITHDREW.

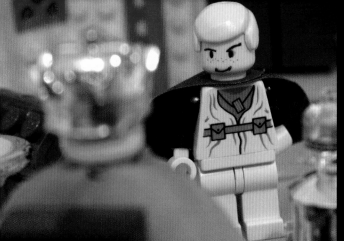

EHUD APPROACHED HIM WHILE THE KING SAT ALONE
IN THE COOL OF HIS UPSTAIRS ROOM AND SAID, 'I
HAVE A MESSAGE FOR YOU FROM GOD.'

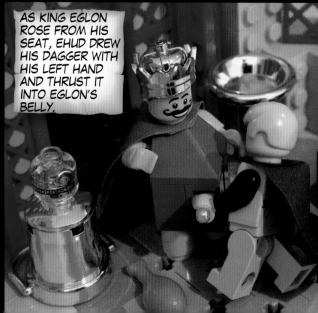

AS KING EGLON
ROSE FROM HIS
SEAT, EHUD DREW
HIS DAGGER WITH
HIS LEFT HAND
AND THRUST IT
INTO EGLON'S
BELLY.

THE HANDLE WENT IN AFTER THE BLADE, AND THE FAT CLOSED OVER IT. EHUD DID NOT PULL THE DAGGER OUT OF HIS BELLY.

EHUD ESCAPED THROUGH THE LATRINE, HAVING LOCKED THE DOORS OF THE UPSTAIRS ROOM BEHIND HIM.

AFTER HE HAD GONE, KING EGLON'S SERVANTS CAME AND FOUND THE DOORS TO THE UPSTAIRS ROOM LOCKED. THEY SAID, 'HE MUST BE RELIEVING HIMSELF IN THE LATRINE.'

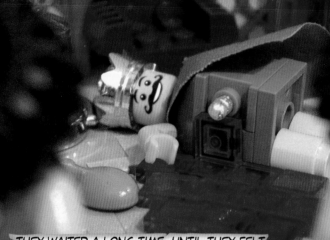

THEY WAITED A LONG TIME, UNTIL THEY FELT EMBARRASSED, AND THEN USED A KEY TO OPEN THE DOORS. AND THERE WAS THEIR MASTER, LYING DEAD ON THE FLOOR.

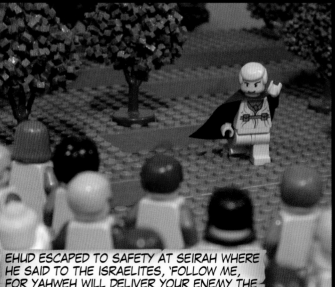

EHUD ESCAPED TO SAFETY AT SEIRAH WHERE HE SAID TO THE ISRAELITES, 'FOLLOW ME, FOR YAHWEH WILL DELIVER YOUR ENEMY THE MOABITES INTO YOUR HANDS!'

THEY FOLLOWED HIM AND CAPTURED THE FORDS OF THE JORDAN RIVER OPPOSITE MOAB.

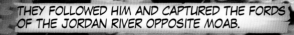

THEY KILLED ABOUT 10,000 MOABITES THAT DAY, ALL STRONG, CAPABLE FIGHTERS. NOT ONE OF THEM ESCAPED.

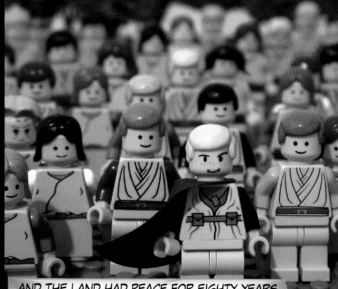

AND THE LAND HAD PEACE FOR EIGHTY YEARS.

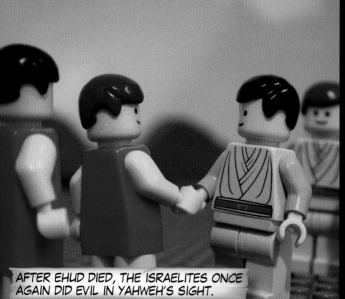

AFTER EHUD DIED, THE ISRAELITES ONCE AGAIN DID EVIL IN YAHWEH'S SIGHT.

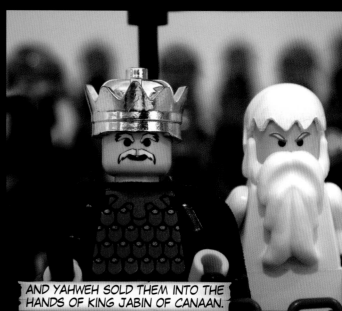

AND YAHWEH SOLD THEM INTO THE HANDS OF KING JABIN OF CANAAN.

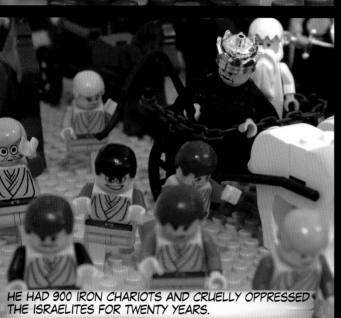

HE HAD 900 IRON CHARIOTS AND CRUELLY OPPRESSED THE ISRAELITES FOR TWENTY YEARS.

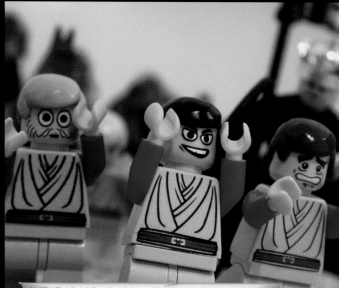

AND THE ISRAELITES CRIED OUT TO YAHWEH.

DEBORAH WAS JUDGE OF ISRAEL AT THE TIME. SHE SUMMONED BARAK OF NAPHTALI AND SAID TO HIM, 'YAHWEH COMMANDS YOU: "TAKE TEN THOUSAND MEN TO MOUNT TABOR. I WILL LURE SISERA, THE GENERAL OF JABIN'S ARMY, AND GIVE HIM INTO YOUR HANDS."'

BARAK SAID TO HER, 'IF YOU GO WITH ME, I WILL GO. BUT IF YOU DO NOT GO WITH ME, I WILL NOT GO.'

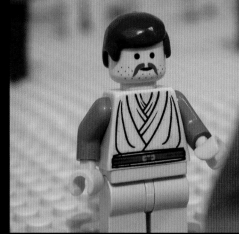

DEBORAH SAID, 'YES, I WILL GO WITH YOU. BUT THE WAY YOU ARE GOING ABOUT THIS, YOU WILL NOT WIN GLORY. YAHWEH WILL GIVE SISERA INTO THE HANDS OF A WOMAN.'

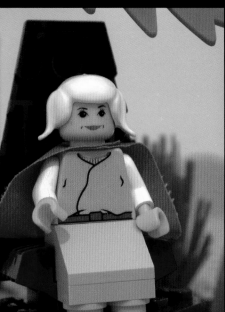

BARAK SUMMONED MEN FROM THE TRIBES OF ZEBULUN AND NAPHTALI, AND 10,000 MEN FOLLOWED HIM.

WHEN SISERA HEARD THAT BARAK WAS ENCAMPED AT MOUNT TABOR, HE SUMMONED HIS NINE HUNDRED IRON CHARIOTS AND ALL HIS TROOPS.

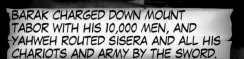

BARAK CHARGED DOWN MOUNT TABOR WITH HIS 10,000 MEN, AND YAHWEH ROUTED SISERA AND ALL HIS CHARIOTS AND ARMY BY THE SWORD.

SISERA LEAPT FROM HIS CHARIOT AND FLED ON FOOT.

SISERA'S ENTIRE ARMY DIED BY THE SWORD. NOT ONE MAN SURVIVED.

SISERA FLED ON FOOT TOWARD THE TENT OF JAEL, AND SHE CAME OUT TO MEET SISERA AND SAID, 'COME, MY LORD, AND REST HERE. DO NOT BE AFRAID.'

SO SISERA ENTERED HER TENT TO REST, AND SHE PUT A BLANKET OVER HIM.

THEN JAEL TOOK A TENT PEG IN ONE HAND AND A HAMMER IN THE OTHER. SHE CREPT UP SOFTLY TO HIM WHILE HE WAS ASLEEP FROM EXHAUSTION.

AND SHE DROVE THE TENT PEG THROUGH HIS TEMPLE. SHE SHATTERED HIS SKULL, CRUSHING HIS HEAD.

AND THE LAND WAS AT PEACE FOR FORTY YEARS.

AGAIN, THE ISRAELITES DID EVIL IN YAHWEH'S SIGHT.

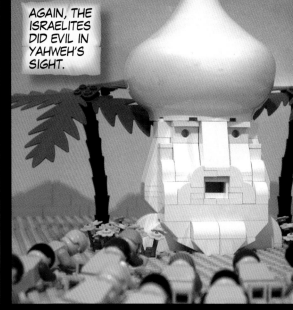

AND YAHWEH SOLD THEM INTO THE HANDS OF THE MIDIANITES FOR SEVEN YEARS.

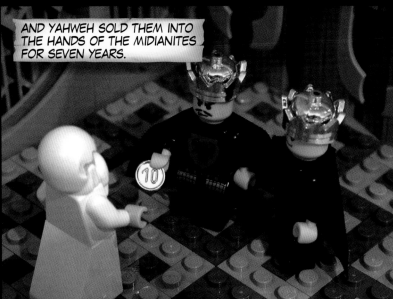

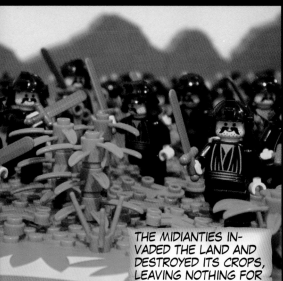

THE MIDIANTIES INVADED THE LAND AND DESTROYED ITS CROPS, LEAVING NOTHING FOR THE ISRAELITES TO EAT.

THE ISRAELITES WERE LEFT SO IMPOVERISHED THAT THEY CRIED OUT TO YAHWEH.

THE SPIRIT OF YAHWEH CAME UPON GIDEON, AND HE BLEW A TRUMPET, SUMMONING THE MEN OF THE ABIEZRITE CLAN TO FOLLOW HIM. HE SENT MESSENGERS THROUGHOUT MANASSEH AND TO THE TRIBES OF ASHER, ZEBULUN, AND NAPHTALI, AND THEY TOO CAME UP TO MEET HIM.

YAHWEH THEN SAID TO GIDEON, 'YOU HAVE TOO MANY MEN WITH YOU FOR ME TO HAND OVER THE MIDIANITES. ANNOUNCE TO THE MEN, "ANYONE TREMBLING WITH FEAR MAY LEAVE."'

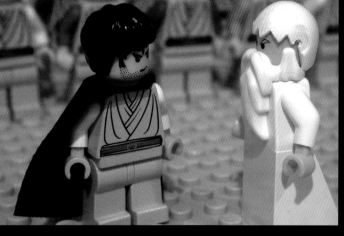

AND 22,000 MEN LEFT.

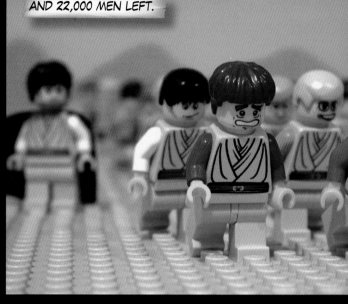

10,000 MEN REMAINED AND YAHWEH SAID TO GIDEON, 'THERE ARE STILL TOO MANY MEN. BRING THEM DOWN TO THE WATER, AND I WILL SORT THEM OUT FOR YOU THERE.'

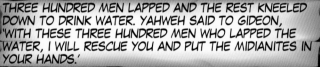

SO HE BROUGHT THE MEN DOWN TO THE WATER, AND THEN YAHWEH SAID TO GIDEON, 'SEPARATE THOSE WHO LAP UP THE WATER LIKE DOGS FROM THOSE WHO KNEEL DOWN TO DRINK.'

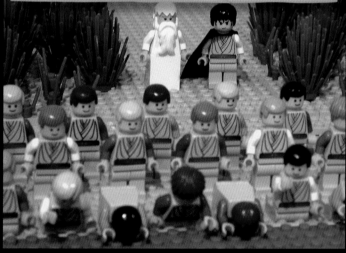

THREE HUNDRED MEN LAPPED AND THE REST KNEELED DOWN TO DRINK WATER. YAHWEH SAID TO GIDEON, 'WITH THESE THREE HUNDRED MEN WHO LAPPED THE WATER, I WILL RESCUE YOU AND PUT THE MIDIANITES IN YOUR HANDS.'

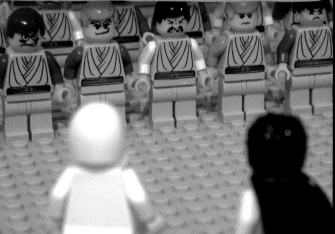

GIDEON DIVIDED THE THREE HUNDRED MEN INTO THREE GROUPS, GIVING EACH A TRUMPET AND AN EMPTY JAR WITH A TORCH INSIDE.

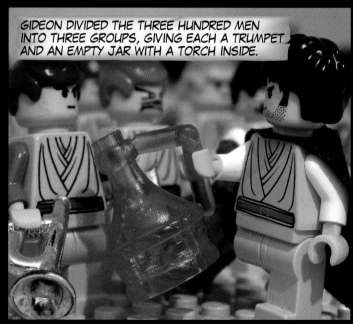

THE MIDIANITES WERE CAMPED BELOW IN THE VALLEY. GIDEON SAID TO THE MEN, 'WHEN I GET TO THE EDGE OF THE CAMP AND I BLOW MY TRUMPET, YOU ALSO BLOW THE TRUMPETS ALL AROUND THE CAMP AND SHOUT.'

GIDEON AND THE HUNDRED MEN WITH HIM REACHED THE EDGE OF THE CAMP. THEY BLEW THEIR TRUMPETS AND BROKE THE JARS THAT WERE IN THEIR HANDS.

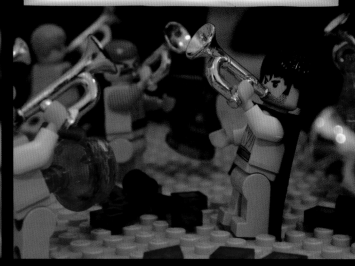

THROUGHOUT THE CAMP, YAHWEH CAUSED THE MIDIANITES TO ATTACK ONE ANOTHER WITH THEIR SWORDS.

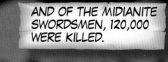
AND OF THE MIDIANITE SWORDSMEN, 120,000 WERE KILLED.

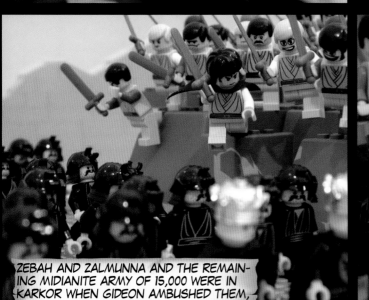
ZEBAH AND ZALMUNNA AND THE REMAINING MIDIANITE ARMY OF 15,000 WERE IN KARKOR WHEN GIDEON AMBUSHED THEM, TAKING THEM BY SURPRISE.

AND HE CAPTURED THE TWO MIDIANITE KINGS, ZEBAH AND ZALMUNNA.

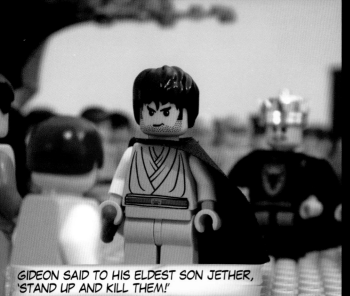

GIDEON SAID TO HIS ELDEST SON JETHER, 'STAND UP AND KILL THEM!'

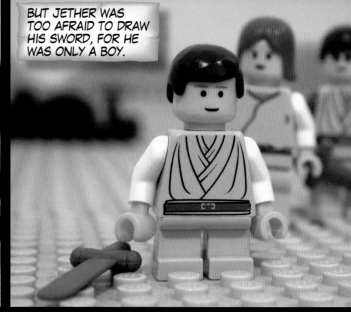

BUT JETHER WAS TOO AFRAID TO DRAW HIS SWORD, FOR HE WAS ONLY A BOY.

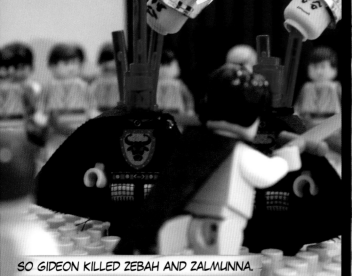

SO GIDEON KILLED ZEBAH AND ZALMUNNA.

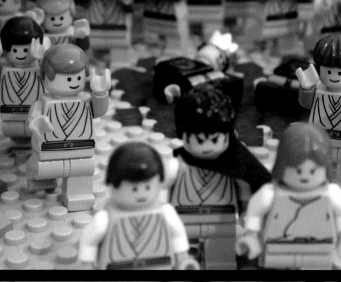

AND THE LAND WAS AT PEACE FOR FORTY YEARS.

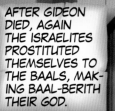

AFTER GIDEON DIED, AGAIN THE ISRAELITES PROSTITUTED THEMSELVES TO THE BAALS, MAKING BAAL-BERITH THEIR GOD.

YAHWEH SOLD THEM INTO THE HANDS OF THE AMMONITES, AND THEY BRUTALLY OPPRESSED THE ISRAELITES FOR EIGHTEEN YEARS.

THEN THE ISRAELITES CRIED OUT TO YAHWEH, SAYING, 'WE HAVE SINNED AGAINST YOU, FORSAKING OUR GOD AND WORSHIPPING THE BAALS.'

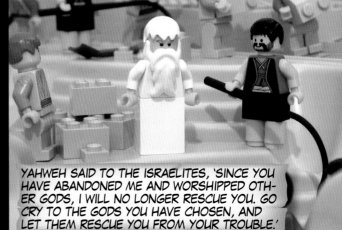

YAHWEH SAID TO THE ISRAELITES, 'SINCE YOU HAVE ABANDONED ME AND WORSHIPPED OTHER GODS, I WILL NO LONGER RESCUE YOU. GO CRY TO THE GODS YOU HAVE CHOSEN, AND LET THEM RESCUE YOU FROM YOUR TROUBLE.'

BUT FINALLY YAHWEH GREW TIRED OF SEEING THE ISRAELITES SUFFER, AND THE SPIRIT OF YAHWEH CAME UPON JEPHTHAH, THE GREAT WARRIOR FROM GILEAD.

JEPHTHAH MADE A VOW TO YAHWEH, SAYING, 'IF YOU DELIVER THE AMMONITES INTO MY HANDS, I WILL OFFER AS A BURNT SACRIFICE TO YAHWEH THE FIRST THING THAT COMES OUT OF THE DOOR OF MY HOUSE TO GREET ME.'

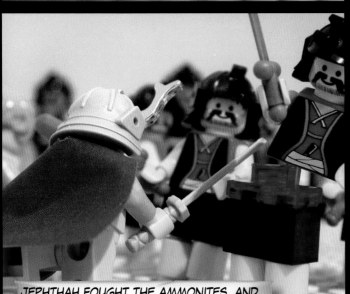

JEPHTHAH FOUGHT THE AMMONITES, AND YAHWEH DELIVERED THEM INTO HIS HANDS.

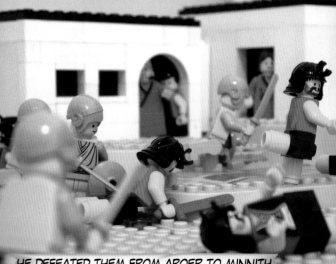

HE DEFEATED THEM FROM AROER TO MINNITH, TWENTY CITIES IN ALL.

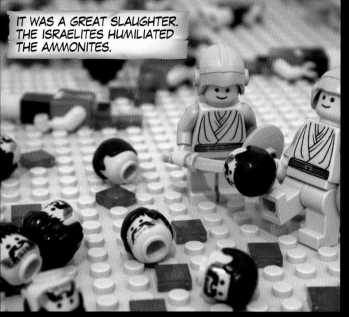

IT WAS A GREAT SLAUGHTER. THE ISRAELITES HUMILIATED THE AMMONITES.

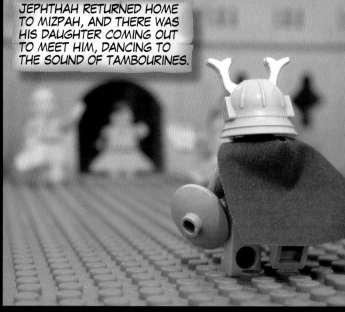

JEPHTHAH RETURNED HOME TO MIZPAH, AND THERE WAS HIS DAUGHTER COMING OUT TO MEET HIM, DANCING TO THE SOUND OF TAMBOURINES.

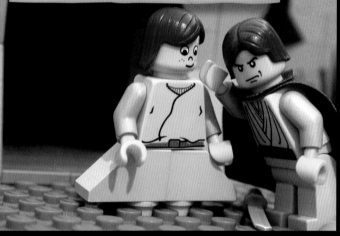

SHE WAS HIS ONLY CHILD, FOR HE HAD NO OTHER SONS OR DAUGHTERS. WHEN HE SAW HER, HE TORE HIS CLOTHES AND SAID, 'OH, MY DAUGHTER, YOU HAVE MADE ME MISERABLE, AND CAUSED ME GREAT TROUBLE.'

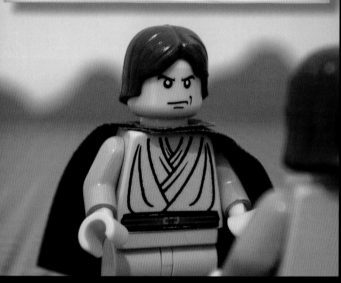

'I HAVE MADE A VOW TO YAHWEH AND CANNOT BREAK IT.'

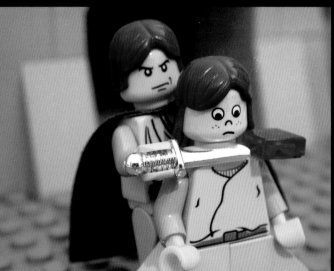

AND SO JEPHTHAH ACTED TO HER ACCORDING TO HIS VOW.

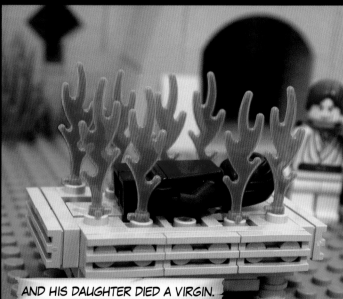

AND HIS DAUGHTER DIED A VIRGIN.

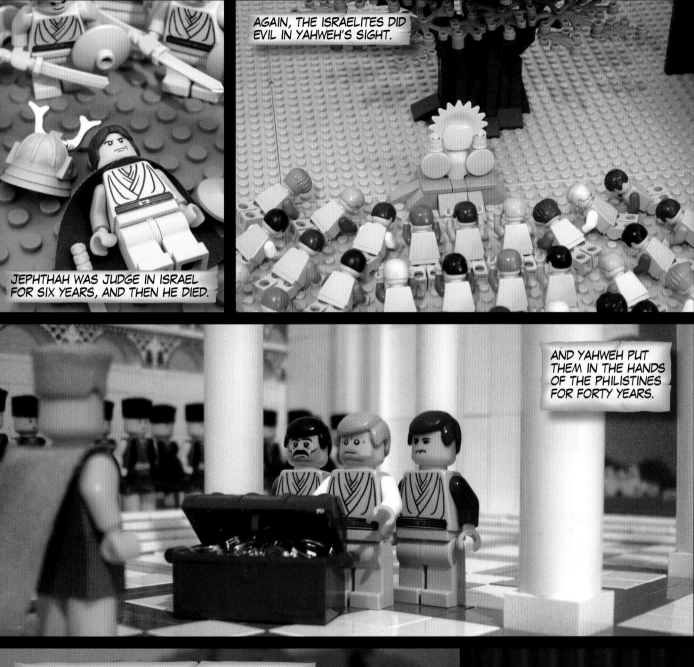

AGAIN, THE ISRAELITES DID EVIL IN YAHWEH'S SIGHT.

JEPHTHAH WAS JUDGE IN ISRAEL FOR SIX YEARS, AND THEN HE DIED.

AND YAHWEH PUT THEM IN THE HANDS OF THE PHILISTINES FOR FORTY YEARS.

THE ANGEL OF YAHWEH APPEARED TO THE WIFE OF MANOAH AND SAID, 'YOU ARE INFERTILE, BUT YOU WILL CONCEIVE AND BEAR A SON. NO RAZOR SHALL TOUCH HIS HEAD, FOR HE WILL BE DEDICATED TO GOD FROM BIRTH. HE WILL RESCUE ISRAEL FROM THE HANDS OF THE PHILISTINES.'

THE WOMAN BORE A SON AND NAMED HIM SAMSON.

THE CHILD GREW, AND
YAHWEH BLESSED HIM.

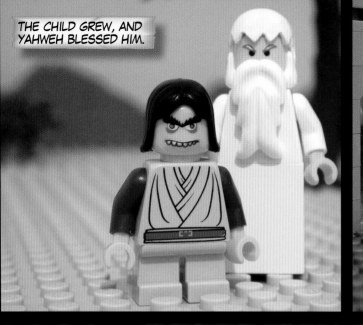

SAMSON WENT DOWN TO TIMNAH
WHERE HE NOTICED A WOMAN, ONE
OF THE PHILISTINE GIRLS.

HE RETURNED HOME AND
TOLD HIS FATHER AND MOTH-
ER, 'I NOTICED A PHILISTINE
GIRL AT TIMNAH. NOW GO
GET HER TO BE MY WIFE.'

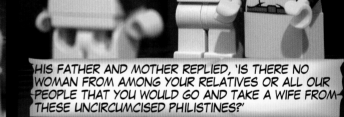

HIS FATHER AND MOTHER REPLIED, 'IS THERE NO
WOMAN FROM AMONG YOUR RELATIVES OR ALL OUR
PEOPLE THAT YOU WOULD GO AND TAKE A WIFE FROM
THESE UNCIRCUMCISED PHILISTINES?'

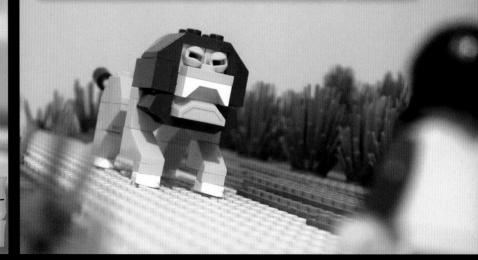

SAMSON HEADED DOWN TO TIMNAH, BUT AS HE APPROACHED THE
VINEYARDS, HE SAW A ROARING YOUNG LION COMING AT HIM.

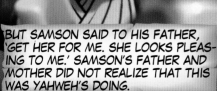

BUT SAMSON SAID TO HIS FATHER,
'GET HER FOR ME. SHE LOOKS PLEAS-
ING TO ME.' SAMSON'S FATHER AND
MOTHER DID NOT REALIZE THAT THIS
WAS YAHWEH'S DOING.

YAHWEH'S SPIRIT SEIZED HIM, AND HE TORE THE LION APART WITH HIS BARE HANDS AS EASILY AS IF IT WERE A YOUNG GOAT.

SAMSON DID NOT TELL HIS FATHER OR MOTHER WHAT HE HAD DONE, BUT CONTINUED ON TO TIMNAH AND TALKED WITH THE GIRL AND FOUND HER PLEASING.

LATER, SAMSON WAS ON HIS WAY BACK TO MARRY HER WHEN HE TURNED TO LOOK AT THE LION'S CARCASS, AND IN IT WAS A SWARM OF BEES AND SOME HONEY.

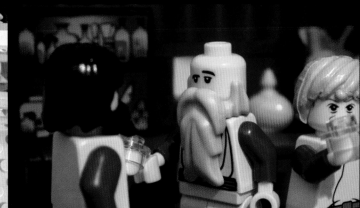

HE SCOOPED OUT SOME HONEY, AND WHEN HE RETURNED TO HIS PARENTS, HE GAVE SOME TO THEM, AND THEY ATE IT. BUT HE DID NOT TELL THEM THAT HE HAD TAKEN THE HONEY FROM THE LION'S CARCASS.

SAMSON'S FATHER WENT DOWN TO THE WOMAN, AND SAMSON THREW A FEAST THERE, AS WAS THE CUSTOM FOR BRIDEGROOMS.

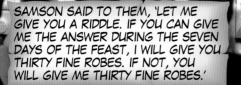

SAMSON SAID TO THEM, 'LET ME GIVE YOU A RIDDLE. IF YOU CAN GIVE ME THE ANSWER DURING THE SEVEN DAYS OF THE FEAST, I WILL GIVE YOU THIRTY FINE ROBES. IF NOT, YOU WILL GIVE ME THIRTY FINE ROBES.'

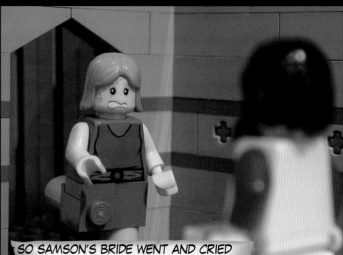

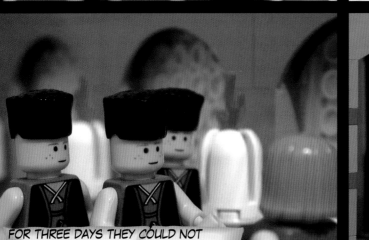

FOR THREE DAYS THEY COULD NOT SOLVE THE RIDDLE, AND ON THE FOURTH DAY THEY SAID TO SAMSON'S BRIDE, 'COAX THE ANSWER TO THE RIDDLE OUT OF YOUR HUSBAND, OR WE WILL BURN YOU AND YOUR FATHER'S FAMILY! DID YOU BRING US HERE TO ROB US?'

SO SAMSON'S BRIDE WENT AND CRIED BEFORE HIM, 'YOU ONLY HATE ME, YOU DO NOT LOVE ME! YOU GAVE THE MEN OF MY PEOPLE A RIDDLE, BUT YOU HAVE NOT TOLD ME THE ANSWER!'

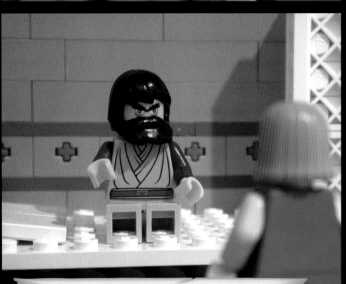

SAMSON SAID TO HER, 'I HAVE NOT EVEN TOLD MY FATHER OR MOTHER, SO WHY SHOULD I TELL YOU?'

SHE CRIED BEFORE HIM THE SEVEN DAYS OF THE FEAST, UNTIL FINALLY ON THE SEVENTH DAY SHE HAD PERSISTED SO MUCH THAT HE TOLD HER THE ANSWER.

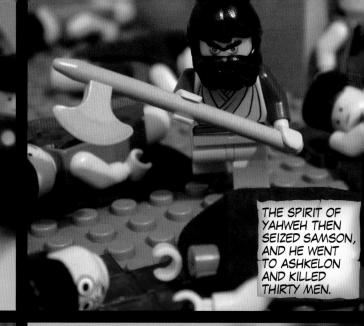

SHE TOLD THE ANSWER TO HER PEOPLE, AND BEFORE SUNSET ON THE SEVENTH DAY, THE MEN OF THE TOWN SAID TO HIM, 'WHAT IS SWEETER THAN HONEY? WHAT IS STRONGER THAN A LION?'

THE SPIRIT OF YAHWEH THEN SEIZED SAMSON, AND HE WENT TO ASHKELON AND KILLED THIRTY MEN.

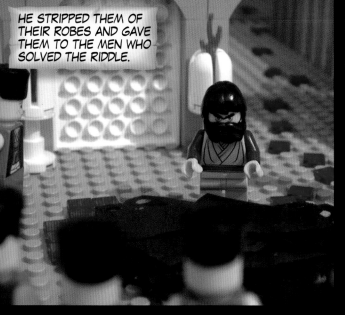

HE STRIPPED THEM OF THEIR ROBES AND GAVE THEM TO THE MEN WHO SOLVED THE RIDDLE.

SAMSON WAS FURIOUS AND WENT BACK HOME.

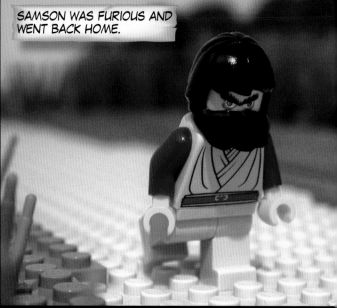

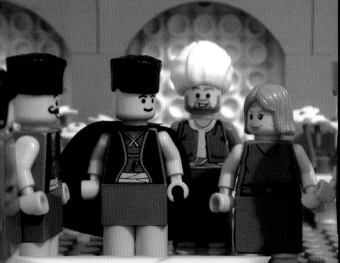

SAMSON'S BRIDE WAS GIVEN TO THE ATTEN-DANT WHO HAD SERVED AS HIS BEST MAN.

LATER ON, DURING THE WHEAT HARVEST, SAMSON TOOK A YOUNG GOAT AND WENT TO VISIT HIS BRIDE. HE SAID, 'LET ME LAY WITH MY WIFE IN HER BEDROOM.'

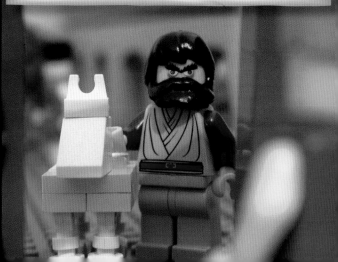

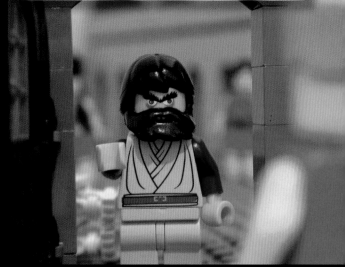

BUT HER FATHER SAID, 'I THOUGHT YOU HATED HER, SO I GAVE HER TO YOUR BEST MAN. HER YOUNGER SISTER IS MORE ATTRACTIVE. TAKE HER INSTEAD.'

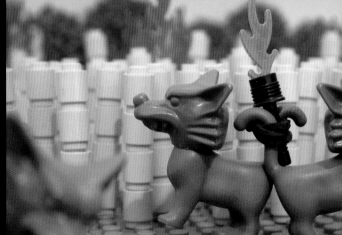

SAMSON SAID TO THEM, 'THIS TIME, WHEN I HURT THE PHILISTINES, I WILL NOT BE TO BLAME!'

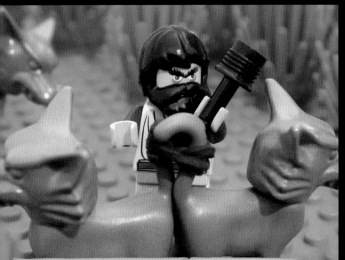

SAMSON WENT AND CAUGHT THREE HUNDRED JACKALS, TURNED THEM TAIL TO TAIL, AND TIED A TORCH BETWEEN EACH PAIR OF TAILS.

HE LIT THE TORCHES AND TURNED THE JACKALS LOOSE ON THE PHILISTINES' GRAIN FIELDS, THUS BURNING THEIR STANDING GRAIN, THEIR BUNDLED GRAIN, AND THEIR VINEYARDS AS WELL.

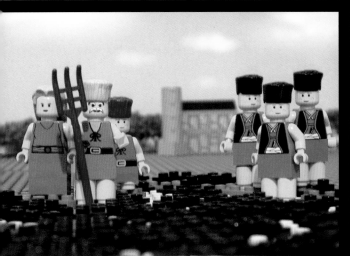

THE PHILISTINES ASKED, 'WHO HAS DONE THIS?' AND THEY WERE TOLD, 'SAMSON WHO MARRIED THE GIRL FROM TIMNAH, BECAUSE HIS WIFE WAS GIVEN TO HIS BEST MAN.'

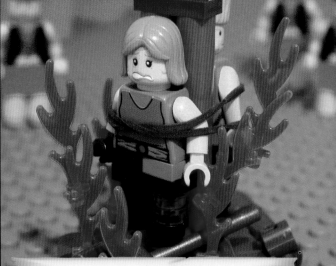

SO THE PHILISTINES WENT AND BURNT TO DEATH THE GIRL FROM TIMNAH AND HER FATHER.

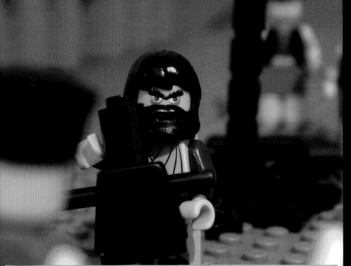

THEN SAMSON SAID TO THEM, 'BECAUSE YOU HAVE DONE THIS, I WILL NOT STOP UNTIL I HAVE HAD MY REVENGE!'

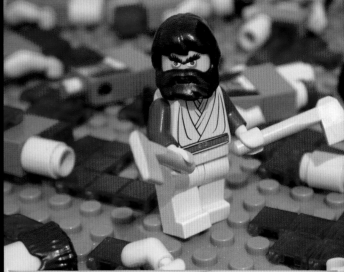

SAMSON CUT THEM TO PIECES IN A GREAT SLAUGHTER.

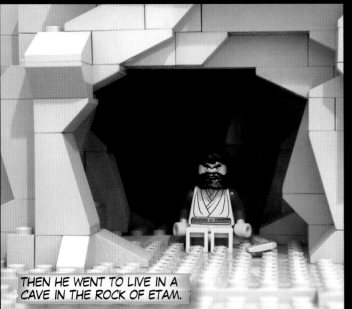

THEN HE WENT TO LIVE IN A CAVE IN THE ROCK OF ETAM.

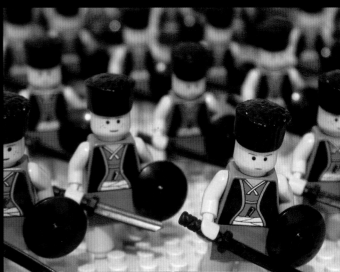

THE PHILISTINES MARCHED INTO JUDAH AND PREPARED TO ATTACK THE TOWN OF LEHI.

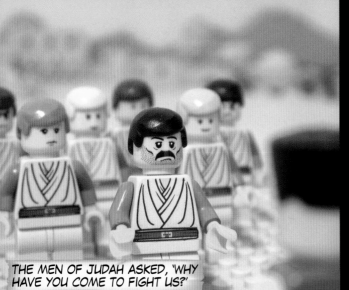

THE MEN OF JUDAH ASKED, 'WHY HAVE YOU COME TO FIGHT US?'

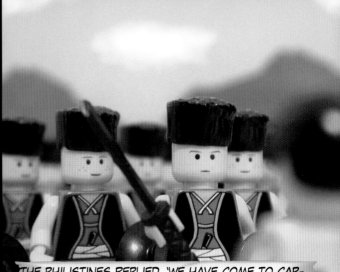

THE PHILISTINES REPLIED, 'WE HAVE COME TO CAPTURE SAMSON AND TREAT HIM AS HE TREATED US.'

SO THE MEN OF JUDAH SAID TO SAMSON, 'WE HAVE COME TO CAPTURE YOU AND HAND YOU OVER TO THE PHILISTINES.'

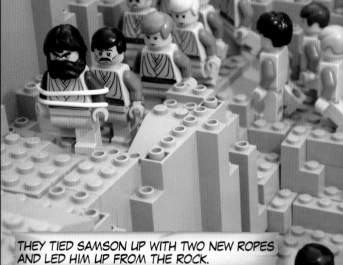

THEY TIED SAMSON UP WITH TWO NEW ROPES AND LED HIM UP FROM THE ROCK.

ARRIVING AT LEHI, THE PHILISTINES SHOUTED AS HE APPROACHED.

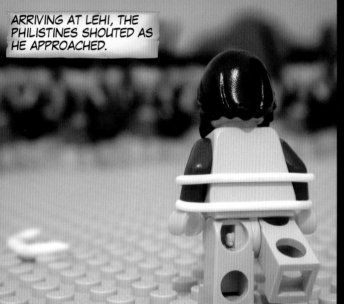

THEN THE SPIRIT OF YAHWEH SEIZED SAMSON, THE ROPES BURNT AWAY LIKE FLAX IN A FIRE, HIS BINDINGS COMING UNDONE. SPOTTING A FRESH JAWBONE OF A DONKEY, SAMSON PICKED IT UP.

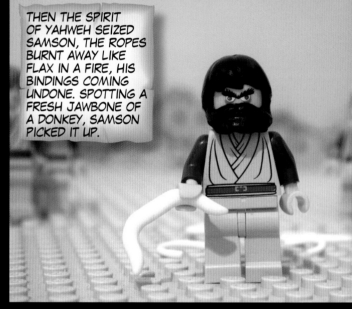

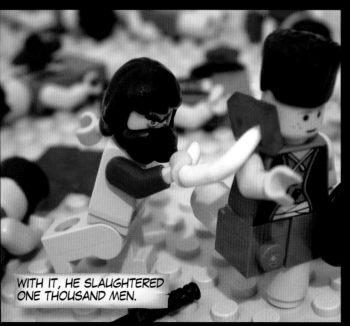

WITH IT, HE SLAUGHTERED ONE THOUSAND MEN.

AFTER THIS, SAMSON FELL IN LOVE WITH A WOMAN NAMED DELILAH IN THE VALLEY OF SOREK.

THE PHILISTINES LEADERS VISITED HER AND SAID, 'ENTICE HIM. FIND OUT WHAT MAKES HIM SO STRONG AND HOW WE CAN OVERPOWER, BIND, AND HUMILI- ATE HIM. AND WE WILL EACH GIVE YOU ELEVEN HUNDRED SILVER PIECES.'

SO DELILAH SAID TO SAMSON, 'TELL ME WHAT MAKES YOU SO STRONG, AND HOW YOU CAN BE OVERPOWERED, BOUND, AND HUMILIATED.'

SAMSON SAID TO HER, 'IF I WERE BOUND WITH SEVEN FRESH BOWSTRINGS NOT YET DRIED, I WOULD BECOME AS WEAK AS ANY OTHER MAN.'

SO THE PHILISTINE LEADERS BROUGHT HER SEVEN FRESH BOWSTRINGS NOT YET DRIED, AND SHE BOUND HIM WITH THEM.

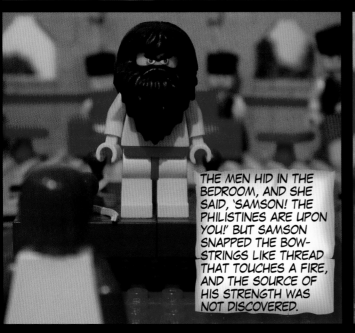

THE MEN HID IN THE BEDROOM, AND SHE SAID, 'SAMSON! THE PHILISTINES ARE UPON YOU!' BUT SAMSON SNAPPED THE BOW- STRINGS LIKE THREAD THAT TOUCHES A FIRE, AND THE SOURCE OF HIS STRENGTH WAS NOT DISCOVERED.

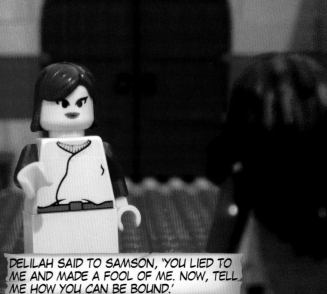

DELILAH SAID TO SAMSON, 'YOU LIED TO ME AND MADE A FOOL OF ME. NOW, TELL ME HOW YOU CAN BE BOUND.'

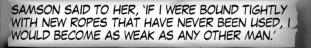

SAMSON SAID TO HER, 'IF I WERE BOUND TIGHTLY WITH NEW ROPES THAT HAVE NEVER BEEN USED, I WOULD BECOME AS WEAK AS ANY OTHER MAN.'

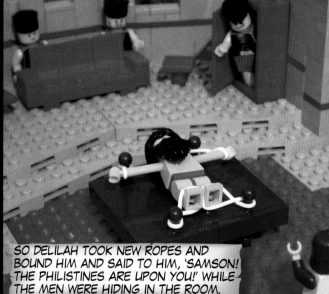

SO DELILAH TOOK NEW ROPES AND BOUND HIM AND SAID TO HIM, 'SAMSON! THE PHILISTINES ARE UPON YOU!' WHILE THE MEN WERE HIDING IN THE ROOM.

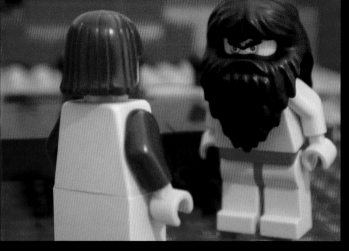

BUT SAMSON SNAPPED OFF THE ROPES LIKE THEY WERE THREADS.

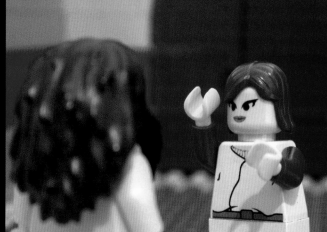

DELILAH SAID TO SAMSON, 'HOW CAN YOU SAY THAT YOU LOVE ME WHEN YOUR HEART IS NOT WITH ME? AGAIN YOU HAVE MADE A FOOL OF ME AND HAVE NOT TOLD ME WHAT MAKES YOU SO STRONG.'

SHE CONTINUED NAGGING WITH SUCH WORDS, DAY AFTER DAY, UNTIL HE BECAME SICK TO DEATH OF IT.

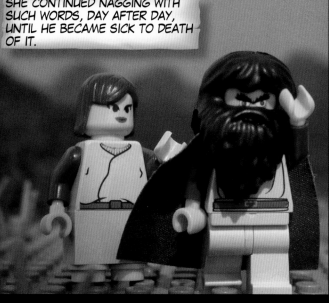

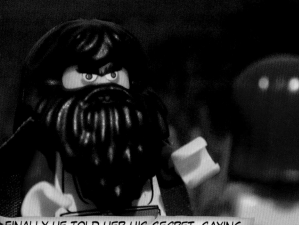

FINALLY HE TOLD HER HIS SECRET, SAYING, 'MY HAIR HAS NEVER BEEN CUT BECAUSE I HAVE BEEN SET APART TO GOD SINCE BIRTH. IF MY HEAD WERE SHAVED, MY STRENGTH WOULD LEAVE ME, AND I WOULD BECOME AS WEAK AS ANY OTHER MAN.'

SO DELILAH LULLED SAMSON TO SLEEP ON HER LAP AND THEN SUMMONED A MAN TO SHAVE OFF HIS HAIR, AND HIS STRENGTH LEFT HIM.

THE PHILISTINES CAPTURED HIM AND GOUGED OUT HIS EYES.

THEY BOUND HIM IN BRONZE SHACKLES AND MADE HIM A GRINDER IN THE PRISON.

THE PHILISTINES GATHERED TO OFFER A GREAT SACRIFICE TO DAGON THEIR GOD, SAYING, 'OUR GOD HAS DELIVERED OUR ENEMY TO US! THE ONE WHO DESTROYED OUR LAND AND KILLED SO MANY OF US!' THEIR SPIRITS RUNNING HIGH, THEY SHOUTED, 'BRING OUT SAMSON!'

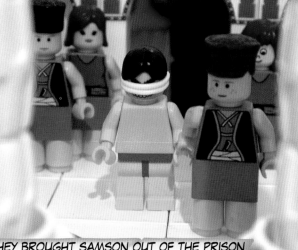

SO THEY BROUGHT SAMSON OUT OF THE PRISON TO ENTERTAIN THEM AND STOOD HIM BETWEEN TWO PILLARS. NOW SAMSON'S HAIR HAD BEGUN TO GROW BACK AFTER IT HAD BEEN SHAVED OFF.

SAMSON SAID TO THE YOUNG MAN WHO HELD HIS HAND, 'PUT ME WHERE I CAN FEEL THE PILLARS THAT SUPPORT THIS TEMPLE, SO I CAN LEAN ON THEM.'

NOW, THE TEMPLE WAS CROWDED WITH MEN AND WOMEN. ALL THE PHILISTINE LEADERS WERE THERE, PLUS ABOUT THREE THOUSAND MEN AND WOMEN ON THE TERRACE TO WATCH SAMSON ENTERTAIN.

THEN SAMSON PUT HIS HANDS ON THE TWO CENTRAL PILLARS THAT SUPPORTED THE TEMPLE AND SAID, 'LET ME DIE WITH THE PHILISTINES!' AS HE PUSHED WITH ALL HIS MIGHT.

THE TEMPLE COLLAPSED ON THE LEADERS AND ALL THE PEOPLE IN IT. AND SO SAMSON KILLED MANY MORE PEOPLE WITH HIS DEATH THAN HE HAD KILLED DURING HIS LIFE.

IN THOSE DAYS, THE TRIBE OF DAN WAS LOOKING FOR A PLACE TO SETTLE. THEY SENT FIVE STRONG MEN TO LAISH TO SPY OUT THE LAND, AND THEY NOTICED THAT THE PEOPLE THERE WERE LIVING UNTROUBLED, PEACEFUL, AND UNSUSPECTING.

SO SIX HUNDRED FULLY ARMED DANITES CAME TO LAISH WHERE THE PEOPLE WERE PEACEFUL AND UNSUSPECTING.

AND THE DANITES STRUCK THEM DOWN WITH THEIR SWORDS.

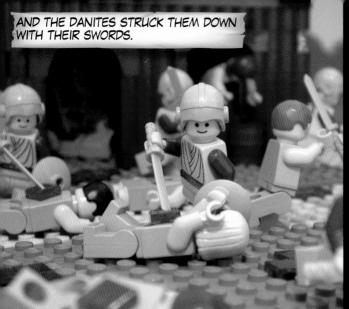

AND THEY BURNED THE CITY WITH FIRE. NO ONE CAME TO THEIR RESCUE.

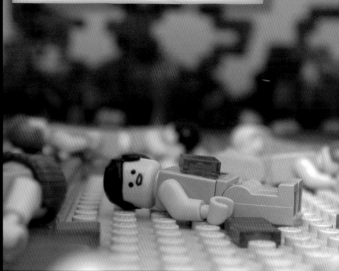

THE DANITES REBUILT THE TOWN AND SETTLED THERE. THEY RENAMED IT DAN AFTER THEIR FOREFATHER, BUT IT USED TO BE CALLED LAISH.

NOW, THERE WAS A LEVITE WHO LIVED IN THE REMOTE AREA OF THE EPHRAIMITE HILL COUNTRY. HE ACQUIRED A CONCUBINE FROM BETHLEHEM IN JUDAH.

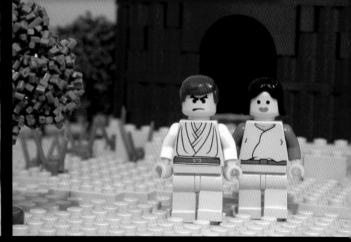

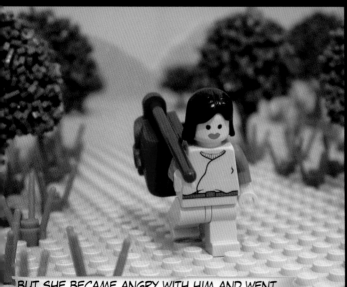

BUT SHE BECAME ANGRY WITH HIM AND WENT HOME TO HER FATHER'S HOUSE IN BETHLEHEM.

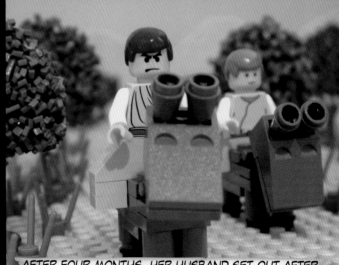

AFTER FOUR MONTHS, HER HUSBAND SET OUT AFTER HER TO PERSUADE HER TO COME BACK, TAKING WITH HIM HIS SERVANT AND TWO DONKEYS.

SHE TOOK HIM INSIDE HER FATHER'S HOUSE, AND THE FATHER WELCOMED HIM IN AND INSISTED HE STAY WITH THEM.

SO THEY ATE A MEAL TOGETHER.

BUT, REFUSING TO STAY THE NIGHT, THE MAN DEPARTED AND WENT TOWARD JEBUS WITH HIS TWO SADDLED DONKEYS AND HIS CONCUBINE.

DAYLIGHT WAS FADING AS THEY APPROACHED JEBUS, AND THE SERVANT SAID TO HIS MASTER, 'COME ON, LET'S STOP AT THIS JEBUSITE CITY AND SPEND THE NIGHT.'

BUT HIS MASTER SAID, 'WE SHOULD NOT STOP IN A CITY OF FOREIGNERS WITH PEOPLE WHO ARE NOT ISRAELITES. WE WILL GO ON TO GIBEAH.'

SO THEY TRAVELED ON TO GIBEAH IN THE LAND OF BENJAMIN TO SPEND THE NIGHT. THEY SAT DOWN IN THE CITY SQUARE, BUT NO ONE TOOK THEM INTO HIS HOUSE FOR THE NIGHT.

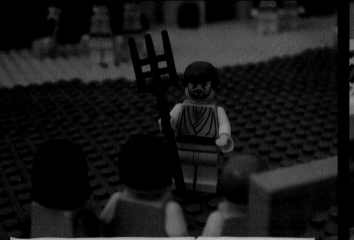

EVENTUALLY, AN OLD MAN CAME BY, RETURNING FROM HIS WORK IN THE FIELDS. HE WAS ALSO FROM THE EPHRAIMITE HILLS, AND HE SAID TO THEM, 'I WILL TAKE CARE OF ALL YOUR NEEDS, JUST DON'T SPEND THE NIGHT IN THE CITY SQUARE.'

SO HE TOOK THEM INTO HIS HOUSE AND FED THE DONKEYS. THEY WASHED THEIR FEET AND ATE AND DRANK.

THEY WERE ENJOYING THEMSELVES WHEN SOME WORTHLESS MEN OF THE TOWN SURROUNDED THE HOUSE AND POUNDED ON THE DOOR, SAYING, 'BRING OUT THE MAN WHO CAME TO YOUR HOUSE SO WE CAN LAY WITH HIM!'

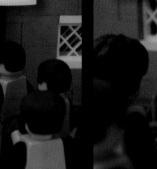

THE OWNER OF THE HOUSE WENT OUTSIDE AND SAID TO THEM, 'NO, MY BROTHERS, DO NOT BE SO WICKED! THIS MAN IS MY GUEST, SO DO NOT DO SUCH A SHAMEFUL THING!'

'HERE IS MY VIRGIN DAUGHTER AND HIS CONCUBINE. ABUSE THEM, AND DO TO THEM WHATEVER YOU WISH, BUT DO NOT DO SUCH A DISGRACEFUL THING TO THIS MAN!'

THE MEN WOULD NOT LISTEN TO HIM, SO THE LEVITE TOOK HIS CONCUBINE AND SENT HER OUTSIDE TO THEM. THE MEN ABUSED HER ALL NIGHT.

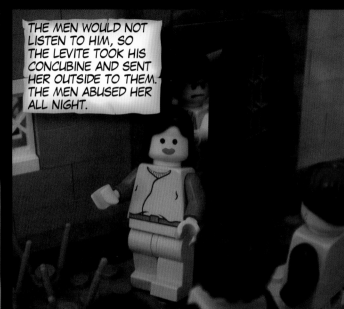

AT DAWN, THEY LET HER GO, AND THE GIRL WENT BACK TO THE HOUSE WHERE HER MASTER WAS STAYING, AND SHE FELL DOWN AND LAY THERE UNTIL MORNING.

WHEN HER MASTER GOT UP IN THE MORNING AND OPENED THE DOOR OF THE HOUSE, THERE WAS HIS CONCUBINE LAYING ON THE DOORSTEP WITH HER HAND ON THE THRESHOLD. 'GET UP. LET'S GO,' HE SAID TO HER, BUT THERE WAS NO RESPONSE.

SO HE PUT HER ON A DONKEY AND HEADED HOME.

WHEN HE REACHED HIS HOUSE, HE TOOK A KNIFE AND CARVED UP HIS CONCUBINE INTO TWELVE PIECES.

AND HE SENT THEM THROUGHOUT THE LAND OF ISRAEL. EVERYONE WHO SAW IT SAID, 'NOTHING LIKE THIS HAS EVER BEEN SEEN OR DONE FROM THE TIME THE ISRAELITES CAME UP FROM EGYPT UNTIL TODAY. TAKE NOTE! CONSIDER IT! DISCUSS IT!'

THEN THE TRIBES OF ISRAEL SENT MEN THROUGHOUT THE TRIBE OF BENJAMIN, SAYING, 'HAND OVER THE WORTHLESS MEN OF GIBEAH SO WE CAN PUT THEM TO DEATH AND PURGE THIS EVIL FROM ISRAEL.'

BUT THE BENJAMINITES WOULD NOT LISTEN TO THEIR ISRAELITE BROTHERS, AND THEY MUSTERED AT GIBEAH TO FIGHT THE ISRAELITES. THERE WERE 26,000 SWORDSMEN.

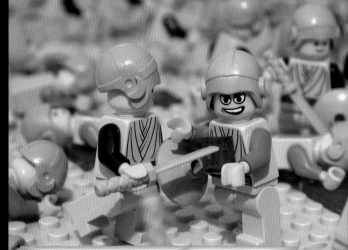

THE ISRAELITES, NOT INCLUDING BENJAMIN, MUSTERED 400,000 SWORDSMEN. THEY WENT UP TO BETHEL AND ASKED GOD, 'WHO SHOULD BE THE FIRST TO ATTACK THE BENJAMINITES?'

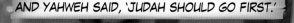

AND YAHWEH SAID, 'JUDAH SHOULD GO FIRST.'

THE NEXT MORNING THE ISRAELITES WENT OUT TO FIGHT THE BENJAMINITES, BUT THAT DAY THE BENJAMINITES KILLED 22,000 ISRAELITES.

THE SECOND DAY THE BENJAMINITES KILLED ANOTHER 18,000 ISRAELITES.

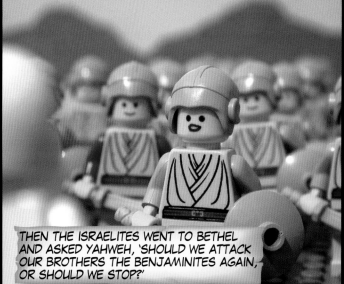

THEN THE ISRAELITES WENT TO BETHEL AND ASKED YAHWEH, 'SHOULD WE ATTACK OUR BROTHERS THE BENJAMINITES AGAIN, OR SHOULD WE STOP?'

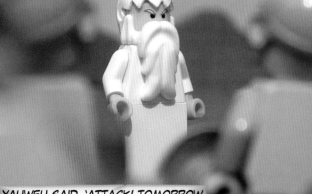

YAHWEH SAID, 'ATTACK! TOMORROW I WILL HAND THEM OVER TO YOU.'

THE NEXT DAY THE ISRAELITES ATTACKED THE BENJAMINITES, AND THE ISRAELITES KILLED 25,100 BEN-JAMINITE SWORDS-MEN, AND THE BEN-JAMINITES SAW THAT THEY WERE DEFEATED.

SIX HUNDRED SURVIVORS FLED INTO THE DESERT TO THE ROCK OF RIMMON WHERE THEY STAYED FOR FOUR MONTHS.

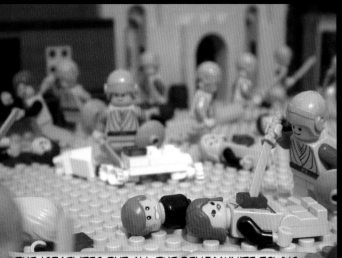

THE ISRAELITES PUT ALL THE BENJAMINITE TOWNS TO THE SWORD, INCLUDING ALL THE PEOPLE, LIVE-STOCK, AND EVERYTHING THEY COULD FIND AND SET FIRE TO ALL THE CITIES THEY CAME ACROSS.

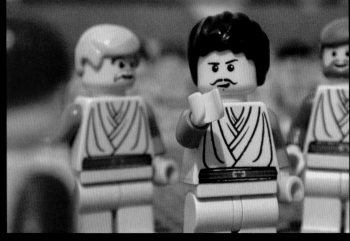

THEN THE ISRAELITES FELT SORRY FOR WHAT HAP-PENED TO THEIR BROTHERS THE BENJAMINITES, AND SAID, 'HOW SHALL WE FIND WIVES FOR THOSE WHO ARE LEFT, SINCE WE TOOK AN OATH BEFORE YAHWEH NOT TO GIVE ANY OF THEM OUR DAUGHTERS AS WIVES?'

SO THE ASSEMBLY SENT 12,000 STRONG FIGHTING MEN TO JABESH-GILEAD WITH THE ORDERS: 'GO AND PUT EVERYONE LIVING THERE TO THE SWORD, INCLUDING THE WOMEN AND CHILDREN.'

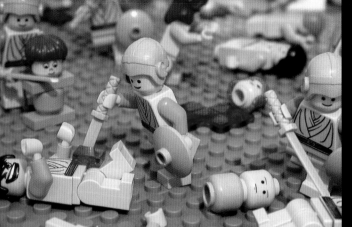

'THIS IS WHAT YOU ARE TO DO: KILL EVERY MALE AND ANY WOMAN WHO IS NOT A VIRGIN.'

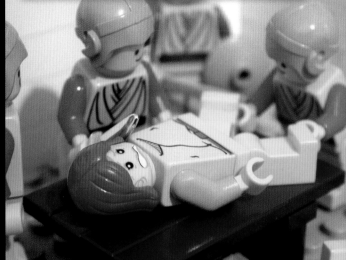

THEY FOUND AT JABESH-GILEAD FOUR HUNDRED YOUNG GIRLS WHO WERE VIRGINS, WHO HAD NEVER LAID WITH A MAN, AND THEY BROUGHT THEM BACK TO THE CAMP.

BUT THERE WERE NOT ENOUGH FOR ALL OF THEM, SO THEY COMMANDED THE BENJAMINITES, SAYING, 'THERE IS AN ANNUAL FESTIVAL TO YAHWEH IN SHILOH, NORTH OF BETHEL.'

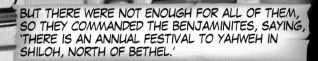

'HIDE IN THE VINEYARDS, AND WHEN YOU SEE GIRLS OF SHILOH COMING OUT TO DANCE, COME OUT, AND EACH OF YOU SEIZE YOURSELF A WIFE.'

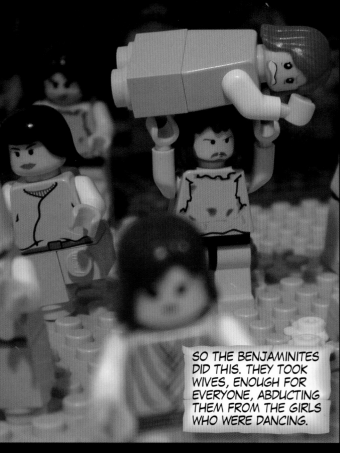

SO THE BENJAMINITES DID THIS. THEY TOOK WIVES, ENOUGH FOR EVERYONE, ABDUCTING THEM FROM THE GIRLS WHO WERE DANCING.

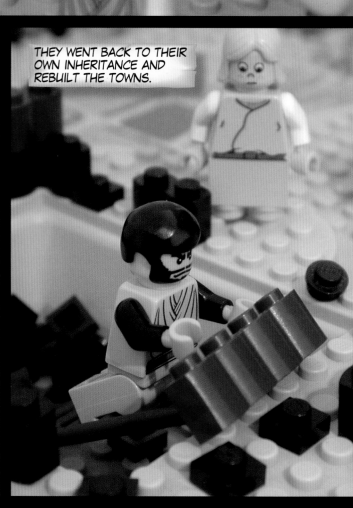

THEY WENT BACK TO THEIR OWN INHERITANCE AND REBUILT THE TOWNS.

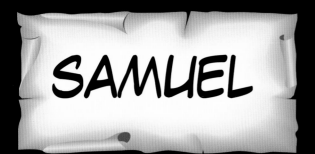

SAMUEL

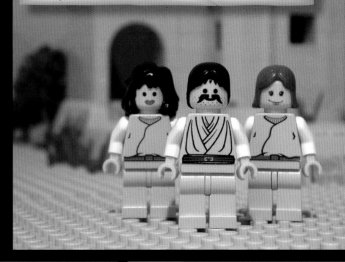

THERE WAS A MAN NAMED ELKANAH FROM THE HIGHLANDS OF EPHRAIM, AND HE HAD TWO WIVES, HANNAH AND PENINNAH. ELKANAH LOVED HANNAH MORE, BUT YAHWEH HAD MADE HER INFERTILE.

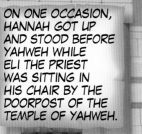

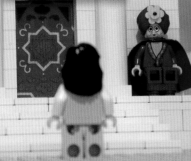

ON ONE OCCASION, HANNAH GOT UP AND STOOD BEFORE YAHWEH WHILE ELI THE PRIEST WAS SITTING IN HIS CHAIR BY THE DOORPOST OF THE TEMPLE OF YAHWEH.

SHE MADE A VOW, SAYING, 'YAHWEH, IF YOU WILL REGARD THE SUFFERING OF YOUR SERVANT AND GIVE HER A SON, I WILL DEDICATE HIM TO YAHWEH ALL THE DAYS OF HIS LIFE, AND NO RAZOR SHALL EVER TOUCH HIS HEAD.'

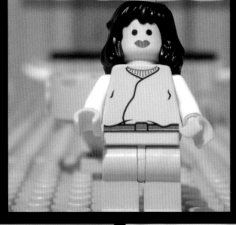

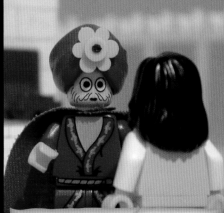

AS HANNAH PRAYED, HER LIPS WERE MOVING, BUT HER VOICE COULD NOT BE HEARD. ELI THOUGHT SHE WAS DRUNK AND SAID TO HER, 'HOW LONG WILL YOU STAY DRUNK? GET RID OF YOUR WINE!'

ELI SAID, 'GO IN PEACE, AND MAY THE GOD OF ISRAEL GRANT WHAT YOU HAVE ASKED HIM.'

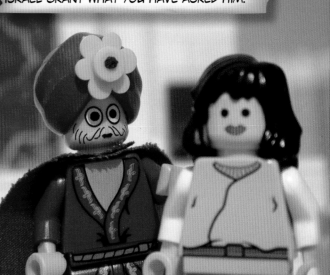

HANNAH REPLIED, 'I HAVE NOT BEEN DRINKING WINE OR BEER! I WAS POURING OUT MY SOUL TO YAHWEH. DO NOT TAKE YOUR SERVANT TO BE A WORTHLESS WOMAN.'

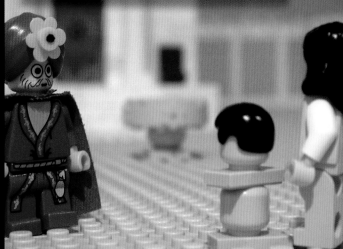

HANNAH GAVE BIRTH TO A SON WHOM SHE NAMED SAMUEL, SAYING, 'BECAUSE I ASKED YAHWEH FOR HIM.'

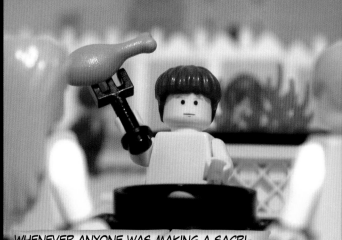

THEN, TAKING THE CHILD TO ELI, SHE SAID, 'THIS IS THE CHILD FOR WHICH I WAS PRAYING. NOW I DEDICATE HIM TO YAHWEH.'

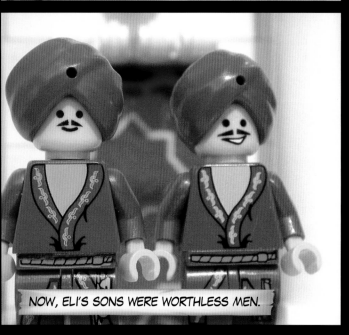

NOW, ELI'S SONS WERE WORTHLESS MEN.

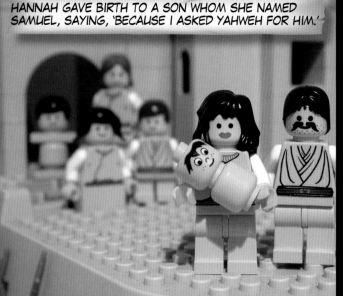

WHENEVER ANYONE WAS MAKING A SACRI-FICE, THE PRIEST'S SERVANT WOULD TAKE A THREE-PRONGED FORK AND JAB IT INTO THE CAULDRON, AND EVERYTHING THAT CAME UP, THE PRIEST WOULD CLAIM FOR HIMSELF.

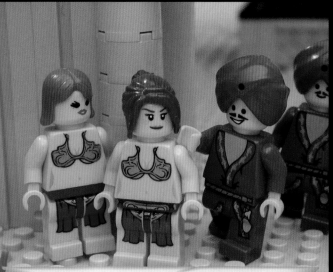

AND THEY WOULD LAY WITH THE WOMEN WHO SERVED AT THE DOORWAY OF THE TENT OF MEETING.

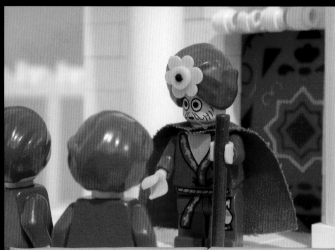

ELI, NOW VERY OLD, HEARD ABOUT EVERYTHING HIS SONS WERE DOING, AND SAID, 'WHY ARE YOU BEHAVING THIS WAY? IF A MAN SINS AGAINST YAHWEH, WHO CAN INTERCEDE FOR HIM?'

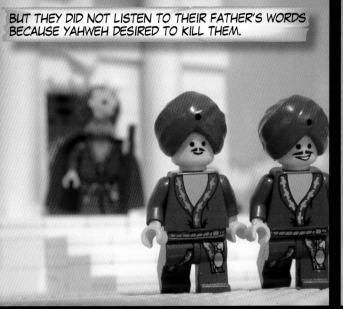

BUT THEY DID NOT LISTEN TO THEIR FATHER'S WORDS BECAUSE YAHWEH DESIRED TO KILL THEM.

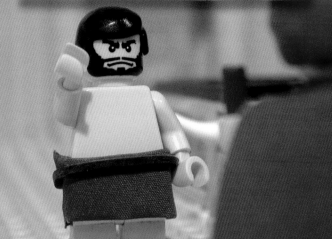

A MAN OF GOD CAME TO ELI AND TOLD HIM, 'YAHWEH SAYS: "I PROMISED THAT YOUR FATHER'S FAMILY WOULD WALK BEFORE ME FOREVER. BUT NOW I SAY, MAY IT NEVER BE SO!"'

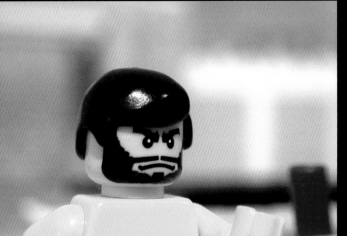

'"NO ONE IN YOUR FAMILY WILL LIVE TO OLD AGE. ANY I DO NOT CUT OFF FROM MY ALTAR WILL BE SPARED ONLY TO BLIND YOUR EYES WITH TEARS AND GRIEF. THEY WILL ALL DIE IN THE PRIME OF THEIR LIVES."'

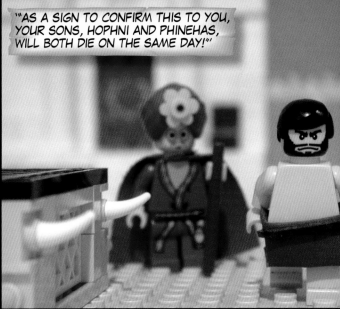

'"AS A SIGN TO CONFIRM THIS TO YOU, YOUR SONS, HOPHNI AND PHINEHAS, WILL BOTH DIE ON THE SAME DAY!"'

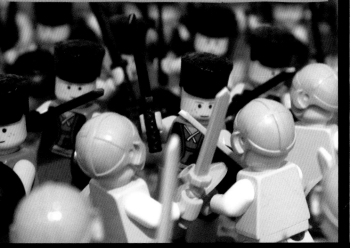

AT THIS TIME, THE ISRAELITES WERE AT WAR AGAINST THE PHILISTINES, AND THE FIGHTING GREW FIERCE. ISRAEL WAS DEFEATED BY THE PHILISTINES, AND ABOUT 4,000 MEN WERE KILLED ON THE BATTLEFIELD.

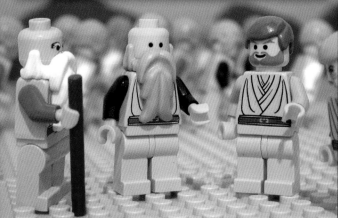

WHEN THE SOLDIERS RETURNED TO CAMP, THE ELDERS OF ISRAEL ASKED, 'WHY DID YAHWEH BRING US DEFEAT TODAY? LET'S BRING THE ARK OF THE COVENANT FROM SHILOH, SO THAT IT WILL SAVE US FROM THE HANDS OF OUR ENEMIES.'

SO THEY BROUGHT THE ARK OF THE COVENANT FROM SHILOH, AND ELI'S SONS, HOPHNI AND PHINEHAS, WERE THERE WITH THE ARK.

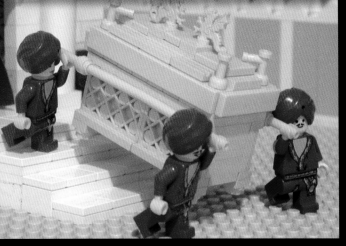

WHEN THE ARK OF THE COVENANT ARRIVED AT THE CAMP, ALL THE ISRAELITES SHOUTED WITH SUCH FORCE THAT THE GROUND SHOOK.

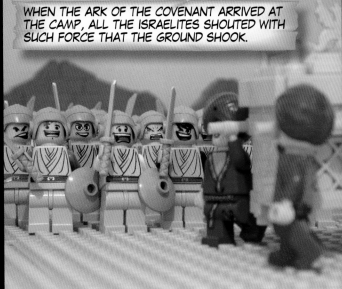

THE PHILISTINES HEARD THE SHOUT AND WERE AFRAID, BUT SAID, 'TAKE COURAGE! BE STRONG, PHILISTINES, OR ELSE WE WILL BECOME SLAVES TO THE HEBREWS! BE MEN AND FIGHT!'

SO THE PHILISTINES FOUGHT.

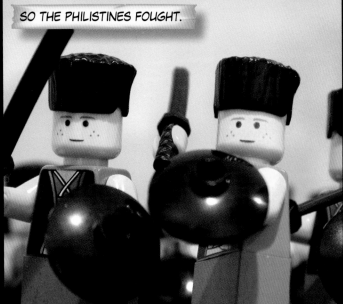

AND ISRAEL WAS DEFEATED.

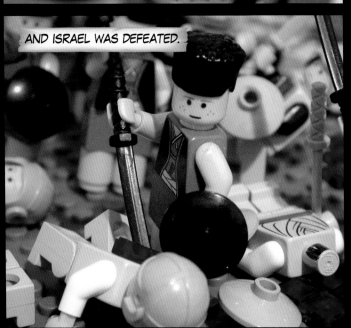

ELI'S SONS, HOPHNI AND PHINEHAS, WERE KILLED.

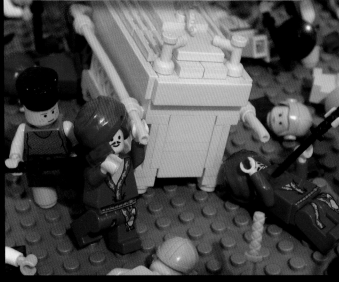

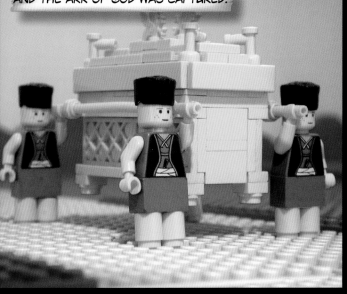

AND THE ARK OF GOD WAS CAPTURED.

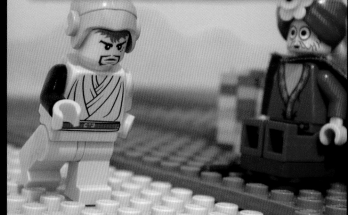

A BENJAMINITE RAN FROM THE BATTLE TO SHILOH, HIS CLOTHES TORN AND DUST ON HIS HEAD. ELI WAS 98 YEARS OLD AND BLIND, SITTING IN HIS CHAIR BY THE SIDE OF THE ROAD. HE ASKED, 'WHAT HAPPENED, MY SON?'

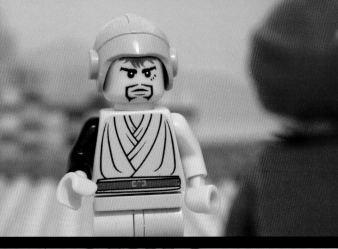

HE SAID TO ELI, 'ISRAEL HAS FLED BEFORE THE PHILISTINES, YOUR TWO SONS WERE KILLED, AND THE ARK OF GOD WAS CAPTURED.'

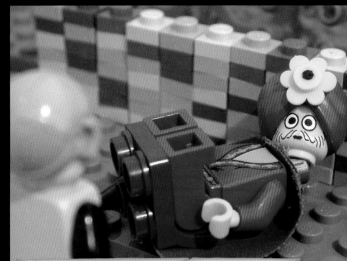

AT THE MENTION OF THE ARK, ELI FELL OVER BACKWARD, BROKE HIS NECK, AND DIED. HE HAD BEEN JUDGE OVER ISRAEL FOR 40 YEARS.

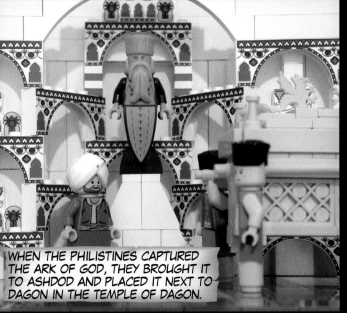

WHEN THE PHILISTINES CAPTURED THE ARK OF GOD, THEY BROUGHT IT TO ASHDOD AND PLACED IT NEXT TO DAGON IN THE TEMPLE OF DAGON.

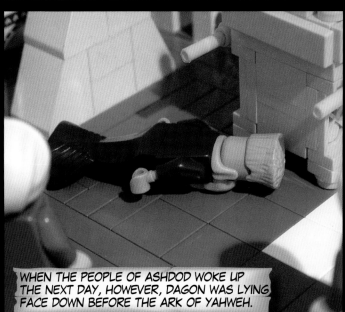

WHEN THE PEOPLE OF ASHDOD WOKE UP THE NEXT DAY, HOWEVER, DAGON WAS LYING FACE DOWN BEFORE THE ARK OF YAHWEH.

YAHWEH DEALT SEVERELY WITH ASHDOD AND THE SURROUNDING TOWNS, AFFLICTING THE PEOPLE WITH TUMORS.

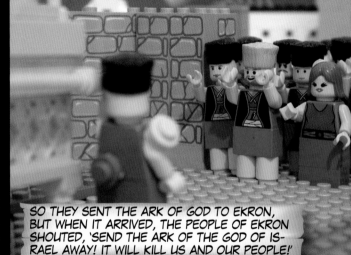

SO THEY SENT THE ARK OF GOD TO EKRON, BUT WHEN IT ARRIVED, THE PEOPLE OF EKRON SHOUTED, 'SEND THE ARK OF THE GOD OF ISRAEL AWAY! IT WILL KILL US AND OUR PEOPLE!'

INDEED, THERE WAS A TERROR OF DEATH THROUGHOUT THE CITY. GOD WAS DEALING WITH THEM SEVERELY, AND THOSE WHO DID NOT DIE WERE AFFLICTED WITH TUMORS.

SO THE PEOPLE TOOK TWO COWS AND HARNESSED THEM TO A CART. THEY PUT THE ARK OF YAHWEH ON THE CART ALONG WITH A BOX AND GOLDEN TUMORS.

THE COWS HEADED STRAIGHT FOR BETH-SHEMESH, MOOING AS THEY WENT, TURNING NEITHER RIGHT NOR LEFT.

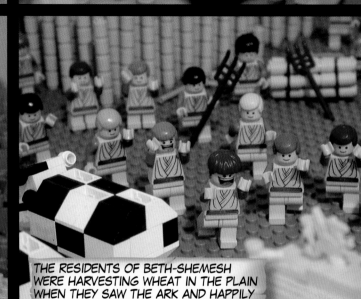

THE RESIDENTS OF BETH-SHEMESH WERE HARVESTING WHEAT IN THE PLAIN WHEN THEY SAW THE ARK AND HAPPILY CAME TO MEET IT.

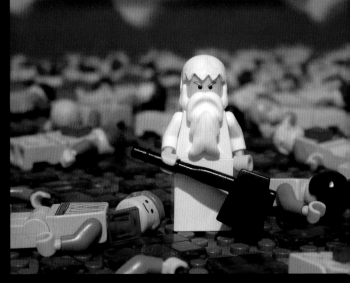

BECAUSE OF THIS, GOD KILLED 50,070 OF THEM.

BUT SOME OF THE PEOPLE OF BETH-SHEMESH LOOKED INSIDE THE ARK.

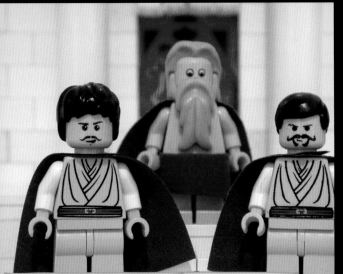

WHEN SAMUEL GREW OLD, HE APPOINTED HIS SONS JOEL AND ABIJAH AS JUDGES OVER ISRAEL.

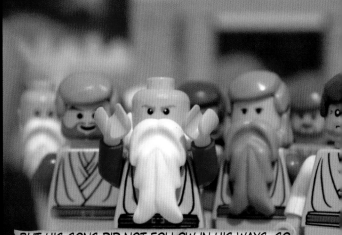

BUT HIS SONS DID NOT FOLLOW IN HIS WAYS, SO THE ELDERS OF ISRAEL CAME TO SAMUEL AND SAID, 'YOU ARE OLD, AND YOUR SONS DO NOT FOLLOW YOUR WAYS, SO APPOINT US A KING TO LEAD US, LIKE ALL THE OTHER NATIONS HAVE.'

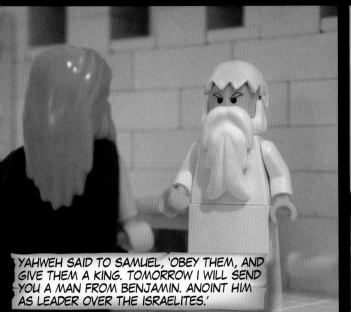

YAHWEH SAID TO SAMUEL, 'OBEY THEM, AND GIVE THEM A KING. TOMORROW I WILL SEND YOU A MAN FROM BENJAMIN. ANOINT HIM AS LEADER OVER THE ISRAELITES.'

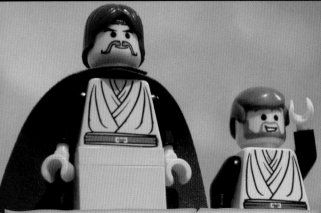

THERE WAS A BENJAMINITE NAMED KISH WHO HAD A SON NAMED SAUL. AMONGST ALL THE ISRAELITES, NO ONE WAS MORE HANDSOME, AND HE STOOD HEAD AND SHOULDERS TALLER THAN ANYONE ELSE. NOW KISH'S DONKEYS WERE LOST, AND KISH SAID TO SAUL, 'TAKE ONE OF THE SLAVES AND GO LOOK FOR THE DONKEYS.'

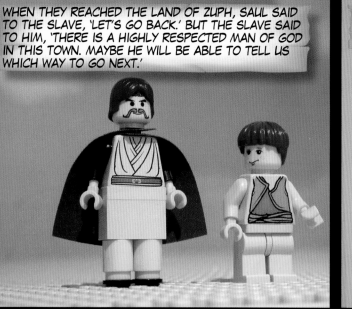

WHEN THEY REACHED THE LAND OF ZUPH, SAUL SAID TO THE SLAVE, 'LET'S GO BACK.' BUT THE SLAVE SAID TO HIM, 'THERE IS A HIGHLY RESPECTED MAN OF GOD IN THIS TOWN. MAYBE HE WILL BE ABLE TO TELL US WHICH WAY TO GO NEXT.'

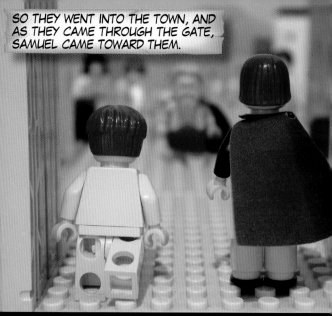

SO THEY WENT INTO THE TOWN, AND AS THEY CAME THROUGH THE GATE, SAMUEL CAME TOWARD THEM.

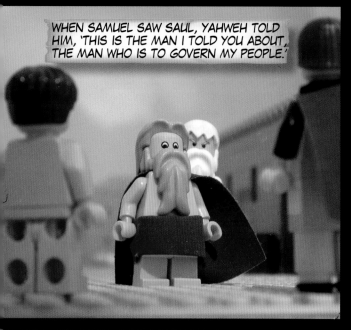

WHEN SAMUEL SAW SAUL, YAHWEH TOLD HIM, 'THIS IS THE MAN I TOLD YOU ABOUT, THE MAN WHO IS TO GOVERN MY PEOPLE.'

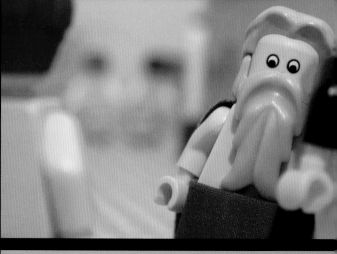
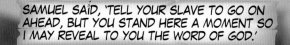

SAMUEL SAID, 'TELL YOUR SLAVE TO GO ON AHEAD, BUT YOU STAND HERE A MOMENT SO I MAY REVEAL TO YOU THE WORD OF GOD.'

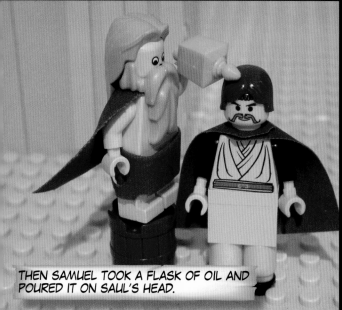

THEN SAMUEL TOOK A FLASK OF OIL AND POURED IT ON SAUL'S HEAD.

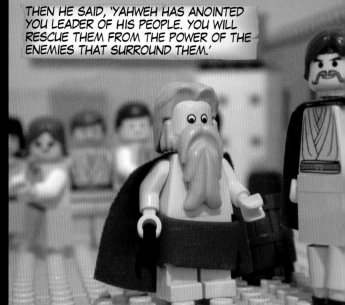

THEN HE SAID, 'YAHWEH HAS ANOINTED YOU LEADER OF HIS PEOPLE. YOU WILL RESCUE THEM FROM THE POWER OF THE ENEMIES THAT SURROUND THEM.'

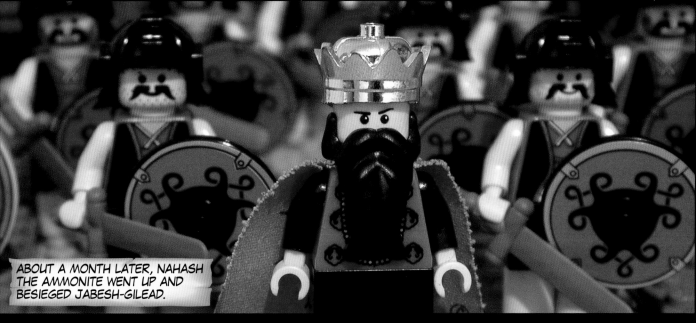

ABOUT A MONTH LATER, NAHASH THE AMMONITE WENT UP AND BESIEGED JABESH-GILEAD.

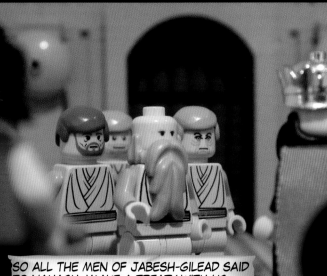

NAHASH REPLIED, 'I WILL MAKE A TREATY WITH YOU ONLY IF I MAY GOUGE OUT THE RIGHT EYE OF EVERY ONE OF YOU, THEREBY DISGRACING ALL OF ISRAEL.'

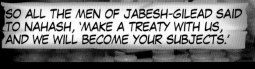

SO ALL THE MEN OF JABESH-GILEAD SAID TO NAHASH, 'MAKE A TREATY WITH US, AND WE WILL BECOME YOUR SUBJECTS.'

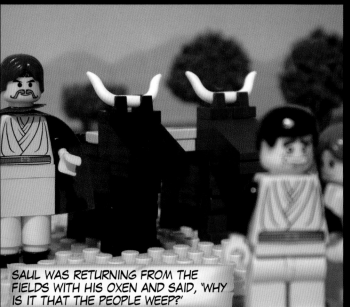

SAUL WAS RETURNING FROM THE FIELDS WITH HIS OXEN AND SAID, 'WHY IS IT THAT THE PEOPLE WEEP?'

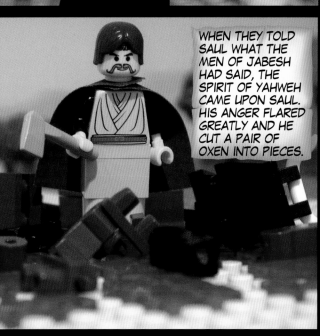

WHEN THEY TOLD SAUL WHAT THE MEN OF JABESH HAD SAID, THE SPIRIT OF YAHWEH CAME UPON SAUL. HIS ANGER FLARED GREATLY AND HE CUT A PAIR OF OXEN INTO PIECES.

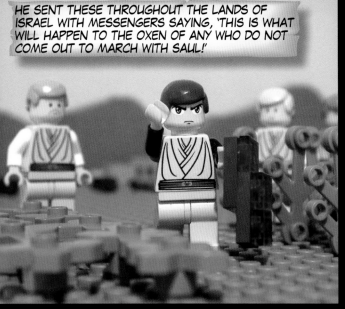

HE SENT THESE THROUGHOUT THE LANDS OF ISRAEL WITH MESSENGERS SAYING, 'THIS IS WHAT WILL HAPPEN TO THE OXEN OF ANY WHO DO NOT COME OUT TO MARCH WITH SAUL!'

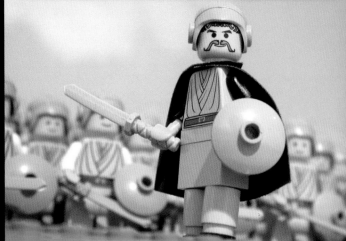

THE PEOPLE CAME OUT AND JOINED AS ONE ARMY. SAUL MUSTERED THEM AT BEZEK, AND THEY NUMBERED 300,000 FROM ISRAEL AND 30,000 FROM JUDAH.

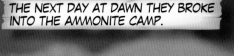
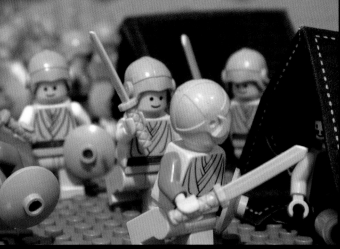

THE NEXT DAY AT DAWN THEY BROKE INTO THE AMMONITE CAMP.

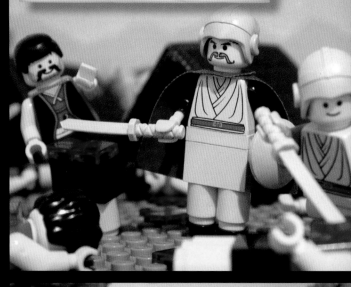

AND THEY SLAUGHTERED THE AMMONITES UNTIL THE MIDDLE OF THE DAY.

SURVIVORS WERE SO SCATTERED THAT NO TWO OF THEM WERE LEFT TOGETHER.

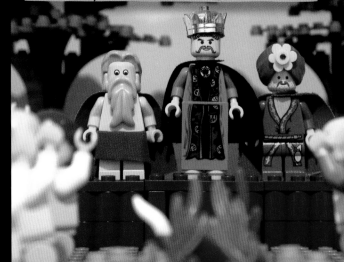

AND THE PEOPLE ALL WENT TO GILGAL WHERE THEY MADE SAUL KING BEFORE YAHWEH, OFFERED SACRIFICES, AND GREATLY REJOICED.

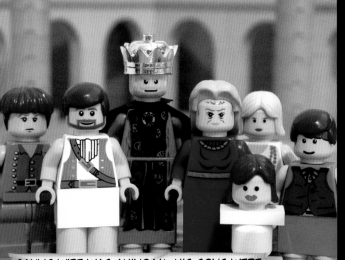

SAUL'S WIFE WAS AHINOAM. HIS SONS WERE JONATHAN, ISHVI, AND MALCHISHUA. HIS DAUGHTERS WERE MERAB AND MICHAL.

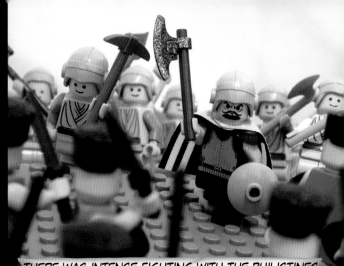

THERE WAS INTENSE FIGHTING WITH THE PHILISTINES THROUGHOUT SAUL'S LIFETIME. THE GENERAL IN CHARGE OF HIS ARMY WAS ABNER.

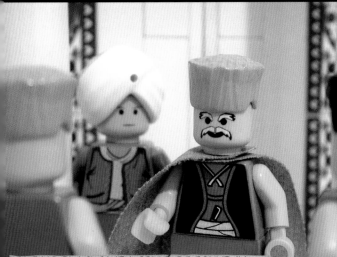

BUT NO BLACKSMITH COULD BE FOUND IN ALL THE LAND OF ISRAEL BECAUSE THE PHILISTINES HAD SAID, 'OTHERWISE THE HE-BREWS WILL MAKE SWORDS AND SPEARS!'

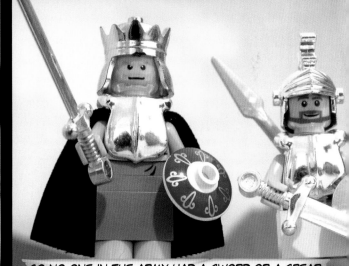

SO NO ONE IN THE ARMY HAD A SWORD OR A SPEAR. ONLY SAUL AND HIS SON JONATHAN HAD THEM.

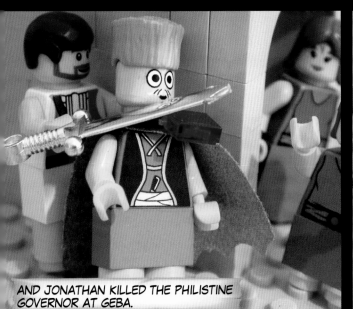

AND JONATHAN KILLED THE PHILISTINE GOVERNOR AT GEBA.

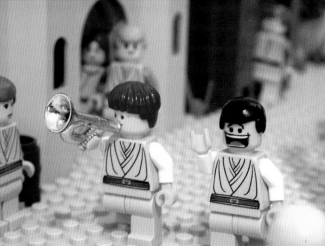

SAUL HAD THE TRUMPETS BLOWN THROUGH-OUT ALL THE LAND, SAYING, 'JONATHAN HAS KILLED THE PHILISTINE GOVERNOR AND MADE THE PHILISTINES DISGUSTED WITH ISRAEL.'

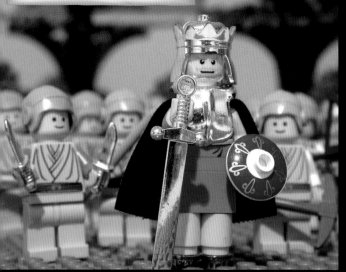

SO THE PEOPLE WERE RALLIED TO JOIN SAUL AT GILGAL.

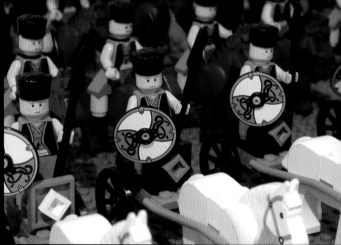

THE PHILISTINES HEARD ABOUT THIS AND MUSTERED TO FIGHT ISRAEL WITH 3,000 CHARIOTS AND 6,000 HORSEMEN.

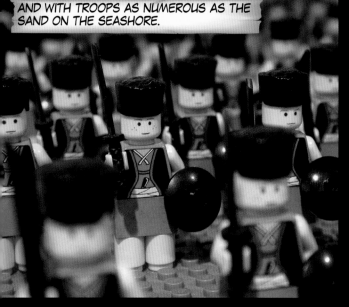

AND WITH TROOPS AS NUMEROUS AS THE SAND ON THE SEASHORE.

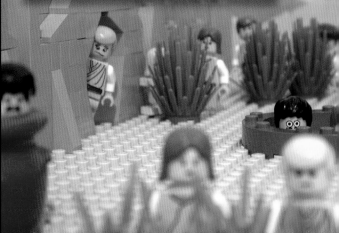

WHEN THE ISRAELITES SAW HOW DESPERATE THEIR SITUATION WAS, THE PEOPLE WERE DISTRESSED AND HID THEMSELVES IN CAVES, THICKETS, ROCKS, WELLS, AND CISTERNS.

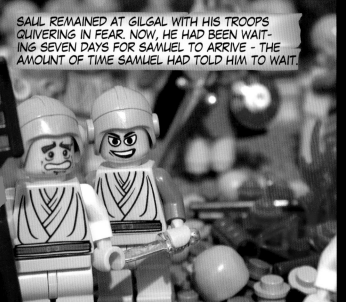

SAUL REMAINED AT GILGAL WITH HIS TROOPS QUIVERING IN FEAR. NOW, HE HAD BEEN WAIT-ING SEVEN DAYS FOR SAMUEL TO ARRIVE - THE AMOUNT OF TIME SAMUEL HAD TOLD HIM TO WAIT.

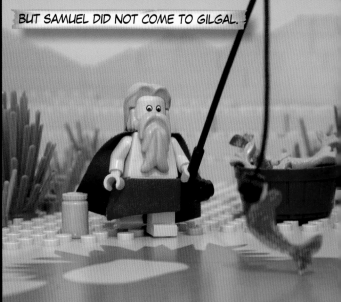

BUT SAMUEL DID NOT COME TO GILGAL.

SEEING THE ARMY DESERTING, AND THAT SAMUEL HAD NOT ARRIVED AT THE TIME HE WAS SUPPOSED TO, SAUL FELT OBLIGED TO OFFER THE BURNT SACRIFICE HIMSELF.

JUST AS HE FINISHED THE BURNT OFFERING, SAMUEL ARRIVED AND SAID, 'WHAT HAVE YOU DONE?'

'YOU HAVE ACTED LIKE A FOOL!' SAID SAMUEL. 'YOU HAVE NOT OBEYED THE COMMAND YAHWEH GAVE YOU. IF ONLY YOU HAD, YAHWEH WOULD HAVE ESTABLISHED YOUR KINGDOM OVER ISRAEL FOREVER!'

'BUT NOW YOUR KINGDOM WILL NOT CONTINUE,' SAID SAMUEL, 'YAHWEH HAS FOUND A MAN AFTER HIS OWN HEART AND APPOINTED HIM LEADER OF HIS PEOPLE.' AND SAMUEL LEFT, CONTINUING ON HIS WAY.

WHILE SAUL WAS ON THE OUTSKIRTS OF GEBA WITH ABOUT SIX HUNDRED TROOPS, JONATHAN SAID TO HIS ARMOR BEARER, 'COME ON, LET'S GO ACROSS TO THE PHILISTINE GARRISON ON THE OTHER SIDE.' BUT HE DID NOT INFORM HIS FATHER.

THERE WAS A ROCKY CLIFF ON EITHER SIDE OF THE PASS BY WHICH JONATHAN SOUGHT TO REACH THE PHILISTINE GARRISON, AND JONATHAN SAID, 'LET'S GO ACROSS TO THE GARRISON OF THESE UNCIRCUMCISED MEN AND PERHAPS YAHWEH WILL DO SOMETHING FOR US.'

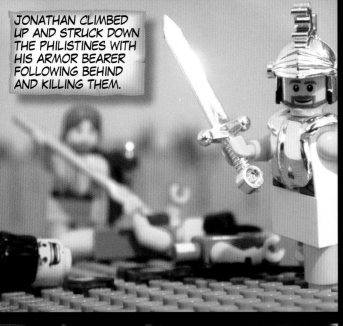

JONATHAN CLIMBED UP AND STRUCK DOWN THE PHILISTINES WITH HIS ARMOR BEARER FOLLOWING BEHIND AND KILLING THEM.

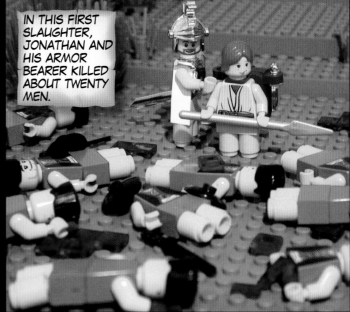

IN THIS FIRST SLAUGHTER, JONATHAN AND HIS ARMOR BEARER KILLED ABOUT TWENTY MEN.

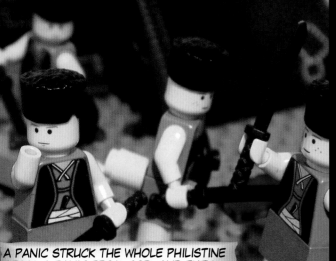

A PANIC STRUCK THE WHOLE PHILISTINE ARMY, A PANIC FROM GOD, AND THEY WERE STRIKING EACH OTHER DOWN WITH THEIR SWORDS IN WILD CONFUSION.

SAUL AND HIS ARMY MARCHED TO WHERE THE FIGHTING WAS, AND THE HEBREWS WHO HAD JOINED THE PHILISTINE ARMY NOW DEFECTED TO THE ISRAELITES WITH SAUL.

THAT DAY, THE ISRAELITES STRUCK DOWN THE PHILISTINES UNTIL THEY WERE UTTERLY EXHAUSTED.

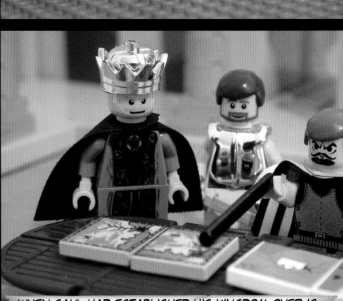

WHEN SAUL HAD ESTABLISHED HIS KINGDOM OVER IS-RAEL, HE FOUGHT AGAINST HIS ENEMIES ON ALL SIDES.

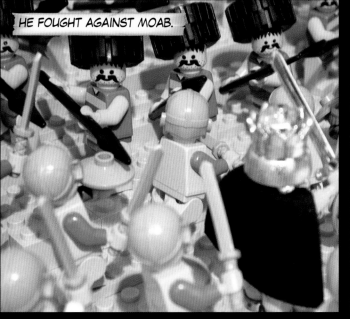

HE FOUGHT AGAINST MOAB.

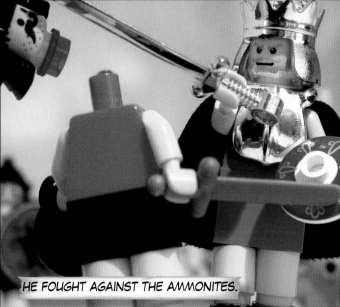

HE FOUGHT AGAINST THE AMMONITES.

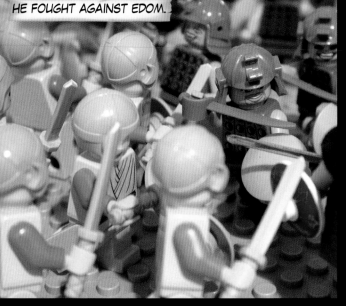

HE FOUGHT AGAINST EDOM.

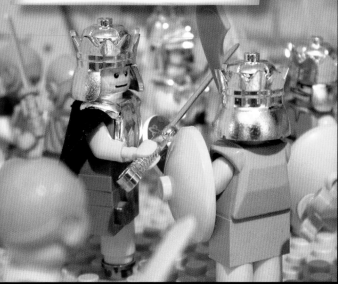

HE FOUGHT AGAINST THE KINGS OF ZOBAH.

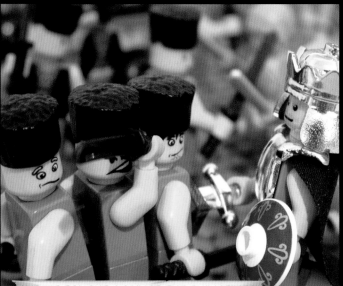

AND HE FOUGHT AGAINST THE PHILISTINES.

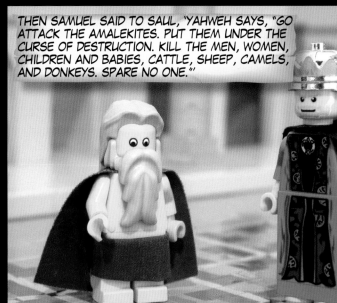

THEN SAMUEL SAID TO SAUL, 'YAHWEH SAYS, "GO ATTACK THE AMALEKITES. PUT THEM UNDER THE CURSE OF DESTRUCTION. KILL THE MEN, WOMEN, CHILDREN AND BABIES, CATTLE, SHEEP, CAMELS, AND DONKEYS. SPARE NO ONE."'

SO SAUL MUSTERED 210,000 TROOPS AND ADVANCED ON THE CITIES OF THE AMALEKITES.

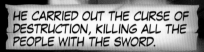

HE CARRIED OUT THE CURSE OF DESTRUCTION, KILLING ALL THE PEOPLE WITH THE SWORD.

SAUL STRUCK DOWN THE AMALEKITES FROM HALVILAH ALL THE WAY TO SHUR, EAST OF EGYPT.

BUT HE TOOK KING AGAG ALIVE, AND THE ARMY SPARED THE BEST OF THE SHEEP AND CATTLE.

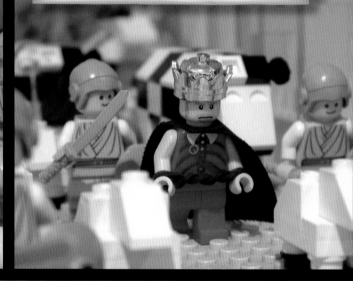

BUT EVERYTHING THAT WAS VILE AND WORTHLESS, THEY PUT UNDER THE CURSE OF DESTRUCTION.

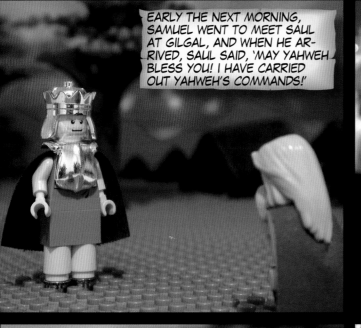

EARLY THE NEXT MORNING, SAMUEL WENT TO MEET SAUL AT GILGAL, AND WHEN HE ARRIVED, SAUL SAID, 'MAY YAHWEH BLESS YOU! I HAVE CARRIED OUT YAHWEH'S COMMANDS!'

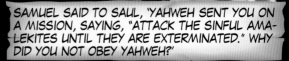

SAMUEL SAID TO SAUL, 'YAHWEH SENT YOU ON A MISSION, SAYING, "ATTACK THE SINFUL AMALEKITES UNTIL THEY ARE EXTERMINATED." WHY DID YOU NOT OBEY YAHWEH?'

SAUL ANSWERED, 'BUT I DID OBEY YAHWEH! I BROUGHT BACK KING AGAG ONLY AFTER EXTERMINATING THE AMALEKITES, AND THE ARMY TOOK THE BEST SHEEP AND CATTLE ONLY TO SACRIFICE TO YAHWEH.'

SAMUEL SAID, 'IS YAHWEH MORE PLEASED BY BURNT SACRIFICES OR BY OBEDIENCE? CERTAINLY OBEDIENCE IS BETTER! BECAUSE YOU HAVE REJECTED YAHWEH'S WORD, HE HAS REJECTED YOU!'

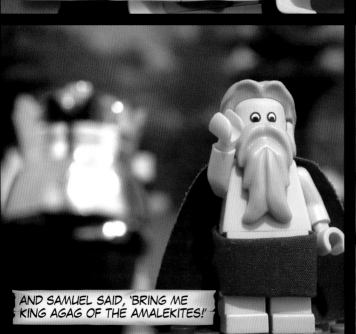

AND SAMUEL SAID, 'BRING ME KING AGAG OF THE AMALEKITES!'

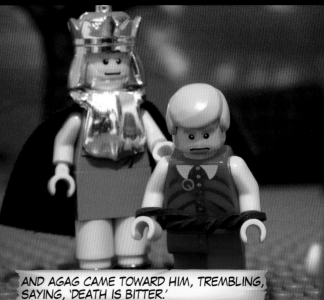

AND AGAG CAME TOWARD HIM, TREMBLING, SAYING, 'DEATH IS BITTER.'

AND SAMUEL HACKED AGAG INTO PIECES BEFORE YAHWEH AT GILGAL.

YAHWEH REGRETTED THAT HE MADE SAUL KING OVER ISRAEL, BUT SAMUEL MOURNED FOR SAUL. YAHWEH SAID TO SAMUEL, 'HOW MUCH LONGER WILL YOU MOURN FOR SAUL? I AM SENDING YOU TO JESSE IN BETHLEHEM, FOR I HAVE CHOSEN A KING FROM AMONG HIS SONS.'

SO SAMUEL DID AS YAHWEH COMMANDED AND HE NEVER SAW SAUL AGAIN TO THE DAY HE DIED. HE WENT TO BETHLEHEM AND THE TOWN ELDERS CAME TO MEET HIM, TREMBLING IN FEAR. THEY ASKED, 'DO YOU COME IN PEACE?'

'YES, IN PEACE,' SAID SAMUEL. 'I HAVE COME TO SACRIFICE TO YAHWEH. PURIFY YOURSELVES, AND COME WITH ME.'

SO HE INVITED JESSE AND HIS SONS TO THE SACRIFICE, AND WHEN THEY ARRIVED, HE NOTICED ELIAB AND THOUGHT, 'SURELY THIS IS YAHWEH'S ANOINTED!'

BUT YAHWEH SAID TO SAMUEL, 'DO NOT CONSIDER HIS HEIGHT OR APPEARANCE, FOR I HAVE REJECTED HIM. PEOPLE LOOK AT APPEARANCES, BUT YAHWEH LOOKS AT THE HEART.'

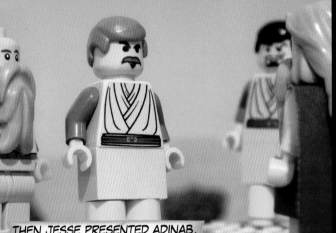

THEN JESSE PRESENTED ADINAB, BUT SAMUEL SAID, 'YAHWEH HAS NOT CHOSEN THIS ONE EITHER.'

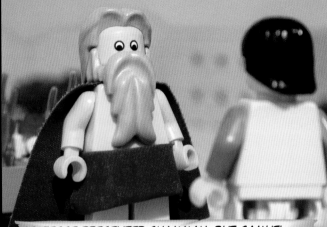

SO JESSE PRESENTED SHAMMAH, BUT SAMUEL SAID, 'YAHWEH HAS NOT CHOSEN THIS ONE EITHER.'

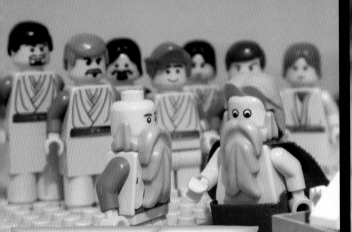

JESSE PRESENTED SEVEN OF HIS SONS TO SAMUEL, BUT SAMUEL SAID TO JESSE, 'DO YOU HAVE ANY OTHER SONS?' JESSE SAID, 'THERE IS STILL THE YOUNGEST. HE IS TENDING THE SHEEP.'

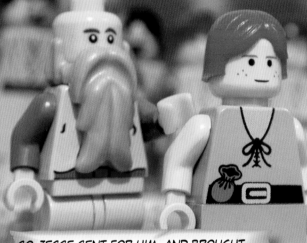

SO JESSE SENT FOR HIM, AND BROUGHT HIM OVER. HE WAS REDDISH WITH BEAUTIFUL EYES AND HANDSOME FEATURES.

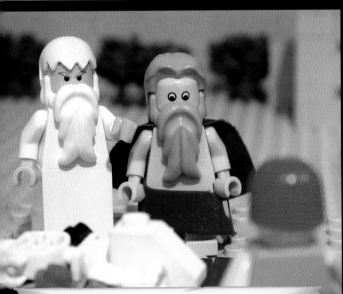

AND YAHWEH SAID, 'GO ANOINT HIM! HE IS THE ONE!'

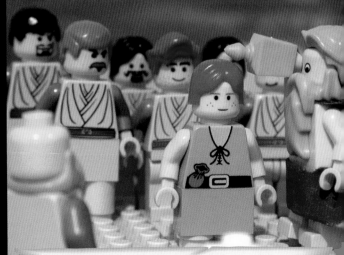

SO SAMUEL TOOK A FLASK OF OLIVE OIL AND ANOINTED HIM IN HIS BROTHERS' PRESENCE, AND THE SPIRIT OF YAHWEH SEIZED DAVID FROM THAT DAY ONWARD.

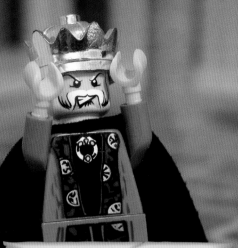

THE SPIRIT OF YAHWEH TURNED AWAY FROM SAUL, AND AN EVIL SPIRIT FROM YAHWEH TORMENTED HIM.

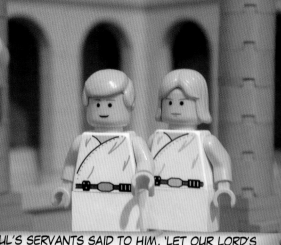

SAUL'S SERVANTS SAID TO HIM, 'LET OUR LORD'S SERVANTS FIND SOMEONE WHO CAN PLAY THE LYRE. WHEN THE EVIL SPIRIT FROM GOD COMES UPON YOU, HE WILL PLAY, AND YOU WILL FEEL BETTER.'

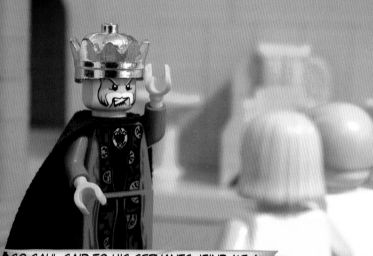

SO SAUL SAID TO HIS SERVANTS, 'FIND ME A MAN WHO PLAYS WELL AND BRING HIM TO ME.'

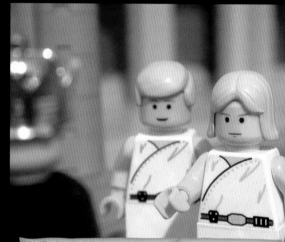

AND ONE OF THE SERVANTS SAID, 'I HAVE SEEN A SON OF JESSE OF BETHLEHEM WHO IS A SKILLED PLAYER, A BRAVE WARRIOR, ELOQUENT, AND HANDSOME. AND YAHWEH IS WITH HIM.'

DAVID CAME TO SAUL AND STOOD BEFORE HIM, AND SAUL LOVED DAVID GREATLY.

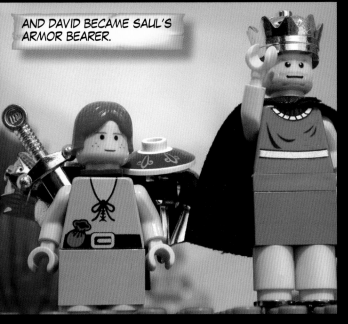

AND DAVID BECAME SAUL'S ARMOR BEARER.

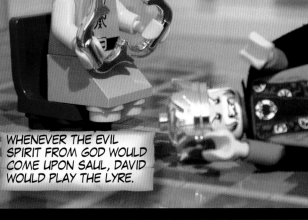

WHENEVER THE EVIL SPIRIT FROM GOD WOULD COME UPON SAUL, DAVID WOULD PLAY THE LYRE.

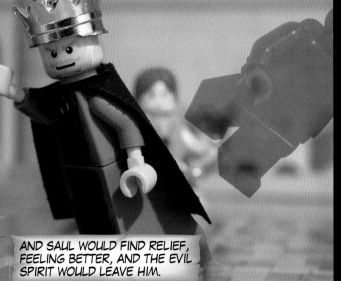

AND SAUL WOULD FIND RELIEF, FEELING BETTER, AND THE EVIL SPIRIT WOULD LEAVE HIM.

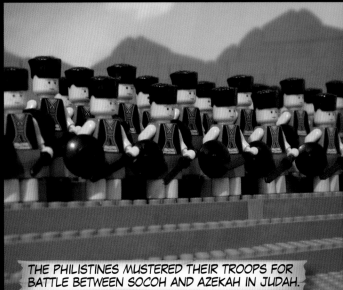

THE PHILISTINES MUSTERED THEIR TROOPS FOR BATTLE BETWEEN SOCOH AND AZEKAH IN JUDAH.

AND SAUL MUSTERED THE ISRAELITE ARMY AND ARRANGED THEIR BATTLE LINE OPPOSITE THE PHILISTINES.

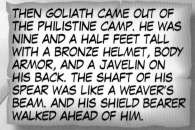

THEN GOLIATH CAME OUT OF THE PHILISTINE CAMP. HE WAS NINE AND A HALF FEET TALL WITH A BRONZE HELMET, BODY ARMOR, AND A JAVELIN ON HIS BACK. THE SHAFT OF HIS SPEAR WAS LIKE A WEAVER'S BEAM. AND HIS SHIELD BEARER WALKED AHEAD OF HIM.

GOLIATH CALLED OUT, 'WHY DO YOU COME OUT AND ALIGN YOUR-SELVES FOR BATTLE? CHOOSE ONE MAN. IF HE IS ABLE TO KILL ME, WE WILL BECOME YOUR SUBJECTS, BUT IF I KILL HIM, YOU WILL BECOME OUR SUBJECTS.'

THE PHILISTINE CAME OUT EVERY MORNING AND EVERY EVENING FOR FORTY DAYS AND TOOK HIS STAND. 'GIVE ME A MAN,' HE SAID, 'AND WE WILL FIGHT IT OUT!'

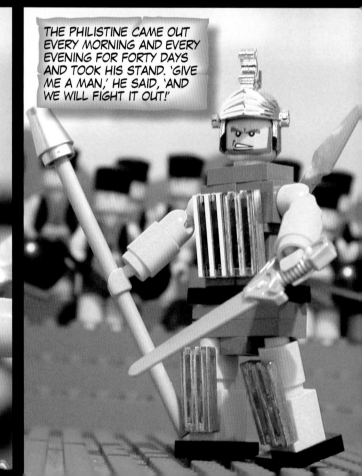

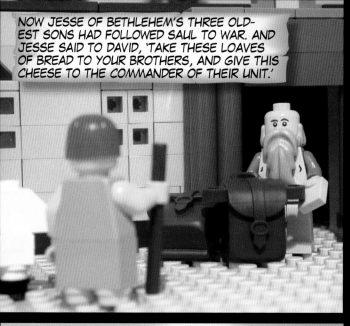

NOW JESSE OF BETHLEHEM'S THREE OLD-EST SONS HAD FOLLOWED SAUL TO WAR. AND JESSE SAID TO DAVID, 'TAKE THESE LOAVES OF BREAD TO YOUR BROTHERS, AND GIVE THIS CHEESE TO THE COMMANDER OF THEIR UNIT.'

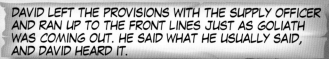
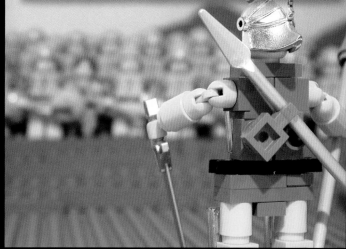

DAVID LEFT THE PROVISIONS WITH THE SUPPLY OFFICER AND RAN UP TO THE FRONT LINES JUST AS GOLIATH WAS COMING OUT. HE SAID WHAT HE USUALLY SAID, AND DAVID HEARD IT.

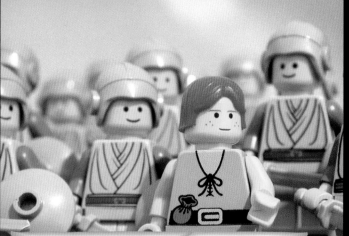

DAVID ASKED THE MEN STANDING NEAR HIM, 'WHO IS THIS UNCIRCUMCISED PHILISTINE TO DEFY THE ARMY OF THE LIVING GOD? WHAT WILL BE DONE FOR THE MAN WHO KILLS THIS PHILISTINE?'

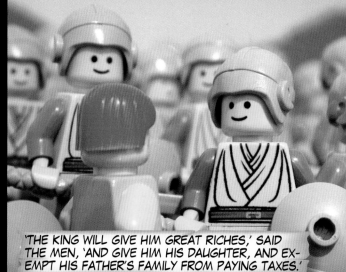

'THE KING WILL GIVE HIM GREAT RICHES,' SAID THE MEN, 'AND GIVE HIM HIS DAUGHTER, AND EX-EMPT HIS FATHER'S FAMILY FROM PAYING TAXES.'

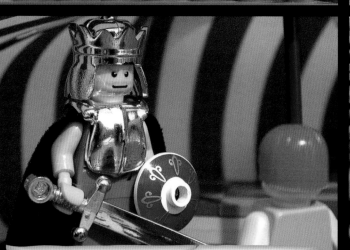

WHAT DAVID SAID WAS REPORTED TO SAUL, AND DA-VID WAS SUMMONED TO HIM. AND SAUL SAID, 'YOU CANNOT GO AGAINST THIS PHILISTINE AND FIGHT HIM, FOR YOU ARE JUST A BOY, AND HE HAS BEEN A WARRIOR SINCE HIS YOUTH.'

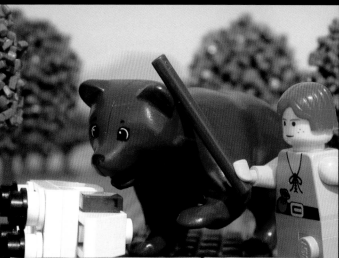

DAVID SAID, 'WHILE TENDING SHEEP, WHEN A LION OR BEAR TOOK ONE OF THE FLOCK, I WOULD CHASE HIM, STRIKE HIM, AND RESCUE IT OUT OF HIS MOUTH.'

'WHEN IT TURNED AGAINST ME, I WOULD GRAB ITS BEARD AND STRIKE AND KILL IT. YOUR SERVANT HAS KILLED BOTH LION AND BEAR THIS WAY.'

'THIS UNCIRCUMCISED PHILISTINE WILL BE LIKE ONE OF THEM FOR CHALLENGING THE ARMY OF THE LIVING GOD.'

SO SAUL SAID TO DAVID, 'GO, AND MAY YAHWEH BE WITH YOU!'

SAUL DRESSED DAVID IN HIS OWN CLOTHES. HE PUT A BRONZE HELMET ON HIS HEAD, GAVE HIM A BREASTPLATE, AND BUCKLED ON HIS SWORD. DAVID TRIED TO WALK AROUND, BUT SAID TO SAUL, 'I CAN'T GO IN THESE, I'M NOT USED TO THEM.'

SO DAVID TOOK HIS STAFF AND PUT FIVE SMOOTH STONES IN HIS SHEPHERD'S BAG. WITH HIS SLING IN HAND, HE WALKED OUT TOWARD THE PHILISTINE.

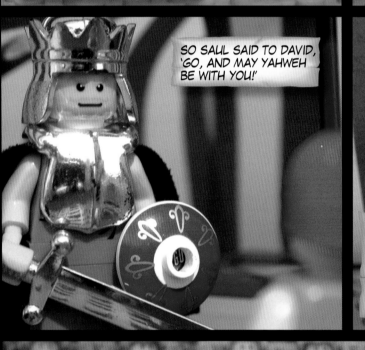

THE PHILISTINE APPROACHED DAVID WITH HIS SHIELD BEARER WALKING AHEAD OF HIM. WHEN HE SAW THAT DAVID WAS ONLY A BOY, REDDISH AND HANDSOME, HE WAS DISDAINFUL, SAYING, 'AM I A DOG, THAT YOU COME AT ME WITH STICKS?'

DAVID SAID TO THE PHILISTINE, 'I COME AGAINST YOU IN THE NAME OF YAHWEH, GOD OF THE ARMY OF ISRAEL. TODAY I WILL KILL YOU AND CUT OFF YOUR HEAD. I WILL GIVE THE CORPSES OF THE PHILISTINE ARMY TO THE BIRDS OF THE SKY AND THE WILD ANIMALS.'

AS THE PHILISTINE APPROACHED, DAVID RAN FORWARD, REACHED INTO HIS BAG FOR A STONE, AND SLUNG IT.

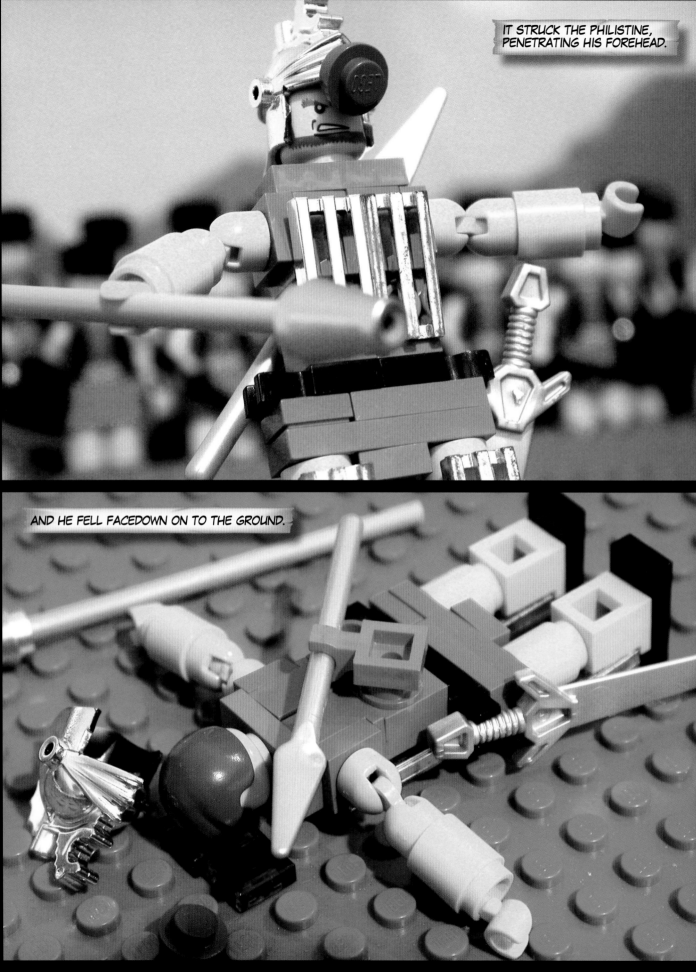

IT STRUCK THE PHILISTINE, PENETRATING HIS FOREHEAD.

AND HE FELL FACEDOWN ON TO THE GROUND.

DAVID RAN AND STOOD OVER HIM. DRAWING THE PHILISTINE'S SWORD FROM ITS SHEATH, HE KILLED HIM, AND HE CUT OFF HIS HEAD WITH THE SWORD.

WHEN THE PHILISTINES SAW THAT THEIR DUELIST WAS DEAD, THEY RAN AWAY, BUT THE MEN OF ISRAEL AND JUDAH CHASED THE PHILISTINES THROUGH THE VALLEY.

THE PHILISTINE DEAD LAY STREWN ALONG THE ROAD FROM EKRON TO GATH.

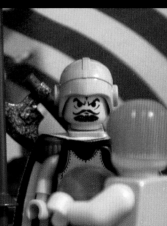

WHEN DAVID RETURNED AFTER KILLING THE PHILISTINE, ABNER TOOK HIM BEFORE SAUL WITH THE HEAD OF THE PHILISTINE STILL IN HIS HANDS. AND SAUL SAID TO HIM, 'WHOSE SON ARE YOU, YOUNG MAN?'

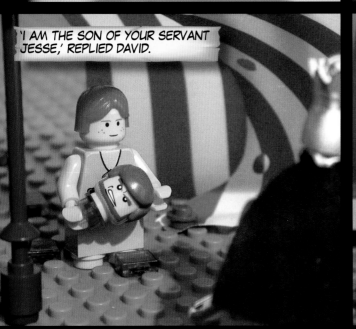

'I AM THE SON OF YOUR SERVANT JESSE,' REPLIED DAVID.

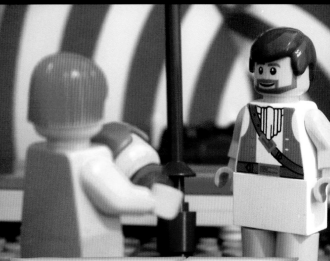

WHEN DAVID HAD FINISHED SPEAKING WITH SAUL, JONATHAN BECAME DEEPLY ATTACHED TO DAVID AND LOVED HIM WITH HIS WHOLE BEING.

WHEN THEY RETURNED, THE WOMEN CAME OUT OF ALL THE TOWNS TO MEET KING SAUL, SINGING AND DANCING WITH TAMBOURINES AND SISTRUMS. THEY SANG, 'SAUL HAS KILLED HIS THOUSANDS AND DAVID HIS TENS OF THOUSANDS.'

SAUL WAS FURIOUS AND HE SAID, 'THEY HAVE GIVEN DAVID TEN THOUSANDS, BUT GIVEN ME MERELY THOUSANDS! WHAT MORE COULD HE HAVE BUT THE KINGDOM?'

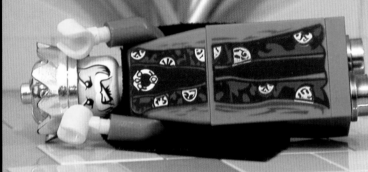

THE NEXT DAY AN EVIL SPIRIT FROM GOD CAME STRONGLY ON SAUL, AND HE WAS IN A PROPHETIC FRENZY IN HIS HOUSE WHILE DAVID PLAYED THE LYRE.

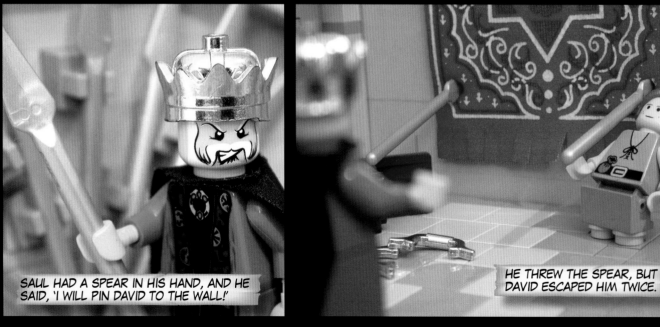

SAUL HAD A SPEAR IN HIS HAND, AND HE SAID, 'I WILL PIN DAVID TO THE WALL!'

HE THREW THE SPEAR, BUT DAVID ESCAPED HIM TWICE.

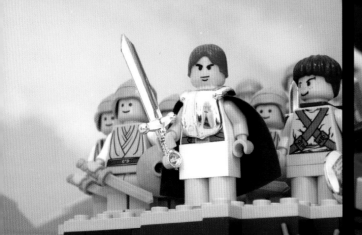

SAUL WAS AFRAID OF DAVID, SO HE REMOVED HIM FROM HIS PRESENCE, MAKING HIM AN ARMY COMMANDER.

DAVID WAS SUCCESSFUL IN EVERY MISSION SAUL SENT HIM ON, FOR YAHWEH WAS WITH HIM.

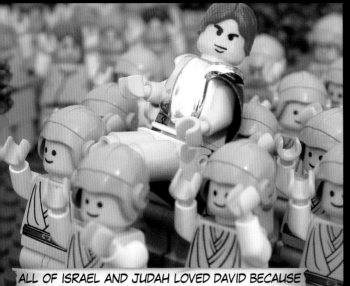

ALL OF ISRAEL AND JUDAH LOVED DAVID BECAUSE HE WAS THEIR LEADER IN BATTLE.

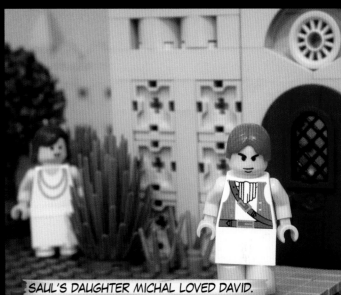

SAUL'S DAUGHTER MICHAL LOVED DAVID.

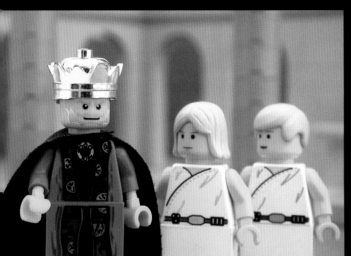

WHEN SAUL WAS TOLD OF THIS, HE WAS PLEASED AND SAID, 'SHE WILL BE A SNARE FOR HIM! TELL DAVID, "THE KING WANTS NO OTHER PRICE FOR THE BRIDE THAN A HUNDRED PHILISTINE FORESKINS."

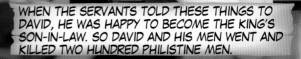

WHEN THE SERVANTS TOLD THESE THINGS TO DAVID, HE WAS HAPPY TO BECOME THE KING'S SON-IN-LAW. SO DAVID AND HIS MEN WENT AND KILLED TWO HUNDRED PHILISTINE MEN.

HE BROUGHT THEIR FORESKINS AND PRESENTED THEM BEFORE THE KING IN FULL NUMBER.

SO SAUL GAVE HIM HIS DAUGHTER MICHAL IN MARRIAGE.

SAUL REALIZED THAT YAHWEH WAS WITH DAVID, AND HE WAS MORE AFRAID OF DAVID THAN EVER. SAUL TOLD JONATHAN AND ALL HIS SERVANTS TO KILL DAVID.

BUT JONATHAN TOOK GREAT DELIGHT IN DAVID, AND SO HE SAID TO HIM, 'MY FATHER SEEKS TO KILL YOU, SO STAY IN A SECRET PLACE AND HIDE YOURSELF. I WILL SPEAK TO HIM, AND IF I FIND OUT ANYTHING, I WILL TELL YOU.'

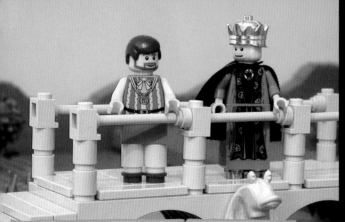

SO JONATHAN SPOKE HIGHLY OF DAVID TO HIS FATHER SAUL, SAYING, 'DAVID HAS NOT SINNED AGAINST YOU, BUT HAS GREATLY BENEFITED YOU. HE RISKED HIS LIFE TO KILL THE PHILISTINE AND YOU WERE HAPPY ABOUT IT. WHY WOULD YOU KILL AN INNOCENT MAN LIKE DAVID FOR NO REASON?'

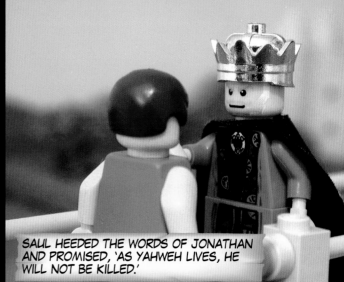

SAUL HEEDED THE WORDS OF JONATHAN AND PROMISED, 'AS YAHWEH LIVES, HE WILL NOT BE KILLED.'

SO JONATHAN SUMMONED DAVID AND BROUGHT HIM BEFORE SAUL. AND DAVID SERVED SAUL AS BEFORE.

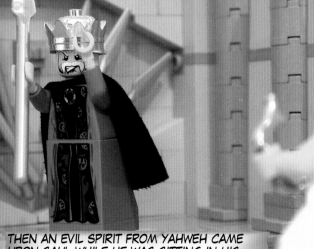

THEN AN EVIL SPIRIT FROM YAHWEH CAME UPON SAUL WHILE HE WAS SITTING IN HIS HOUSE WITH A SPEAR IN HIS HAND AND DAVID WAS PLAYING THE LYRE.

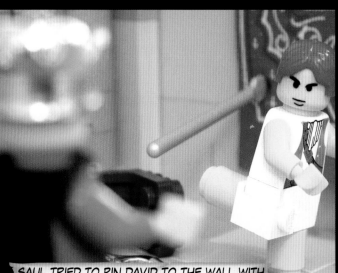

SAUL TRIED TO PIN DAVID TO THE WALL WITH THE SPEAR, BUT DAVID ESCAPED, AND THE SPEAR STUCK INTO THE WALL.

SO SAUL SENT MEN TO WATCH DAVID'S HOUSE AND KILL HIM IN THE MORNING.

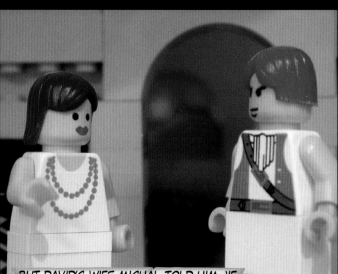

BUT DAVID'S WIFE MICHAL TOLD HIM, 'IF YOU DO NOT SAVE YOURSELF TONIGHT, TOMORROW YOU WILL BE KILLED.'

AND MICHAL LET DAVID DOWN THROUGH A WINDOW, AND HE ESCAPED, FLEEING.

DAVID FLED AND CAME TO JONATHAN. JONATHAN SAID TO DAVID, 'COME ON, LET'S GO OUT INTO THE FIELD.' SO THEY BOTH WENT OUT INTO THE FIELD.

THEY KISSED EACH OTHER.

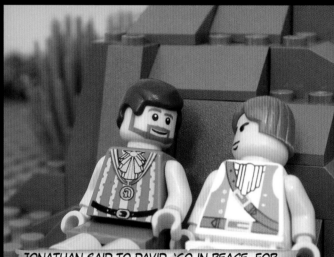

AND THEY WEPT TOGETHER.

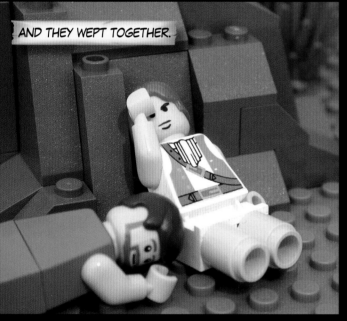

JONATHAN SAID TO DAVID, 'GO IN PEACE, FOR WE HAVE SWORN IN THE NAME OF YAHWEH THAT YAHWEH WILL BOND YOU AND ME AND YOUR DESCENDANTS AND MY DESCENDANTS FOREVER.'

THEN DAVID GOT UP AND LEFT, AND JONATHAN WENT BACK TO THE CITY.

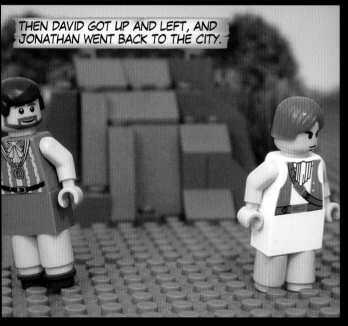

SO DAVID FLED THERE, ESCAPING TO THE CAVES AT ADULLAM.

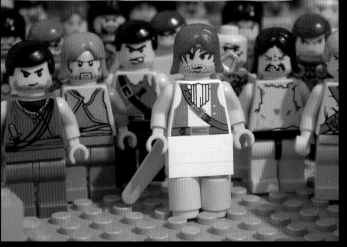

AND ALL THOSE WHO WERE IN TROUBLE, IN DEBT, OR EMBITTERED GATHERED TO HIM, AND DAVID BECAME THEIR LEADER. HE HAD ABOUT 400 MEN WITH HIM.

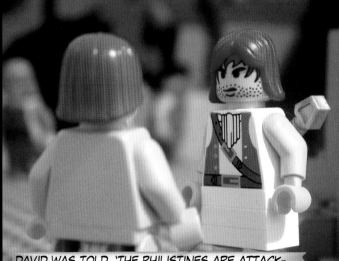

DAVID WAS TOLD, 'THE PHILISTINES ARE ATTACKING KEILAH, LOOTING THE THRESHING FLOORS.'

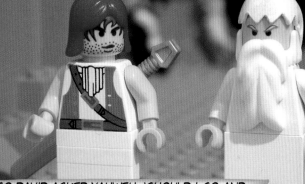

SO DAVID ASKED YAHWEH, 'SHOULD I GO AND STRIKE DOWN THESE PHILISTINES AND RESCUE KEILAH?' AND YAHWEH SAID, 'GO, STRIKE DOWN THE PHILISTINES AND RESCUE KEILAH.'

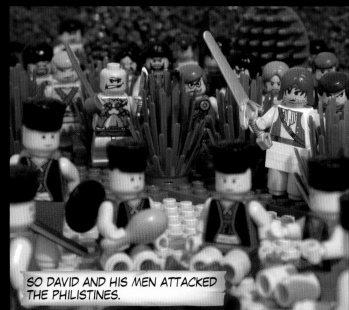

SO DAVID AND HIS MEN ATTACKED THE PHILISTINES.

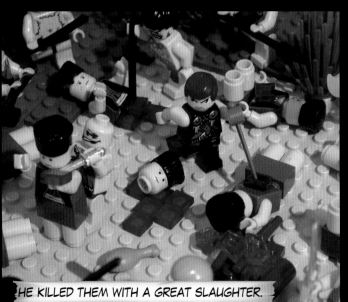

HE KILLED THEM WITH A GREAT SLAUGHTER.

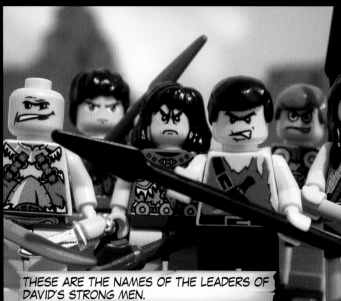

THESE ARE THE NAMES OF THE LEADERS OF DAVID'S STRONG MEN.

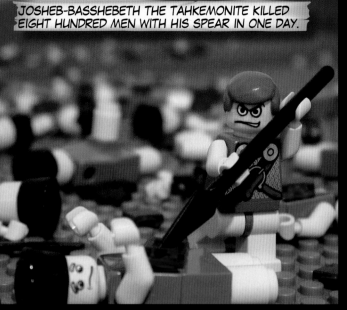

JOSHEB-BASSHEBETH THE TAHKEMONITE KILLED EIGHT HUNDRED MEN WITH HIS SPEAR IN ONE DAY.

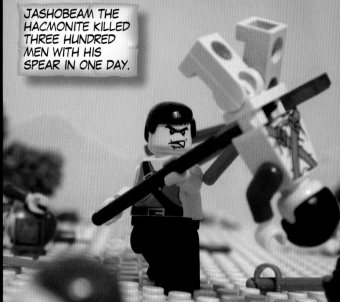

JASHOBEAM THE HACMONITE KILLED THREE HUNDRED MEN WITH HIS SPEAR IN ONE DAY.

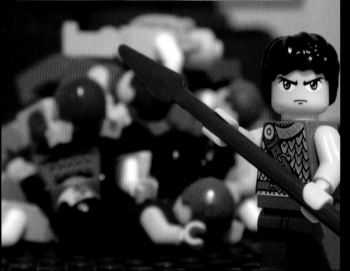

ABISHAI, THE BROTHER OF JOAB, KILLED THREE HUNDRED MEN WITH HIS SPEAR.

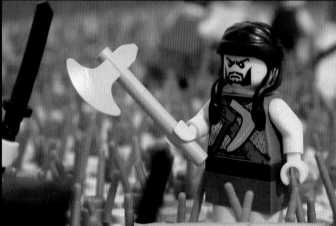

THEN, THERE WAS SHAMMAH THE HARARITE. WHEN THE ARMY RETREATED FROM THE PHILISTINES AT LEHI, HE HELD HIS GROUND IN A FIELD OF LENTILS.

HE DEFEATED THE PHILISTINES WITH YAHWEH, DELIVERING THEM A GREAT VICTORY.

BENAIAH, SON OF JEHOIADA, WAS A STRONG MAN WHO PERFORMED GREAT DEEDS. HE STRUCK DOWN THE TWO SONS OF ARIEL OF MOAB.

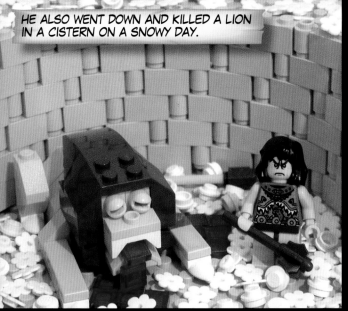

HE ALSO WENT DOWN AND KILLED A LION IN A CISTERN ON A SNOWY DAY.

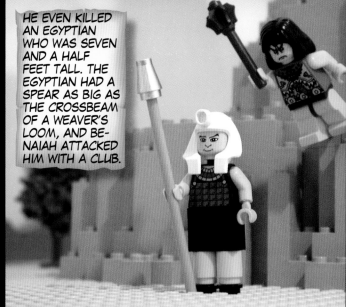

HE EVEN KILLED AN EGYPTIAN WHO WAS SEVEN AND A HALF FEET TALL. THE EGYPTIAN HAD A SPEAR AS BIG AS THE CROSSBEAM OF A WEAVER'S LOOM, AND BE-NAIAH ATTACKED HIM WITH A CLUB.

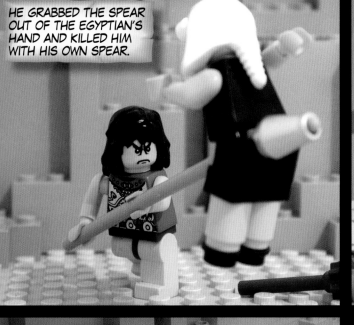

HE GRABBED THE SPEAR OUT OF THE EGYPTIAN'S HAND AND KILLED HIM WITH HIS OWN SPEAR.

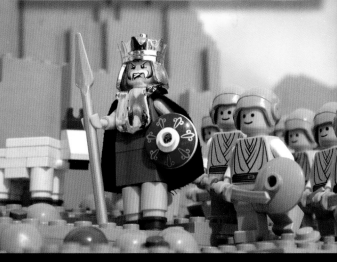

NOW SAUL TOOK 3,000 SELECT MEN FROM ALL OF ISRAEL AND SET OUT TO FIND DAVID AND HIS MEN IN THE REGION OF THE ROCKS AND MOUNTAIN GOATS.

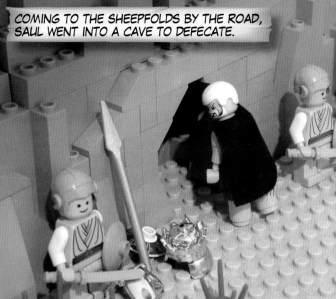

COMING TO THE SHEEPFOLDS BY THE ROAD, SAUL WENT INTO A CAVE TO DEFECATE.

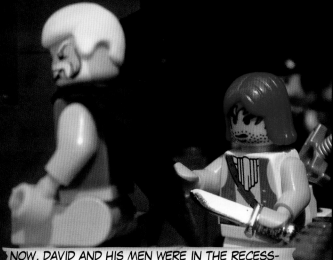

NOW, DAVID AND HIS MEN WERE IN THE RECESS-ES OF THE CAVE, AND DAVID GOT UP AND QUIETLY CUT THE EDGE OFF OF SAUL'S ROBE.

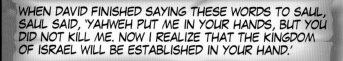

WHEN SAUL LEFT THE CAVE, DAVID CALLED OUT, 'MY LORD, SEE THE EDGE OF YOUR ROBE IN MY HAND! WHEN I CUT OFF THE EDGE OF YOUR ROBE, I DIDN'T KILL YOU. SO REALIZE AND UNDERSTAND THAT EVIL AND REBELLION ARE NOT MY PLAN.'

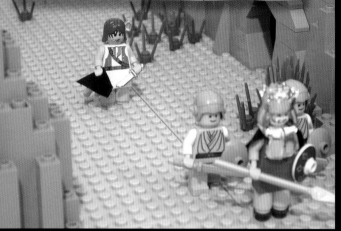

WHEN DAVID FINISHED SAYING THESE WORDS TO SAUL, SAUL SAID, 'YAHWEH PUT ME IN YOUR HANDS, BUT YOU DID NOT KILL ME. NOW I REALIZE THAT THE KINGDOM OF ISRAEL WILL BE ESTABLISHED IN YOUR HAND.'

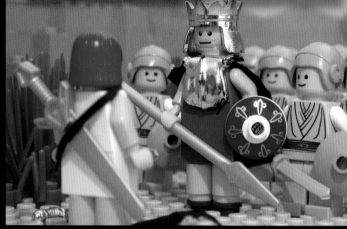

SO SAUL WENT BACK TO HIS HOUSE AND DAVID TO THE STRONGHOLD.

DAVID SAID TO HIMSELF, 'ONE OF THESE DAYS, I'LL BE DESTROYED BY THE HAND OF SAUL. THE BEST THING FOR ME TO DO IS ESCAPE TO THE LAND OF THE PHILISTINES.'

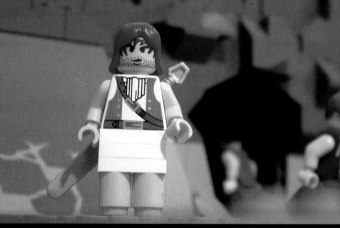

SO DAVID AND HIS MEN, EACH WITH THEIR FAMILIES, CROSSED OVER TO GATH, AND DAVID SETTLED IN GATH WITH HIS TWO WIVES, AHINOAM AND ABIGAIL.

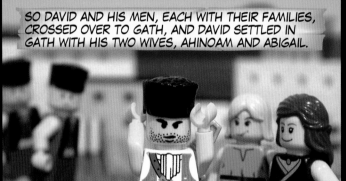

AND DAVID SAID TO KING ACHISH, 'PLEASE GIVE ME ONE OF THE COUNTRY TOWNS TO LIVE IN. FOR WHY SHOULD YOUR SERVANT LIVE IN THE ROYAL CITY WITH YOU?'

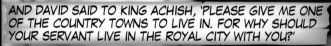

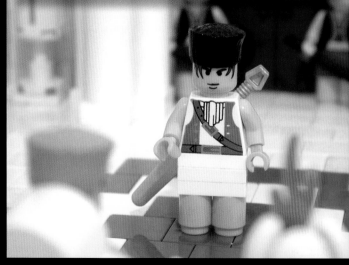

SO ACHISH GAVE HIM ZILKAG ON THAT DAY. THE LENGTH OF TIME THAT DAVID LIVED IN THE PHILISTINE COUNTRYSIDE WAS A YEAR AND FOUR MONTHS.

DAVID AND HIS MEN WOULD GO OUT AND RAID THE GESHURITES, GIRZITES, AND THE AMALEKITES.

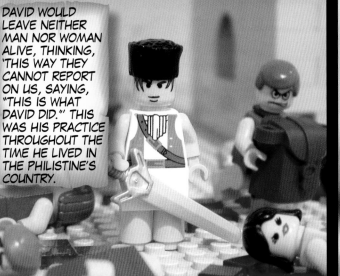

DAVID WOULD LEAVE NEITHER MAN NOR WOMAN ALIVE, THINKING, 'THIS WAY THEY CANNOT REPORT ON US, SAYING, "THIS IS WHAT DAVID DID."' THIS WAS HIS PRACTICE THROUGHOUT THE TIME HE LIVED IN THE PHILISTINE'S COUNTRY.

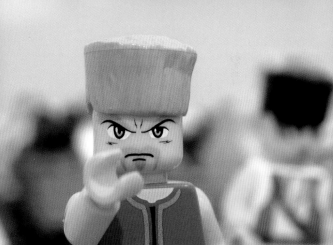

SO ACHISH TRUSTED DAVID, SAYING TO HIMSELF, 'HE HAS BECOME REPUGNANT TO HIS OWN PEOPLE IN ISRAEL. HE WILL PERMANENTLY BE MY SERVANT.'

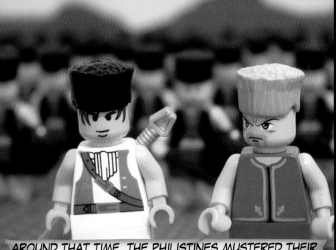

AROUND THAT TIME, THE PHILISTINES MUSTERED THEIR TROOPS TO FIGHT A WAR AGAINST ISRAEL. ACHISH SAID TO DAVID, 'YOU SHOULD UNDERSTAND THAT YOU AND YOUR MEN MUST GO WITH ME INTO THE BATTLE.'

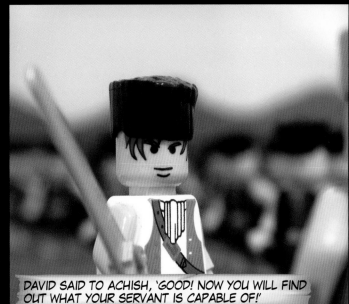

DAVID SAID TO ACHISH, 'GOOD! NOW YOU WILL FIND OUT WHAT YOUR SERVANT IS CAPABLE OF!'

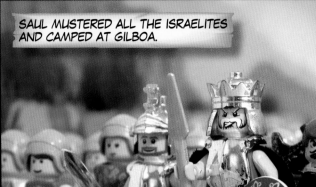
SAUL MUSTERED ALL THE ISRAELITES AND CAMPED AT GILBOA.

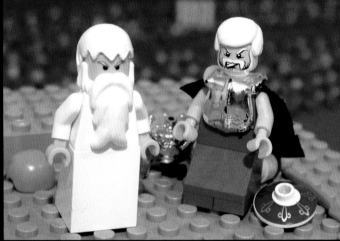
WHEN SAUL SAW THE CAMP OF THE PHILISTINES, HE WAS COMPLETELY TERRIFIED, SO HE INQUIRED OF YAHWEH. BUT YAHWEH DID NOT ANSWER HIM.

NOW SAMUEL WAS DEAD AND BURIED, SO SAUL SAID TO HIS SERVANTS, 'FIND ME A WOMAN WHO IS A NEC-ROMANCER SO THAT I MAY GO AND INQUIRE OF HER.'

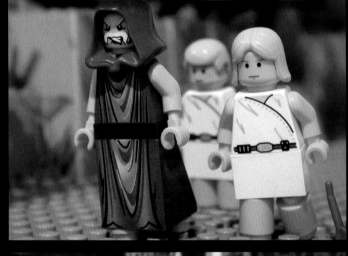
HIS SERVANTS TOLD HIM, 'THERE IS A WOMAN WHO IS A NECROMANCER IN ENDOR.' SO SAUL DIS-GUISED HIMSELF WITH OTHER CLOTHING AND SET OUT ACCOMPANIED BY TWO OF HIS MEN.

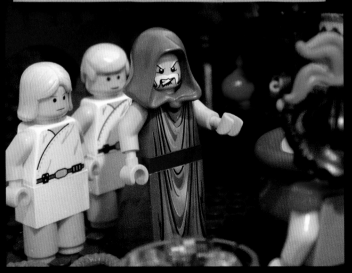
THEY CAME TO THE WOMAN AT NIGHT AND SAID, 'USE DIVINATION TO CONJURE THE PERSON I TELL YOU TO.'

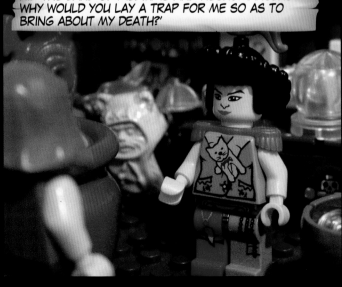
BUT THE WOMAN SAID, 'DON'T YOU KNOW THAT SAUL RID THE LAND OF MEDIUMS AND NECROMANCERS? WHY WOULD YOU LAY A TRAP FOR ME SO AS TO BRING ABOUT MY DEATH?'

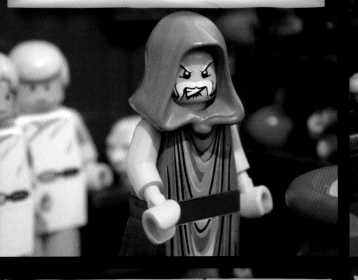

SO SAUL SWORE AN OATH BY YAHWEH, SAYING, 'AS SURELY AS YAHWEH LIVES, YOU WILL NOT BE PUNISHED FOR THIS MATTER. NOW CONJURE SAMUEL FOR ME!'

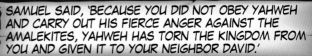

WHEN THE WOMAN SAW SAMUEL, SHE CRIED OUT LOUDLY. WHEN SAUL RE-ALIZED IT WAS SAMUEL, HE BOWED TO THE GROUND. SAMUEL SAID TO SAUL, 'WHY HAVE YOU DISTURBED ME BY BRINGING ME UP?'

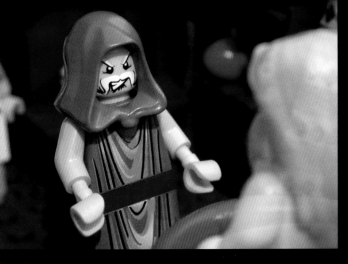

SAUL SAID, 'THE PHILISTINES ARE ATTACKING, AND GOD HAS TURNED AWAY FROM ME. HE DOES NOT ANSWER ME, SO I HAVE CALLED ON YOU TO TELL ME WHAT TO DO.'

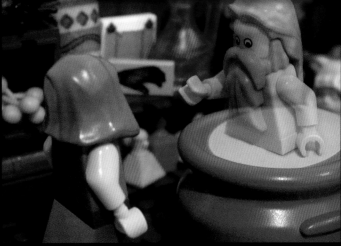

SAMUEL SAID, 'BECAUSE YOU DID NOT OBEY YAHWEH AND CARRY OUT HIS FIERCE ANGER AGAINST THE AMALEKITES, YAHWEH HAS TORN THE KINGDOM FROM YOU AND GIVEN IT TO YOUR NEIGHBOR DAVID.'

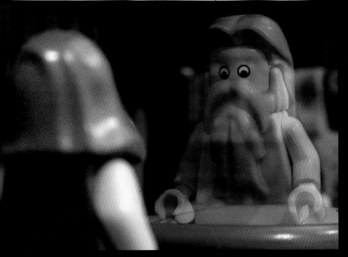

'TOMORROW, BOTH YOU AND YOUR SONS WILL DIE, AND YAHWEH WILL HAND THE ARMY OF ISRAEL OVER TO THE PHILISTINES.'

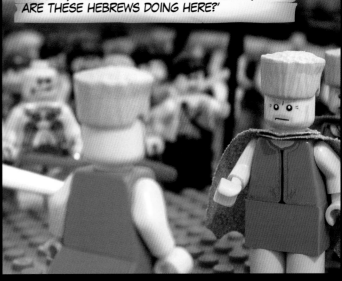

WHILE THE PHILISTINES WERE REVIEWING THEIR TROOPS, THE PHILISTINE LEADERS ASKED, 'WHAT ARE THESE HEBREWS DOING HERE?'

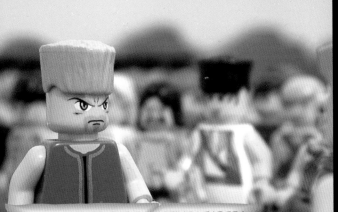

ACHISH SAID TO THE PHILISTINE LEADERS, 'THIS IS DAVID, SERVANT OF KING SAUL OF ISRAEL, WHO HAS BEEN WITH ME FOR YEARS. SINCE THE DAY HE DESERTED, I'VE FOUND NO FAULT WITH HIM.'

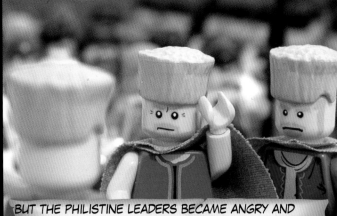

BUT THE PHILISTINE LEADERS BECAME ANGRY AND SAID, 'SEND HIM BACK, FOR IN BATTLE HE MIGHT TURN ON US! ISN'T THIS DAVID OF WHOM THEY SANG, "SAUL HAS KILLED HIS THOUSANDS, BUT DAVID HIS TENS OF THOUSANDS?" WHAT BETTER WAY TO PLEASE HIS LORD THAN WITH THE HEADS OF OUR MEN?'

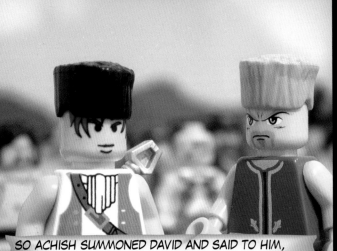

SO ACHISH SUMMONED DAVID AND SAID TO HIM, 'YOU ARE AN UPRIGHT MAN, AND I FIND NO FAULT WITH YOU, BUT THE PHILISTINE LEADERS DO NOT AP- PROVE OF YOU. SO TURN BACK, AND GO IN PEACE.'

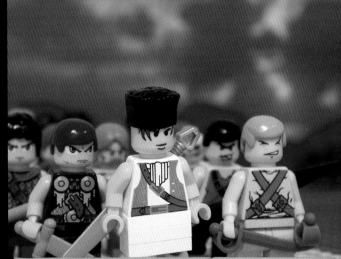

SO EARLY THE NEXT MORNING, DAVID AND HIS MEN SET OUT TO RETURN TO THE LAND OF THE PHILISTINES.

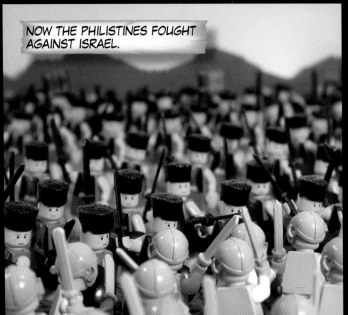

NOW THE PHILISTINES FOUGHT AGAINST ISRAEL.

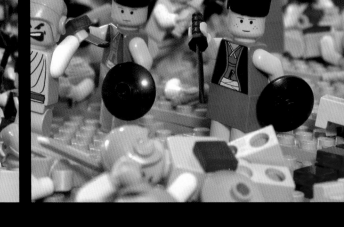

THE ISRAELITES FLED FROM THE PHILISTINES, AND MANY OF THEM FELL DEAD ON MOUNT GILBOA.

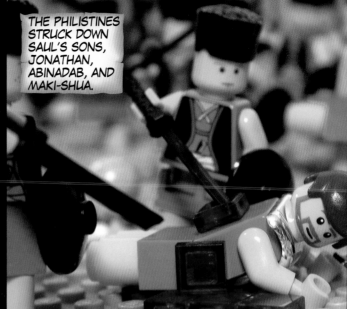

THE PHILISTINES WERE CLOSE ON THE HEELS OF SAUL.

THE PHILISTINES STRUCK DOWN SAUL'S SONS, JONATHAN, ABINADAB, AND MAKI-SHUA.

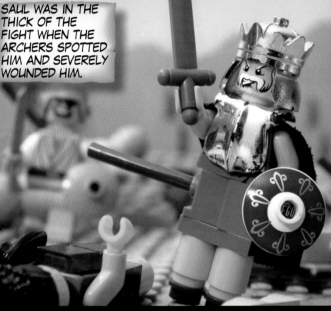

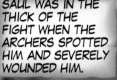

SAUL WAS IN THE THICK OF THE FIGHT WHEN THE ARCHERS SPOTTED HIM AND SEVERELY WOUNDED HIM.

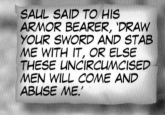

SAUL SAID TO HIS ARMOR BEARER, 'DRAW YOUR SWORD AND STAB ME WITH IT, OR ELSE THESE UNCIRCUMCISED MEN WILL COME AND ABUSE ME.'

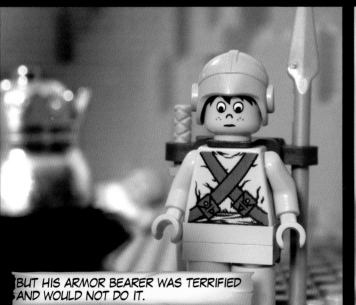

BUT HIS ARMOR BEARER WAS TERRIFIED AND WOULD NOT DO IT.

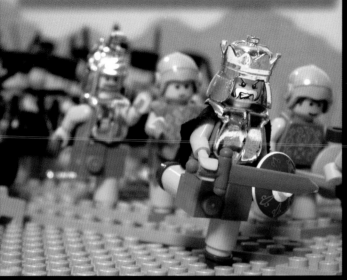

SO SAUL TOOK HIS SWORD AND FELL ON IT. SAUL DIED BECAUSE HE WAS NOT FAITHFUL TO YAHWEH AND DID NOT SEEK YAHWEH'S GUIDANCE. SO YAHWEH KILLED HIM.

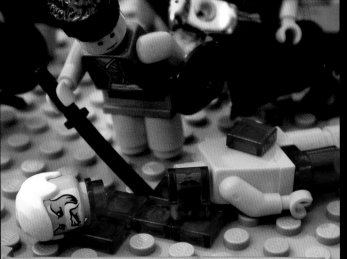

THE NEXT DAY, THE PHILISTINES DISCOVERED SAUL AND HIS THREE SONS LYING DEAD ON MOUNT GILBOA. THEY STRIPPED HIS CORPSE AND CUT OFF SAUL'S HEAD.

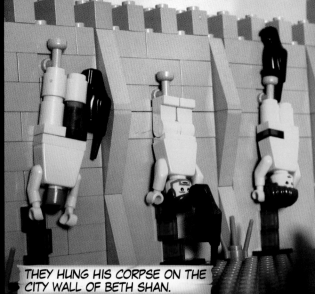

THEY HUNG HIS CORPSE ON THE CITY WALL OF BETH SHAN.

AND THEY PUT HIS ARMOR AND HIS HEAD IN THE TEMPLE OF DAGON.

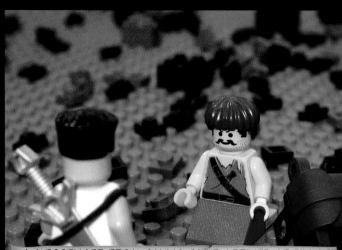

A MESSENGER FROM SAUL'S CAMP ARRIVED AT ZIKLAG WITH HIS CLOTHES TORN AND DIRT ON HIS HEAD. HE THREW HIMSELF PROSTRATE BEFORE DAVID, SAYING, 'THE ARMY FLED THE BATTLE AND MANY FELL DEAD. EVEN SAUL AND HIS SON JONATHAN ARE DEAD!'

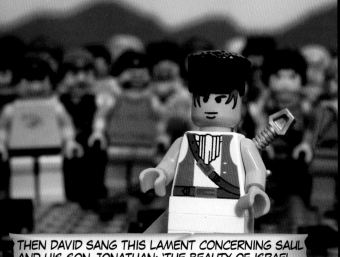

THEN DAVID SANG THIS LAMENT CONCERNING SAUL AND HIS SON JONATHAN: 'THE BEAUTY OF ISRAEL LIES SLAIN! HOW THE MIGHTY HAVE FALLEN!'

'I GRIEVE OVER YOU, MY BROTHER, JONATHAN. YOUR LOVE WAS DEARER TO ME THAN THE LOVE OF A WOMAN!'

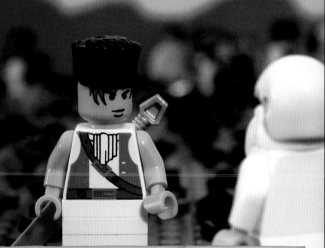

THEN DAVID ASKED YAHWEH, 'SHOULD I GO UP TO ONE OF THE CITIES OF JUDAH? WHERE SHOULD I GO?' AND YAHWEH REPLIED, 'TO HEBRON.'

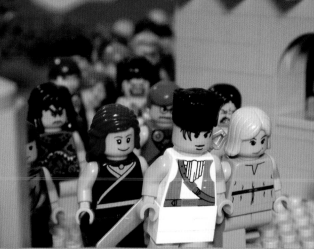

SO DAVID AND HIS TWO WIVES, AHINOAM AND ABIGAIL, AND THE MEN WHO WERE WITH HIM AND THEIR FAMILIES, SETTLED IN THE CITIES OF HEBRON.

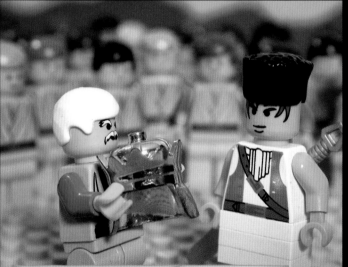

AND THE MEN OF JUDAH CAME AND ANOINTED DAVID AS KING OVER THE PEOPLE OF JUDAH.

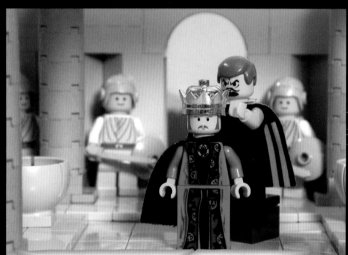

SAUL'S ARMY GENERAL, ABNER, TOOK SAUL'S SON ISHBAAL TO MAHANAIM AND APPOINTED HIM KING OVER ALL ISRAEL. SAUL'S SON, ISHBAAL, WAS 40 YEARS OLD WHEN HE BECAME KING OF ISRAEL.

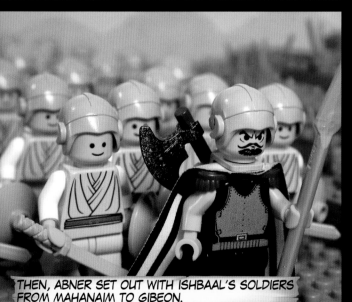

THEN, ABNER SET OUT WITH ISHBAAL'S SOLDIERS FROM MAHANAIM TO GIBEON.

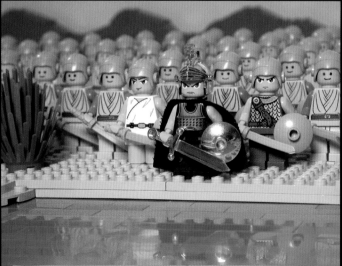

AND JOAB SET OUT WITH DAVID'S SOLDIERS AND CONFRONTED HIM AT THE POOL OF GIBEON.

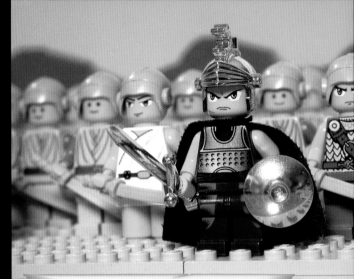

ONE GROUP TOOK POSITION ON ONE SIDE OF THE POOL, AND THE OTHER GROUP TOOK POSITION ON THE OTHER SIDE OF THE POOL. THEN, ABNER SAID TO JOAB, 'LET'S HAVE SOME OF THE MEN COME FORWARD AND FIGHT BEFORE US.'

AND JOAB SAID, 'LET THEM COME FORWARD!'

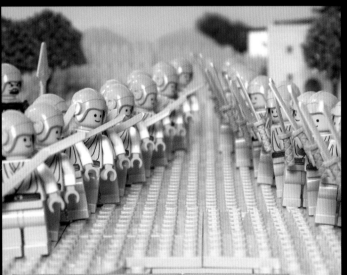

SO THEY CROSSED OVER, TWELVE BELONGING TO ISHBAAL AND TWELVE TO DAVID.

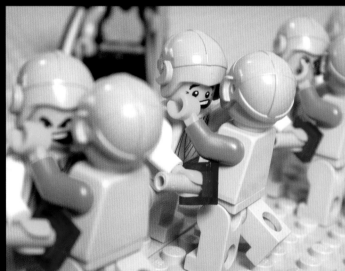

AND EACH GRABBED THE HEAD OF HIS OPPONENT AND THRUST HIS SWORD INTO HIS SIDE.

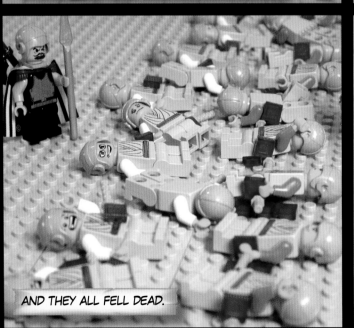

AND THEY ALL FELL DEAD.

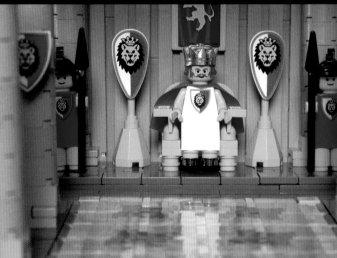

DAVID REIGNED AS KING IN HEBRON FOR SEVEN YEARS AND SIX MONTHS WHILE WAR CONTINUED BETWEEN THE HOUSE OF SAUL AND THE HOUSE OF DAVID.

NOW, SAUL'S SON HAD TWO MEN IN CHARGE OF RAID-ING UNITS, BROTHERS, RECAB AND BAANAH. DURING THE HOTTEST PART OF THE DAY, ISHBAAL WAS ENJOYING HIS MIDDAY REST, AND THEY ENTERED THE INNER HOUSE.

THEY STABBED HIM IN THE STOMACH, THEN THEY CUT OFF HIS HEAD.

RECAB AND BAANAH BROUGHT THE HEAD OF ISHBAAL TO DAVID, SAYING, 'LOOK! THE HEAD OF YOUR ENEMY WHO SOUGHT YOUR LIFE! YAHWEH HAS GRANTED VENGEANCE TO MY LORD!'

DAVID TOLD RECAB AND BAANAH, 'WHEN WORTHLESS MEN KILL AN INNOCENT MAN AS HE SLEEPS IN HIS OWN HOUSE, SHOULD I NOT REQUIRE HIS BLOOD FROM YOUR HANDS AND RID THE EARTH OF YOU?'

THEN DAVID COM-MANDED HIS SOL-DIERS, AND THEY CUT OFF THEIR HANDS AND FEET. AND THEY HUNG THEM NEAR THE POOL IN HEBRON.

KING DAVID MADE A COVENANT WITH THE ELDERS OF ISRAEL AT HEBRON, AND THEY ANOINTED DAVID KING OVER ISRAEL. DAVID WAS 30 YEARS OLD WHEN HE BECAME KING.

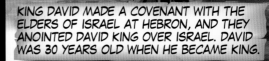

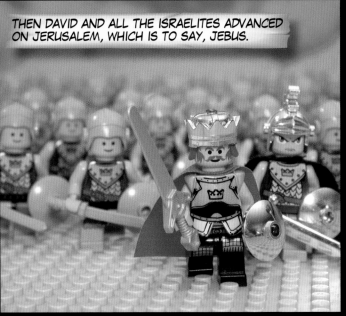

THEN DAVID AND ALL THE ISRAELITES ADVANCED ON JERUSALEM, WHICH IS TO SAY, JEBUS.

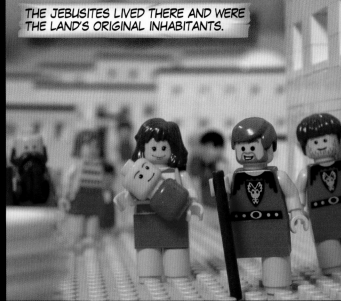

THE JEBUSITES LIVED THERE AND WERE THE LAND'S ORIGINAL INHABITANTS.

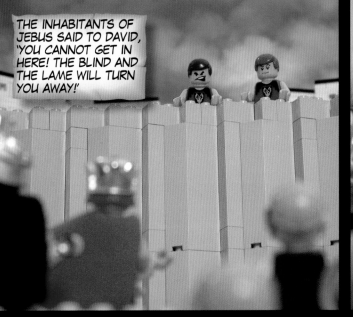

THE INHABITANTS OF JEBUS SAID TO DAVID, 'YOU CANNOT GET IN HERE! THE BLIND AND THE LAME WILL TURN YOU AWAY!'

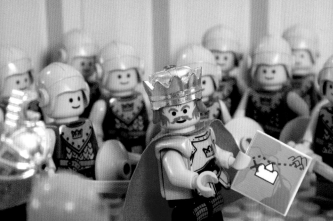

DAVID SAID ON THAT DAY, 'WHOEVER ATTACKS MUST USE THE WATER TUNNEL TO GET TO THE BLIND AND LAME WHO DAVID HATES WITH HIS ENTIRE BEING! WHOEVER KILLS A JEBUSITE FIRST WILL BECOME MY COMMANDING GENERAL!'

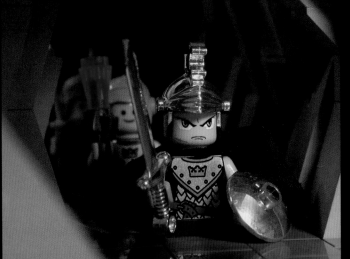

SO JOAB ATTACKED FIRST.

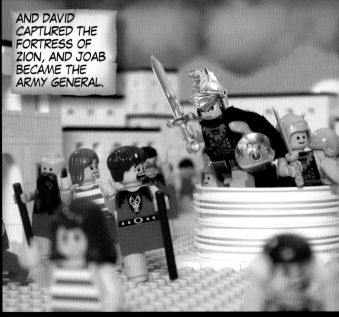

AND DAVID CAPTURED THE FORTRESS OF ZION, AND JOAB BECAME THE ARMY GENERAL.

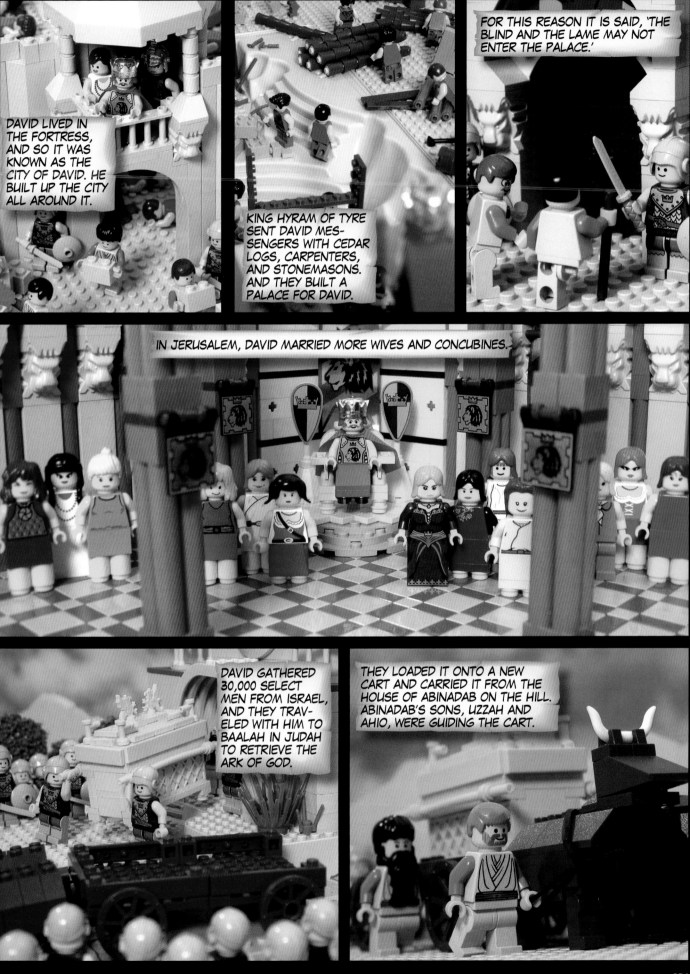

DAVID LIVED IN THE FORTRESS, AND SO IT WAS KNOWN AS THE CITY OF DAVID. HE BUILT UP THE CITY ALL AROUND IT.

KING HYRAM OF TYRE SENT DAVID MESSENGERS WITH CEDAR LOGS, CARPENTERS, AND STONEMASONS. AND THEY BUILT A PALACE FOR DAVID.

FOR THIS REASON IT IS SAID, 'THE BLIND AND THE LAME MAY NOT ENTER THE PALACE.'

IN JERUSALEM, DAVID MARRIED MORE WIVES AND CONCUBINES.

DAVID GATHERED 30,000 SELECT MEN FROM ISRAEL, AND THEY TRAVELED WITH HIM TO BAALAH IN JUDAH TO RETRIEVE THE ARK OF GOD.

THEY LOADED IT ONTO A NEW CART AND CARRIED IT FROM THE HOUSE OF ABINADAB ON THE HILL. ABINADAB'S SONS, UZZAH AND AHIO, WERE GUIDING THE CART.

AND DAVID AND ALL ISRAEL WERE EN-THUSIASTICALLY CELEBRATING: SINGING, AND PLAYING ZITHERS, TAMBOURINES, RATTLES, AND CYMBALS.

WHEN THEY CAME TO THE THRESHING FLOOR AT NACON, THE OXEN STUM-BLED, SO UZZAH REACHED OUT AND STEADIED THE ARK OF GOD.

THE ANGER OF YAHWEH BLAZED AGAINST UZZAH, AND HE KILLED HIM FOR HAVING TOUCHED THE ARK.

DAVID WAS ANGRY BECAUSE YAHWEH ATTACKED UZZAH, AND HE CALLED THAT PLACE OUTBURST-AGAINST-UZZAH. AND THAT REMAINS ITS NAME TO THIS DAY.

SO DAVID DID NOT MOVE THE ARK TO THE CITY OF DAVID. HE LEFT IT AT THE HOUSE OF OBED-EDOM, THE GITTITE.

THE ARK OF YAHWEH STAYED IN THE HOUSE OF OBED-EDOM FOR THREE MONTHS, AND DAVID WAS TOLD, 'YAHWEH HAS BLESSED THE FAMILY OF OBED-EDOM AND EVERYTHING HE OWNS BECAUSE OF THE ARK OF GOD.'

SO THEN DAVID WAS HAPPY TO BRING THE ARK TO THE CITY OF DAVID. ALL ISRAEL WAS SHOUTING AND BLOWING TRUMPETS, AND DAVID DANCED ENTHUSIASTICALLY BEFORE YAHWEH, WEARING A LOINCLOTH.

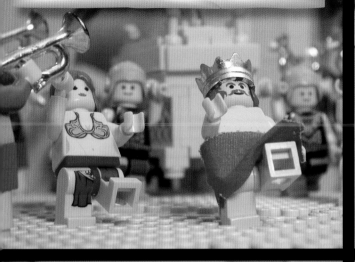

AS THE ARK OF YAHWEH ENTERED THE CITY OF DAVID, SAUL'S DAUGHTER, MICHAL, LOOKED OUT THE WINDOW.

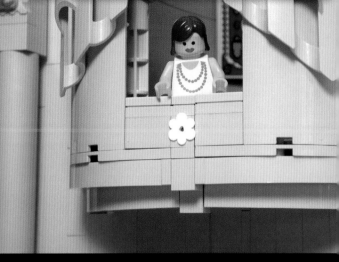

WHEN SHE SAW KING DAVID LEAPING AND DANCING BEFORE THE LORD, SHE WAS APPALLED BY HIM.

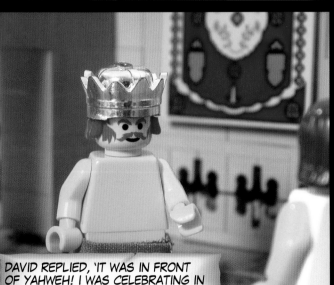

WHEN DAVID WENT HOME, SAUL'S DAUGHTER, MICHAL, SAID, 'WHAT HONOR THE KING OF ISRAEL HAS BROUGHT HIMSELF TODAY! HE HAS EXPOSED HIMSELF IN FRONT OF THE SLAVE GIRLS LIKE A FOOL!'

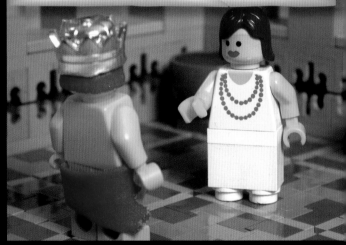

DAVID REPLIED, 'IT WAS IN FRONT OF YAHWEH! I WAS CELEBRATING IN FRONT OF YAHWEH WHO CHOSE ME OVER YOUR FATHER AND HIS FAMILY!'

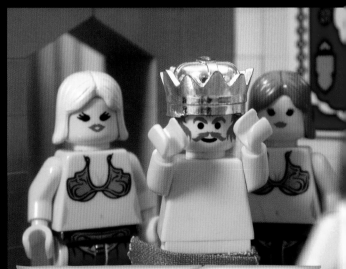

'AND I AM PREPARED TO HUMILIATE MYSELF EVEN MORE THAN THIS! BUT AMONGST THE SLAVE GIRLS YOU MENTIONED, LET ME BE HONORED!'

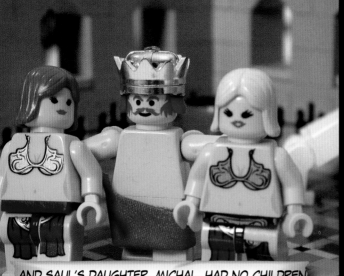

AND SAUL'S DAUGHTER, MICHAL, HAD NO CHILDREN TO THE DAY SHE DIED.

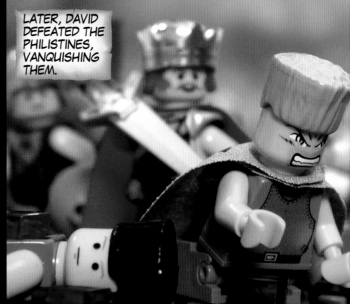

LATER, DAVID DEFEATED THE PHILISTINES, VANQUISHING THEM.

HE TOOK GATH AND THE SURROUNDING TOWNS AWAY FROM THE PHILISTINES.

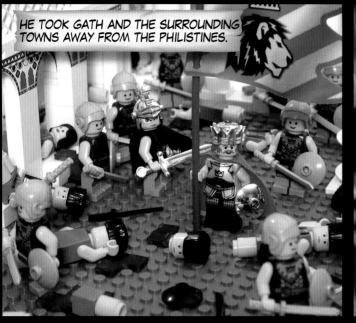

AND DAVID DEFEATED THE MOABITES.

THEN, HE MADE THEM LIE ON THE GROUND, AND HE USED A ROPE TO MEASURE THEM OFF. EVERY TWO LENGTHS OF THEM WERE PUT TO DEATH, AND EACH THIRD LENGTH WAS ALLOWED TO LIVE.

DAVID FOUGHT AGAINST KING HADADEZER OF ZOBAH AS HE SOUGHT TO RESTORE HIS CONTROL ALONG THE EUPHRATES RIVER.

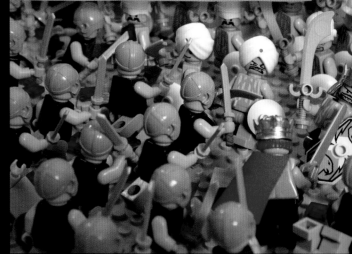

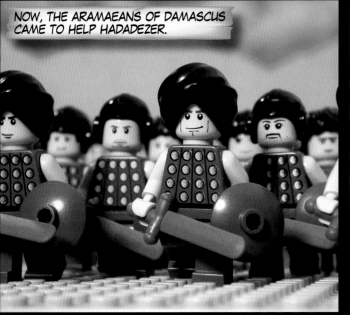

NOW, THE ARAMAEANS OF DAMASCUS CAME TO HELP HADADEZER.

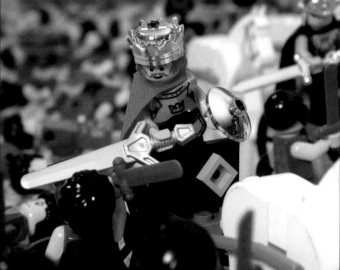

AND DAVID STRUCK DOWN 22,000 OF THEM.

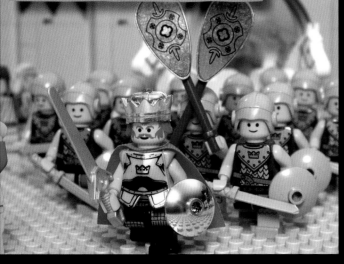

DAVID TOOK THE GOLDEN SHIELDS WHICH HADADEZER'S SERVANTS HAD CARRIED AND BROUGHT THEM TO JERUSALEM.

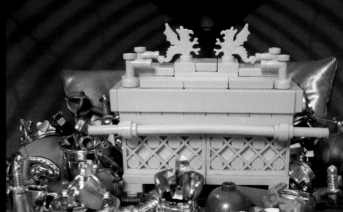

KING DAVID DEDICATED THESE THINGS TO YAHWEH, ALONG WITH THE SILVER AND GOLD THAT HE HAD TAKEN AWAY FROM EDOM, MOAB, THE AMMONITES, THE PHILISTINES, AND AMALEK.

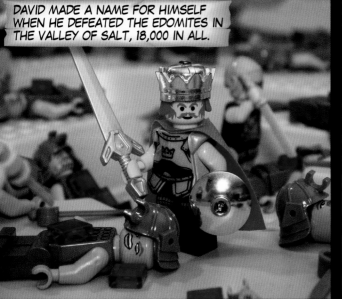

DAVID MADE A NAME FOR HIMSELF WHEN HE DEFEATED THE EDOMITES IN THE VALLEY OF SALT, 18,000 IN ALL.

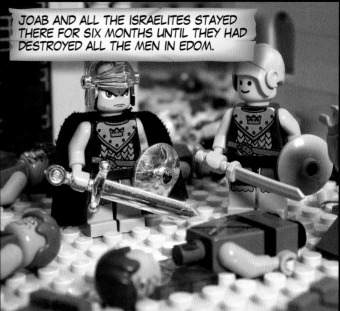

JOAB AND ALL THE ISRAELITES STAYED THERE FOR SIX MONTHS UNTIL THEY HAD DESTROYED ALL THE MEN IN EDOM.

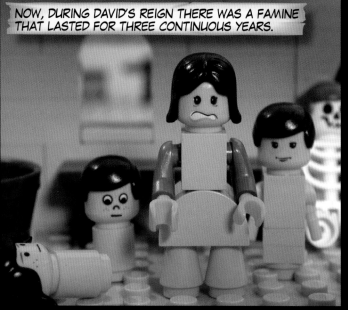

NOW, DURING DAVID'S REIGN THERE WAS A FAMINE THAT LASTED FOR THREE CONTINUOUS YEARS.

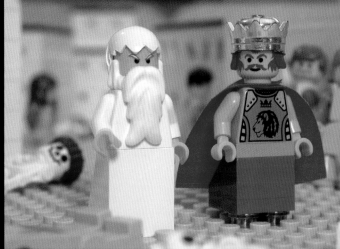

SO DAVID SOUGHT THE FACE OF YAHWEH, AND YAHWEH SAID, 'IT IS BECAUSE OF SAUL AND HIS BLOODY FAMILY, BECAUSE HE KILLED THE GIBEONITES.'

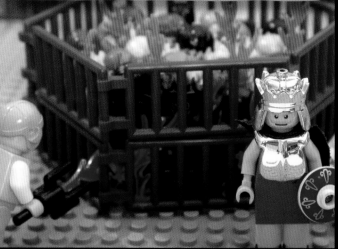

THE GIBEONITES WERE NOT ISRAELITES, BUT THE ISRAELITES HAD VOWED TO SPARE THEM. HOWEVER, IN HIS ZEAL FOR THE PEOPLE OF ISRAEL AND JUDAH, SAUL HAD SOUGHT TO ANNIHILATE THEM.

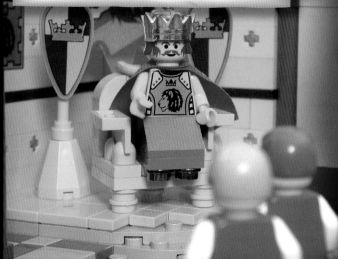

SO THE KING SUMMONED THE GIBEONITES AND ASKED, 'HOW CAN I MAKE AMENDS SO THAT YOU WILL BLESS YAHWEH'S INHERITANCE?'

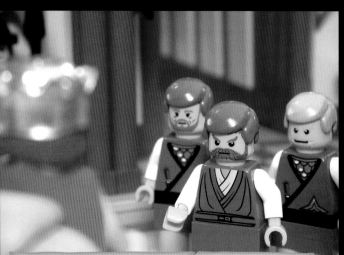

THEY REPLIED, 'HAND OVER TO US SEVEN SONS OF THE MAN WHO SOUGHT TO DISMEMBER AND ANNIHILATE US, AND WE WILL DISMEMBER THEM BEFORE YAHWEH AT GIBEON.'

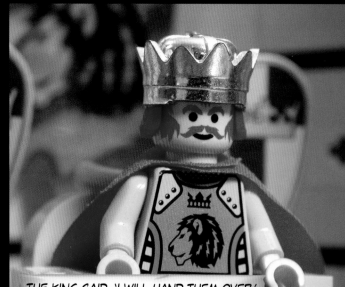

THE KING SAID, 'I WILL HAND THEM OVER.'

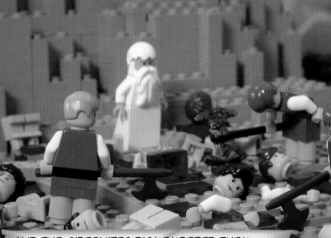

THE KING TOOK SAUL'S TWO SONS ARMONI AND ME-PHIBAAL, WHOSE MOTHER WAS RIZPAH, ALONG WITH THE FIVE SONS OF SAUL'S DAUGHTER MERAB, AND HE HANDED THEM OVER TO THE GIBEONITES.

AND THE GIBEONITES DISMEMBERED THEM BEFORE YAHWEH ON THE MOUNTAIN. THE SEVEN OF THEM DIED TOGETHER. THEY WERE KILLED ON THE FIRST DAYS OF HARVEST.

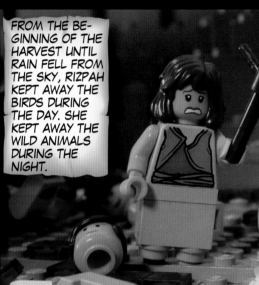

FROM THE BE-GINNING OF THE HARVEST UNTIL RAIN FELL FROM THE SKY, RIZPAH KEPT AWAY THE BIRDS DURING THE DAY. SHE KEPT AWAY THE WILD ANIMALS DURING THE NIGHT.

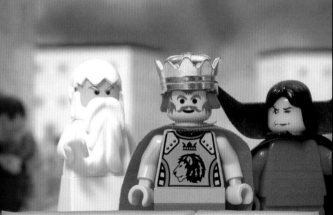

AGAIN, YAHWEH'S ANGER BLAZED AGAINST ISRAEL, AND HE INCITED DAVID AGAINST THEM, SAYING, 'GO AND TAKE A CENSUS OF ISRAEL AND JUDAH!' AND SATAN ROSE UP AGAINST ISRAEL AND INCITED DAVID TO TAKE A CENSUS OF ISRAEL.

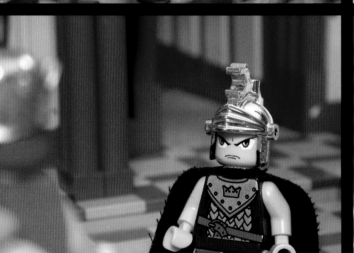

AFTER NINE MONTHS, JOAB RETURNED TO JERUSALEM AND REPORTED THE TOTAL NUMBER OF THE PEOPLE TO THE KING. THERE WERE 800,000 MEN IN ISRAEL ABLE TO WIELD A SWORD AND 500,000 MEN IN JUDAH.

BUT THEN DAVID FELT VERY GUILTY AFTER HE HAD TAKEN A CENSUS OF THE PEOPLE AND SAID TO YAH-WEH, 'I HAVE SINNED GREATLY BY DOING THIS! YAH-WEH, I BEG YOU TO TAKE AWAY THE GUILT OF YOUR SERVANT, FOR I HAVE DONE A VERY FOOLISH THING!'

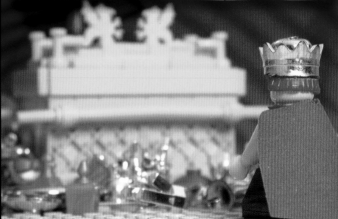

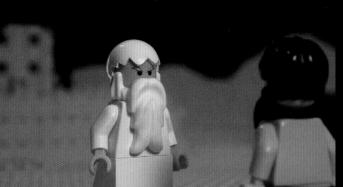

BY THE MORNING, WHEN DAVID GOT UP, THE WORD OF YAHWEH HAD COME TO GAD THE PROPHET: 'GO AND TELL DAVID, "THIS IS WHAT YAHWEH SAYS: 'I AM OFFERING YOU THREE OPTIONS. CHOOSE ONE, AND I WILL INFLICT IT AGAINST YOU.'"'

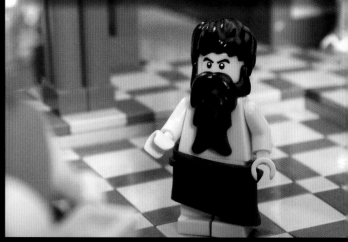

GAD SAID TO DAVID, 'SHALL THERE BE THREE YEARS OF FAMINE ON YOUR LAND? THREE MONTHS OF FLEE-ING FROM YOUR ENEMIES AS THEY PURSUE YOU? OR THREE DAYS OF PLAGUE ON YOUR LAND?'

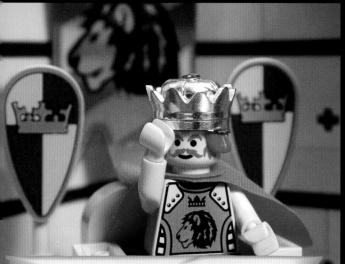

DAVID SAID TO GAD, 'I AM DISTRAUGHT! BUT LET US FALL INTO GOD'S HANDS RATHER THAN INTO THE HANDS OF MEN, FOR GOD IS VERY MERCIFUL.'

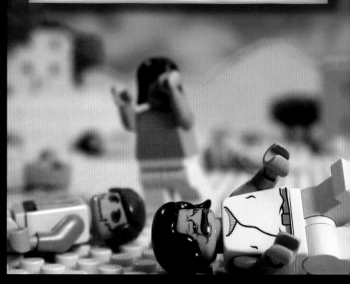

SO YAHWEH SENT A PLAGUE THROUGHOUT ISRAEL.

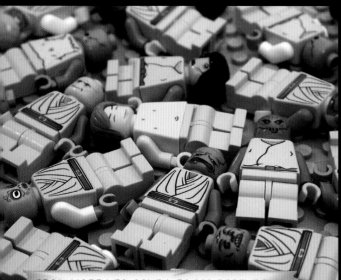

FROM NORTH TO SOUTH, 70,000 PEOPLE DIED.

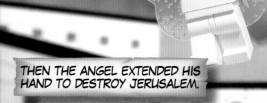

THEN THE ANGEL EXTENDED HIS HAND TO DESTROY JERUSALEM.

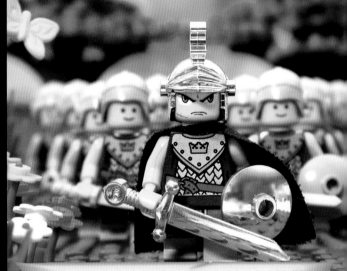

BUT YAHWEH WAS GRIEVED OVER THE DISASTER, AND HE SAID TO THE ANGEL WHO WAS DESTROYING THE PEOPLE, 'THAT IS ENOUGH. HOLD BACK YOUR HAND.'

IN SPRINGTIME, THE TIME WHEN KINGS GO OFF TO WAR, DAVID SENT OUT JOAB AND ALL THE ISRAELITES.

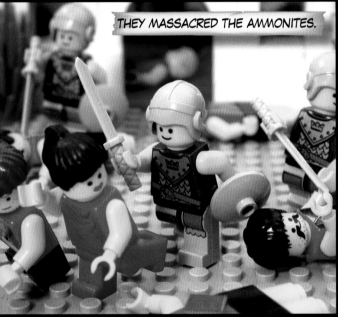

THEY MASSACRED THE AMMONITES.

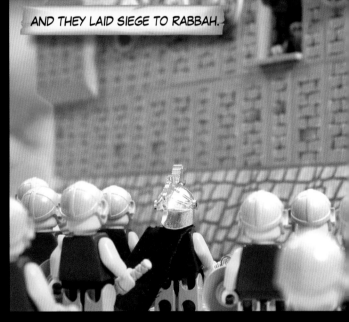

AND THEY LAID SIEGE TO RABBAH.

DAVID REMAINED IN JERUSALEM, AND LATE ONE AFTERNOON, HE WAS WALKING ALONG THE ROOF OF THE PALACE.

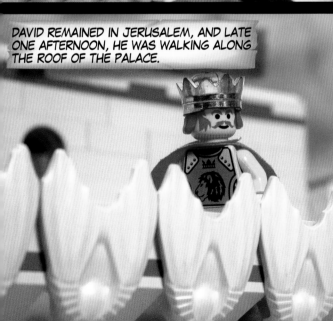

FROM THE ROOF, HE SAW A WOMAN BATHING. THE WOMAN WAS VERY BEAUTIFUL. DAVID SENT SOMEONE TO INQUIRE ABOUT THE WOMAN, AND HE WAS TOLD, 'ISN'T THIS BATHSHEBA, THE WIFE OF URIAH THE HITTITE?'

DAVID SENT MESSENGERS TO FETCH HER, AND SHE CAME TO HIM. HE LAID WITH HER, AND SHE BECAME PREGNANT.

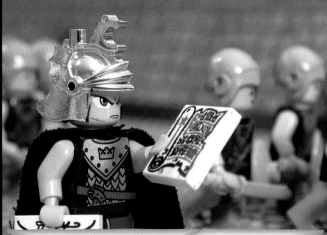

SO DAVID WROTE A LETTER TO JOAB, AND IN IT HE WROTE, 'PUT URIAH IN THE FRONT WHERE THE FIGHTING IS FIERCEST, THEN WITHDRAW SO HE WILL BE STRUCK DOWN AND KILLED.'

WITH THE CITY UNDER SIEGE, JOAB PUT URIAH AT A PLACE WHERE HE KNEW THE STRONGEST DEFENDERS WERE.

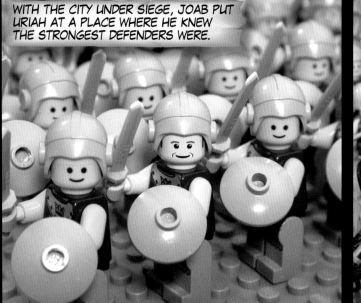

AND WHEN THE MEN OF THE CITY CAME OUT TO FIGHT, SOME OF DAVID'S MEN FELL DEAD, AND URIAH THE HITTITE DIED.

WHEN URIAH'S WIFE HEARD THAT HER HUSBAND URIAH WAS DEAD, SHE MOURNED FOR HER HUSBAND.

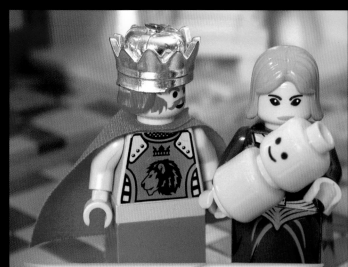

WHEN THE PERIOD OF MOURNING WAS OVER, DAVID HAD HER BROUGHT TO THE PALACE, AND SHE BECAME HIS WIFE. AND SHE BORE HIM A SON.

BUT WHAT DAVID HAD DONE WAS EVIL IN THE EYES OF YAHWEH, AND YAHWEH STRUCK THE CHILD THAT URIAH'S WIFE HAD BORNE TO DAVID.

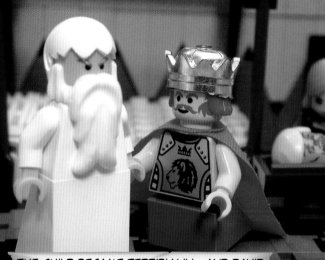

THE CHILD BECAME TERRIBLY ILL, AND DAVID PLEADED WITH YAHWEH FOR THE CHILD.

A WEEK LATER, THE CHILD DIED.

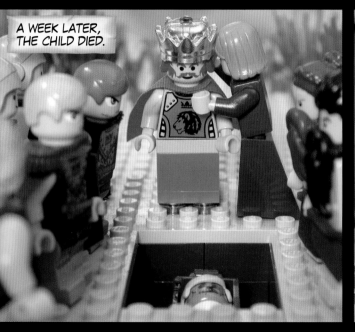

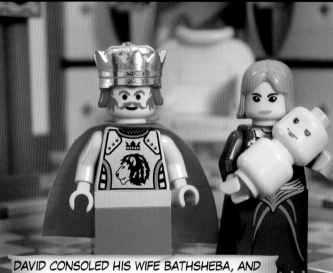

DAVID CONSOLED HIS WIFE BATHSHEBA, AND HE LAID WITH HER. SHE GAVE BIRTH TO A SON, AND HE NAMED HIM SOLOMON.

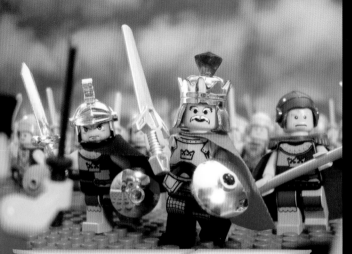

WAR BROKE OUT AGAIN BETWEEN THE PHILISTINES AND ISRAEL, AND DAVID WENT DOWN WITH HIS ARMY AND FOUGHT THE PHILISTINES.

DAVID BECAME EXHAUSTED, AND ONE OF THE DESCENDANTS OF THE GIANTS, ISHBI-BENOB, WHOSE BRONZE SPEARHEAD WEIGHED THREE HUNDRED SHEKELS, SAID HE WOULD KILL DAVID.

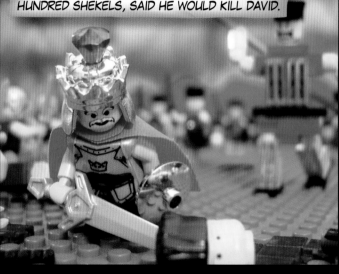

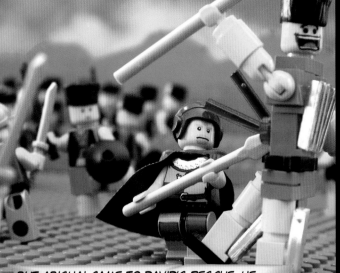

BUT ABISHAI CAME TO DAVID'S RESCUE. HE STRUCK THE PHILISTINE DOWN AND KILLED HIM.

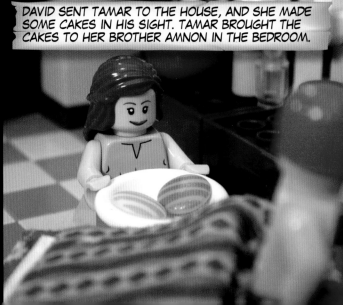

THEN DAVID'S MEN VOWED TO HIM, 'YOU MUST NEVER AGAIN GO OUT WITH US TO BATTLE, SO YOU WILL NOT EXTINGUISH THE LAMP OF ISRAEL.'

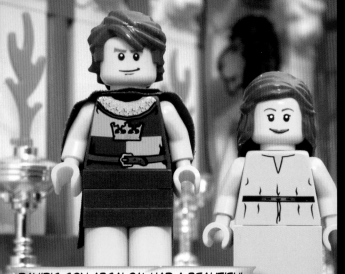

DAVID'S SON ABSALOM HAD A BEAUTIFUL SISTER WHOSE NAME WAS TAMAR.

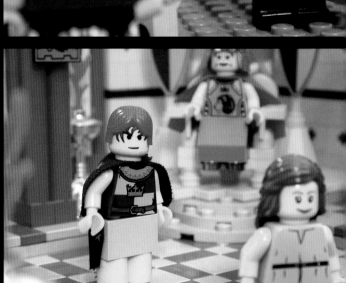

DAVID'S SON AMNON FELL IN LOVE WITH TAMAR. AMNON BECAME TORMENTED TO THE POINT OF ILLNESS OVER HIS SISTER, FOR SHE WAS A VIRGIN, AND SO IT WAS NOT AN OPTION TO DO ANYTHING TO HER.

NOW, AMNON LAY DOWN AND PRETENDED TO BE SICK, AND WHEN THE KING CAME TO SEE HIM, AMNON SAID, 'PLEASE, LET MY SISTER TAMAR COME AND MAKE A COUPLE OF CAKES IN MY SIGHT. THEN, I WILL EAT FROM HER HAND.'

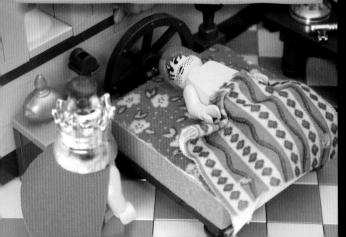

DAVID SENT TAMAR TO THE HOUSE, AND SHE MADE SOME CAKES IN HIS SIGHT. TAMAR BROUGHT THE CAKES TO HER BROTHER AMNON IN THE BEDROOM.

BUT AS SHE WAS OFFERING THE FOOD TO HIM, AMNON GRABBED HER AND SAID TO HER, 'COME, LAY WITH ME, MY SISTER!'

TAMAR SAID TO HIM, 'NO, MY BROTHER! DO NOT RAPE ME, FOR SUCH IS NOT DONE IN ISRAEL! SPEAK TO THE KING, AND HE WILL NOT WITHHOLD ME FROM YOU!'

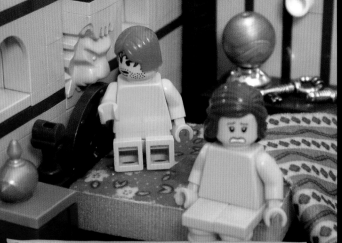
BUT AMNON WOULD NOT LISTEN TO HER, AND HE RAPED HER. THEN AMNON HATED HER. HE HATED HER EVEN MORE THAN HE HAD BEEN IN LOVE WITH HER. HE SAID TO HER, 'GET UP AND GO!'

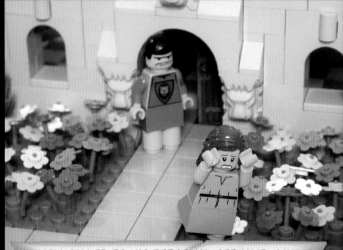
AMNON CALLED TO HIS PERSONAL SERVANT, SAYING, 'TAKE HER OUT OF HERE!' SO HIS SERVANT TOOK HER OUTSIDE, AND TAMAR WENT AWAY, WAILING WITH HER HANDS ON HER HEAD.

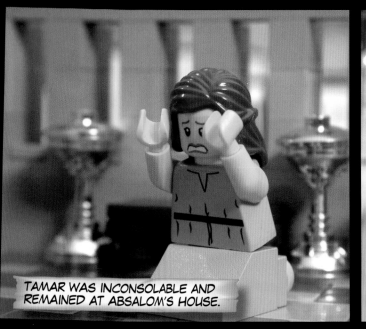
TAMAR WAS INCONSOLABLE AND REMAINED AT ABSALOM'S HOUSE.

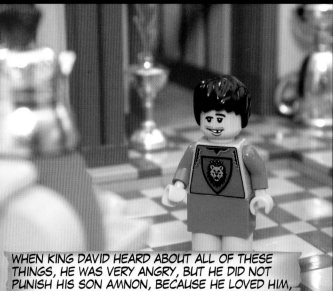
WHEN KING DAVID HEARD ABOUT ALL OF THESE THINGS, HE WAS VERY ANGRY, BUT HE DID NOT PUNISH HIS SON AMNON, BECAUSE HE LOVED HIM, FOR HE WAS HIS FIRSTBORN.

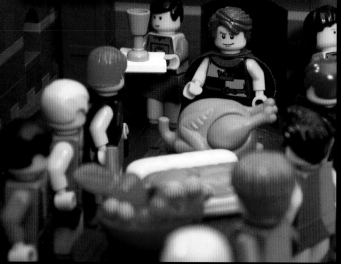

TWO YEARS LATER, WHEN ABSALOM WAS AT BAAL HAZOR WITH THE SHEEP-SHEARERS, HE INVITED ALL THE KING'S SONS THERE.

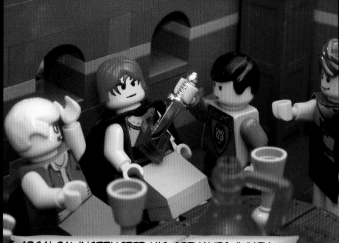

ABSALOM INSTRUCTED HIS SERVANTS, 'WHEN AMNON IS GOOD AND DRUNK, AND I SAY, "STRIKE AMNON DOWN," THEN KILL HIM.' SO ABSALOM'S SERVANTS DID JUST AS HE INSTRUCTED.

IN ALL OF ISRAEL THERE WAS NO ONE MORE PRAISED FOR HIS BEAUTY THAN ABSALOM. FROM HEAD TO TOE, HE LOOKED PERFECT.

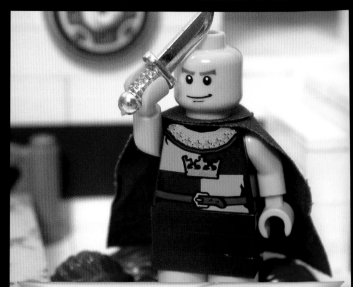

AT THE END OF EVERY YEAR, HE WOULD SHAVE HIS HEAD, BECAUSE OTHERWISE HIS HAIR BECAME TOO HEAVY.

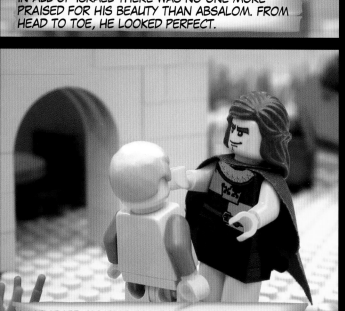

WHENEVER ANYONE CAME UP TO ABSALOM TO PROSTRATE HIMSELF, HE WOULD EXTEND TO THEM HIS HAND, EMBRACE THEM, AND KISS THEM.

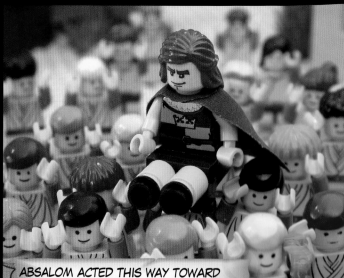

ABSALOM ACTED THIS WAY TOWARD EVERYONE IN ISRAEL. AND SO ABSALOM WON THE HEARTS OF ALL ISRAEL.

AFTER FOUR YEARS, ABSALOM WENT TO HEBRON WITH 200 MEN AND SENT MESSENGERS THROUGHOUT ISRAEL, TELLING THEM, 'AS SOON AS YOU HEAR THE TRUMPET, SHOUT THAT ABSALOM IS KING AT HEBRON!'

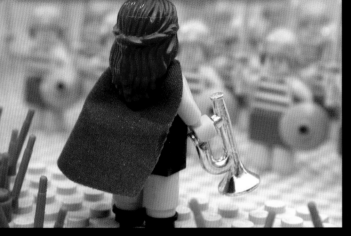

ABSALOM'S SUPPORTERS GREW IN NUMBER, AND A MESSENGER TOLD DAVID, 'THE HEARTS OF THE ISRAELITES ARE WITH ABSALOM!'

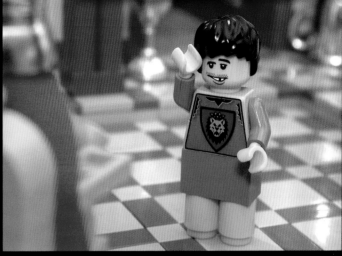

DAVID SAID TO ALL HIS SERVANTS IN JERUSALEM, 'WE MUST FLEE IMMEDIATELY, OR NONE OF US WILL ESCAPE! ABSALOM WILL BRING DISASTER ON US AND PUT THE CITY TO THE SWORD!'

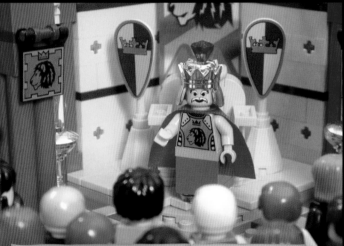

THE KING AND HIS ENTIRE ROYAL COURT SET OUT ON FOOT WITH ALL HIS SERVANTS. ALL HIS OFFICERS WERE WITH HIM AND THE 600 MEN FROM GATH WHO WERE IN DAVID'S SERVICE.

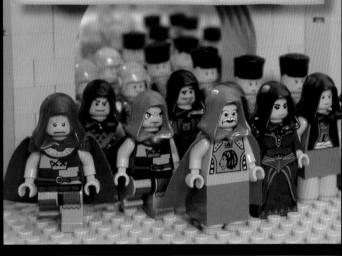

AS DAVID WAS GOING UP THE MOUNT OF OLIVES, HE WAS WEEPING WITH HIS HEAD COVERED AND HIS FEET BARE. DAVID WAS TOLD, 'AHITHOPHEL HAS SIDED WITH ABSALOM.'

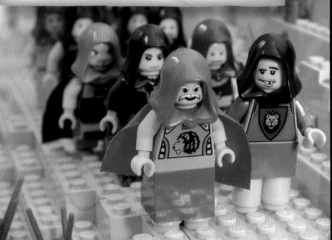

ABSALOM AND THE MEN OF ISRAEL ARRIVED IN JERUSALEM, AND AHITHOPHEL WAS WITH THEM.

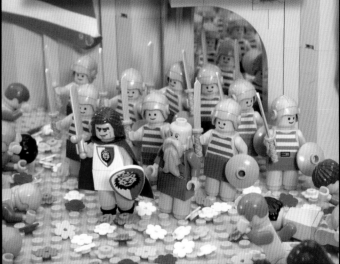

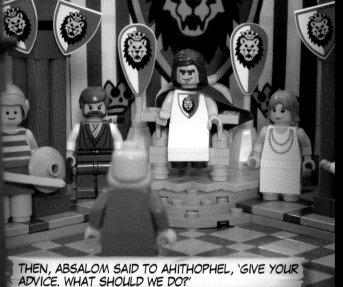

THEN, ABSALOM SAID TO AHITHOPHEL, 'GIVE YOUR ADVICE. WHAT SHOULD WE DO?'

AHITHOPHEL SAID TO ABSALOM, 'LAY WITH YOUR FATHER'S CONCUBINES. ALL ISRAEL WILL HEAR THAT YOU HAVE MADE YOURSELF REPULSIVE TO YOUR FATHER, AND THIS WILL SHORE UP SUPPORT FOR YOU.'

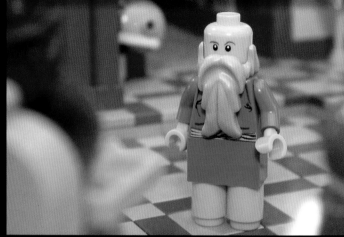

SO THEY SET UP A TENT FOR ABSALOM ON THE ROOF, AND HE LAID WITH HIS FATHER'S CONCUBINES, AND ALL THE ISRAELITES SAW THIS.

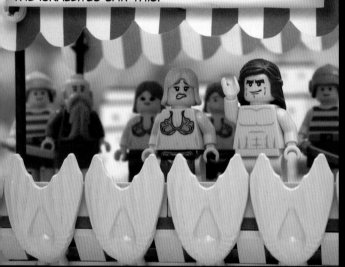

ABSALOM MADE AMASA THE GENERAL OF THE ARMY, AND ABSALOM AND ALL THE MEN OF ISRAEL CROSSED THE JORDAN.

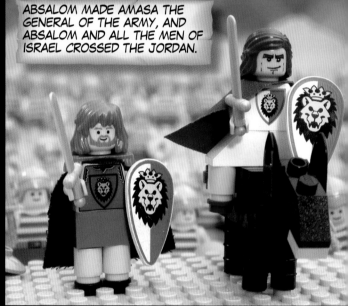

DAVID ASSEMBLED THE ARMY AT MAHANAIM AND SAID TO HIS ARMY COMMANDERS: 'FOR MY SAKE, DEAL GENTLY WITH THE YOUNG MAN, ABSALOM.' AND THE ENTIRE ARMY HEARD HIM GIVE THIS COMMAND.

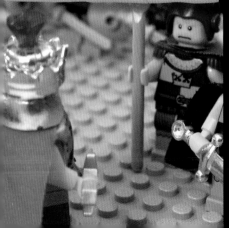

SO THE ARMY MARCHED OUT TO FIGHT AGAINST THE ISRAELITES, AND THE BATTLE TOOK PLACE IN THE FOREST OF EPHRAIM.

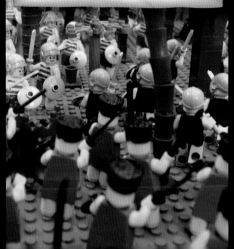

THE ISRAELITE ARMY WAS DEFEATED THERE BY DAVID'S MEN. THE SLAUGHTER WAS GREAT THAT DAY - 20,000 SOLDIERS WERE KILLED.

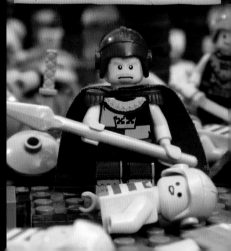

AND ABSALOM'S HEAD GOT CAUGHT IN THE OAK. HE WAS SUSPENDED IN MIDAIR WHILE THE MULE KEPT GOING. AND ONE MAN SAW THIS.

AS ABSALOM WAS RIDING HIS MULE, IT WENT UNDER THE BRANCHES OF A LARGE OAK TREE.

HE REPORTED IT TO JOAB, SAYING, 'I SAW ABSALOM HANGING IN AN OAK TREE.'

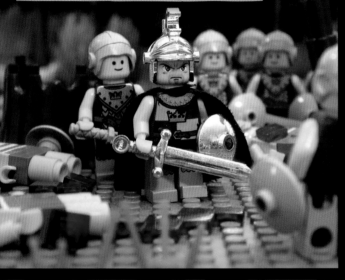

JOAB TOOK THREE DAGGERS AND THRUST THEM INTO THE MIDDLE OF ABSALOM WHILE HE WAS STILL ALIVE IN THE MIDDLE OF THE OAK TREE.

TEN SOLDIERS WHO WERE JOAB'S ARMOR BEARERS THEN FINISHED HIM OFF.

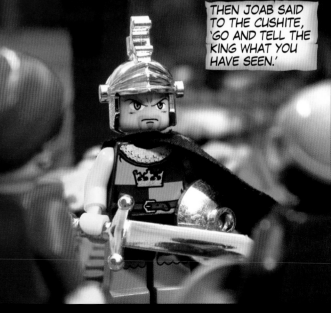

THEN JOAB SAID TO THE CUSHITE, 'GO AND TELL THE KING WHAT YOU HAVE SEEN.'

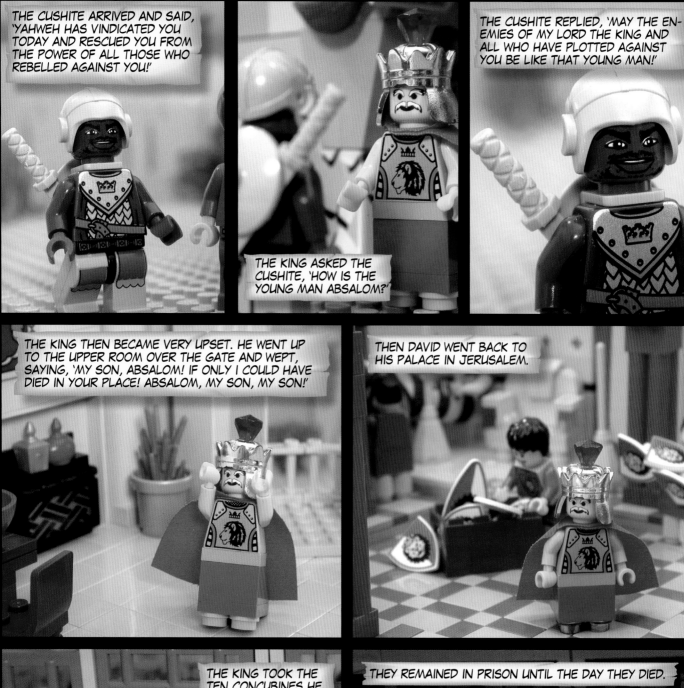

THE CUSHITE ARRIVED AND SAID, 'YAHWEH HAS VINDICATED YOU TODAY AND RESCUED YOU FROM THE POWER OF ALL THOSE WHO REBELLED AGAINST YOU!'

THE KING ASKED THE CUSHITE, 'HOW IS THE YOUNG MAN ABSALOM?'

THE CUSHITE REPLIED, 'MAY THE ENEMIES OF MY LORD THE KING AND ALL WHO HAVE PLOTTED AGAINST YOU BE LIKE THAT YOUNG MAN!'

THE KING THEN BECAME VERY UPSET. HE WENT UP TO THE UPPER ROOM OVER THE GATE AND WEPT, SAYING, 'MY SON, ABSALOM! IF ONLY I COULD HAVE DIED IN YOUR PLACE! ABSALOM, MY SON, MY SON!'

THEN DAVID WENT BACK TO HIS PALACE IN JERUSALEM.

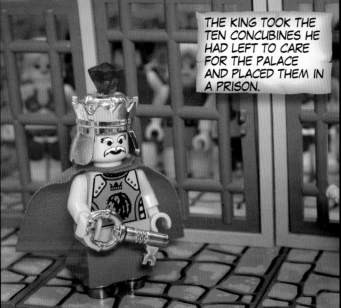

THE KING TOOK THE TEN CONCUBINES HE HAD LEFT TO CARE FOR THE PALACE AND PLACED THEM IN A PRISON.

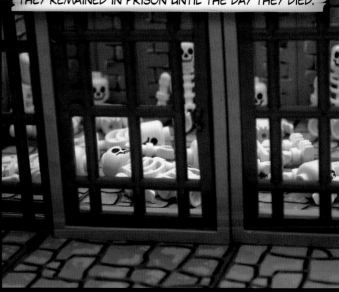

THEY REMAINED IN PRISON UNTIL THE DAY THEY DIED.

KINGS

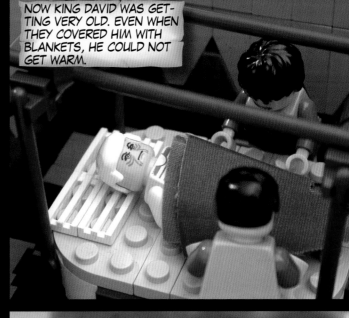

NOW KING DAVID WAS GETTING VERY OLD. EVEN WHEN THEY COVERED HIM WITH BLANKETS, HE COULD NOT GET WARM.

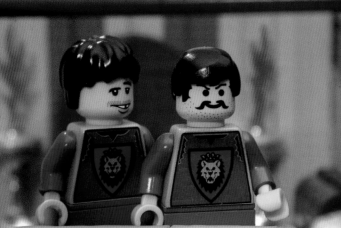

HIS SERVANTS SAID TO HIM, 'A YOUNG VIRGIN MUST BE FOUND TO ATTEND TO THE KING AND COMFORT HIM. SHE WILL LIE ON HIS CHEST SO THE KING MAY GET WARM.'

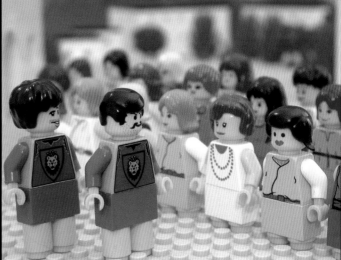

SO THEY SEARCHED THROUGH ALL THE LANDS OF ISRAEL FOR A BEAUTIFUL YOUNG WOMAN.

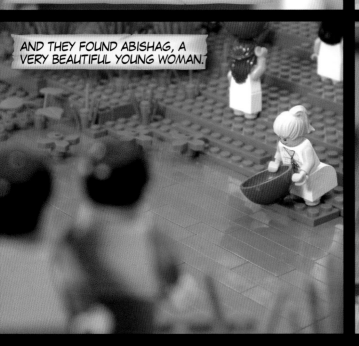

AND THEY FOUND ABISHAG, A VERY BEAUTIFUL YOUNG WOMAN.

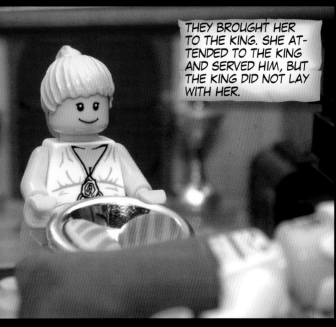

THEY BROUGHT HER TO THE KING. SHE ATTENDED TO THE KING AND SERVED HIM, BUT THE KING DID NOT LAY WITH HER.

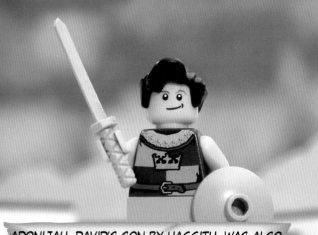

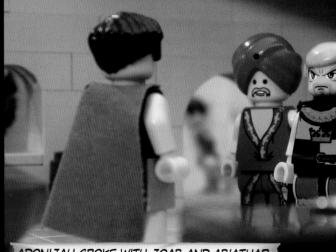

ADONIJAH, DAVID'S SON BY HAGGITH, WAS ALSO VERY HANDSOME. HE WAS BORN RIGHT AFTER ABSALOM. HE WAS NOW LIFTING HIMSELF UP, SAYING, 'I WILL BE KING.'

ADONIJAH SPOKE WITH JOAB AND ABIATHAR, THE PRIEST, AND THEY SUPPORTED HIM.

NATHAN, THE PROPHET, SAID TO SOLOMON'S MOTHER, BATHSHEBA, 'HAVE YOU HEARD THAT HAGGITH'S SON, ADONIJAH, HAS BECOME KING UNBEKNOWNST TO OUR MASTER DAVID?'

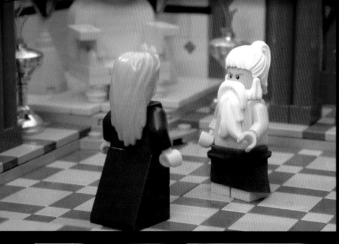

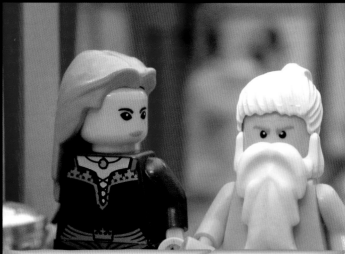

'HERE IS HOW YOU CAN SAVE THE LIFE OF YOUR SON, SOLOMON. GO TO KING DAVID AND SAY, "O KING, DID YOU NOT SOLEMNLY PROMISE YOUR SERVANT, 'SOLOMON WILL SIT ON MY THRONE AND BE KING AFTER ME'?"'

SHE REPLIED, 'MY MASTER, YOU SWORE AN OATH BY YAHWEH, "SOLOMON WILL BE KING AFTER ME AND SIT ON MY THRONE." BUT NOW ADONIJAH HAS BECOME KING WITHOUT YOUR KNOWLEDGE!'

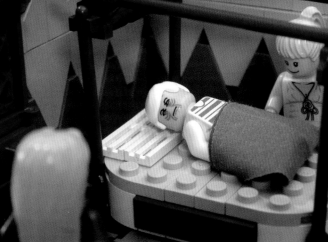

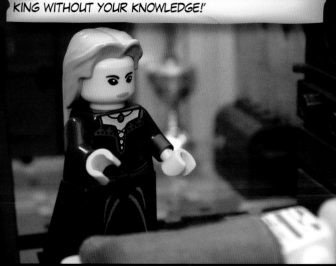

SO BATHSHEBA CAME TO THE KING IN HIS PRIVATE QUARTERS. NOW, THE KING WAS VERY OLD, AND ABISHAG WAS ATTENDING TO THE KING. AND THE KING SAID, 'WHAT DO YOU WANT?'

KING DAVID RESPONDED, 'AS SURELY AS YAHWEH LIVES, I WILL KEEP THE OATH I SWORE TO YOU BY YAHWEH THE GOD OF ISRAEL. SOLOMON WILL SIT ON MY THRONE AND BE KING AFTER ME.'

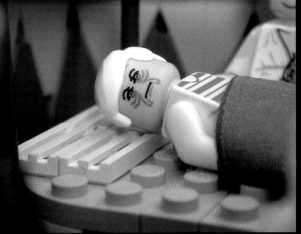

SO ZADOK, THE PRIEST, AND NATHAN, THE PROPHET, PUT SOLOMON ON A MULE AND LED HIM DOWN TO THE SPRING OF GIHON. ZADOK TOOK THE HORN OF OIL AND ANOINTED SOLOMON. THEY SOUNDED THE TRUMPET AND SHOUTED, 'LONG LIVE KING SOLOMON!'

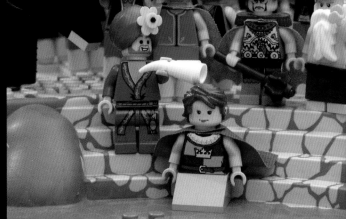

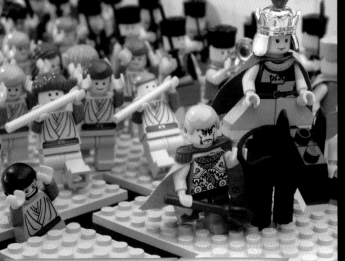

ALL THE PEOPLE CAME UP AFTER HIM, PLAYING FLUTES AND CELEBRATING SO LOUDLY THAT THE GROUND SPLIT OPEN AT THE SOUND OF THEM.

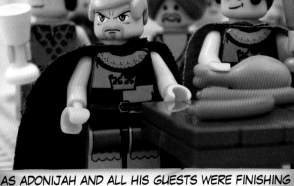

AS ADONIJAH AND ALL HIS GUESTS WERE FINISHING THEIR FEAST, THEY HEARD THE TRUMPET AND JOAB ASKED, 'WHY IS THE CITY SO NOISY?'

AS HE WAS SPEAKING, JONATHAN, THE SON OF ABIA-THAR THE PRIEST, ARRIVED AND SAID, 'KING DAVID HAS MADE SOLOMON KING AND SENT WITH HIM ZADOK, NA-THAN, BENAIAH, AND THE KERETHITES AND PELETHITES!'

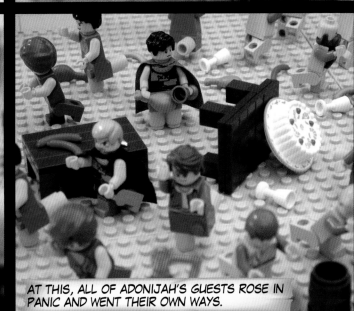

AT THIS, ALL OF ADONIJAH'S GUESTS ROSE IN PANIC AND WENT THEIR OWN WAYS.

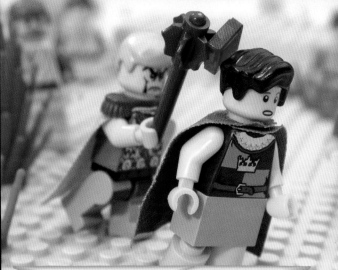

AND KING SOLOMON SENT OUT BENAIAH, AND HE STRUCK DOWN ADONIJAH, AND ADONIJAH DIED.

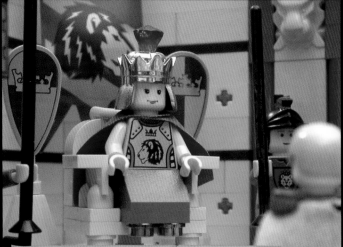

WHEN KING SOLOMON WAS TOLD THAT JOAB HAD FLED TO THE TABERNACLE OF YAHWEH AND WAS BESIDE THE ALTAR, HE COMMANDED BENAIAH, 'GO AND KILL HIM.'

SO BENAIAH WENT AND KILLED JOAB.

AT GIBEON, YAHWEH APPEARED TO SOLOMON IN A DREAM AND SAID, 'ASK ME FOR WHATEVER YOU WANT ME TO GIVE TO YOU.'

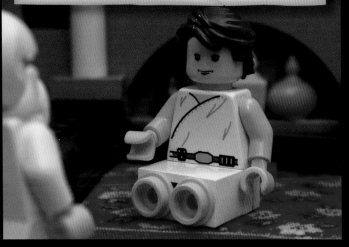

SOLOMON SAID, 'YOUR CHOSEN PEOPLE ARE A GREAT NATION, TOO NUMEROUS TO COUNT, AND I AM YOUNG AND INEXPERIENCED. SO GIVE YOUR SERVANT A DISCERNING HEART TO KNOW RIGHT FROM WRONG.'

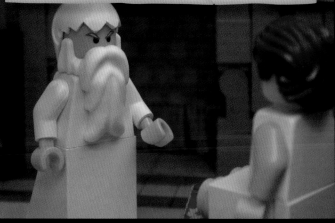

THIS PLEASED YAHWEH, AND GOD SAID TO HIM, 'BECAUSE YOU HAVE NOT ASKED FOR LONG LIFE OR RICHES OR FOR THE LIFE OF YOUR ENEMIES, INDEED, I GIVE YOU A WISE AND DISCERNING HEART, SUPERIOR TO ANYONE WHO HAS LIVED BEFORE YOU OR TO ANYONE WHO WILL LIVE AFTER YOU.'

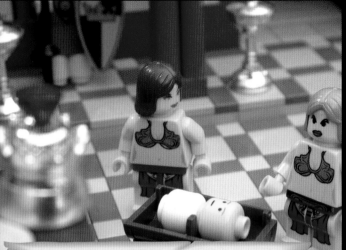

TWO FEMALE PROSTITUTES CAME TO THE KING, AND ONE OF THE WOMEN SAID, 'MY LORD, THIS WOMAN AND I LIVE IN THE SAME HOUSE. THREE DAYS AFTER I GAVE BIRTH, THIS WOMAN ALSO HAD A BABY.'

'THIS WOMAN'S SON DIED BECAUSE SHE LAY ON HIM.'

'SO IN THE MIDDLE OF THE NIGHT, SHE TOOK MY SON WHILE YOUR SERVANT WAS ASLEEP, AND LAID HER DEAD SON AT MY BREAST.'

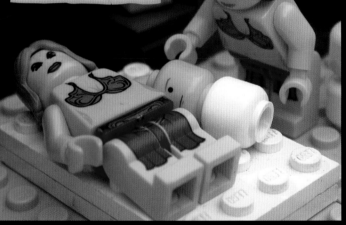

'WHEN I WOKE UP, I SAW THAT MY SON WAS DEAD, BUT LOOKING CLOSELY I REALIZED THAT IT WAS NOT THE SON TO WHOM I HAD GIVEN BIRTH.'

THE OTHER WOMAN SAID, 'NO, THE LIVING SON IS MINE, AND THE DEAD ONE IS YOURS!' BUT THE FIRST WOMAN SAID, 'NO, THE DEAD SON IS YOURS AND THE LIVING SON IS MINE!' AND THEY WENT ON ARGUING BEFORE THE KING.

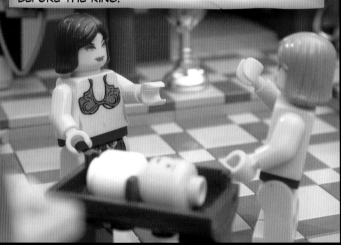

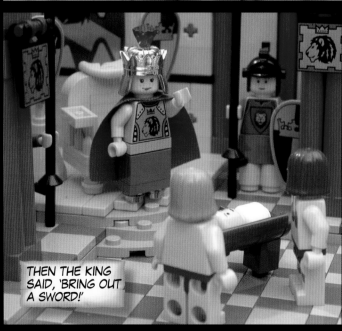

THEN THE KING SAID, 'BRING OUT A SWORD!'

253

SO THEY BROUGHT A SWORD BEFORE THE KING, AND HE SAID, 'CUT THE LIVING CHILD IN TWO, AND GIVE HALF TO EACH MOTHER.'

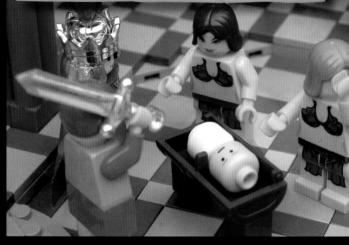

BUT THEN THE MOTHER WHOSE SON WAS ALIVE WAS FILLED WITH COMPASSION FOR HER SON AND SAID, 'MY LORD, GIVE HER THE LIVING CHILD, JUST DON'T KILL HIM!' BUT THE OTHER WOMAN SAID, 'LET IT BE NEITHER OF OURS! CUT IT!'

THEN THE KING RESPONDED, 'GIVE THE FIRST WOMAN THE LIVING CHILD. DO NOT KILL HIM. SHE IS HIS MOTHER.'

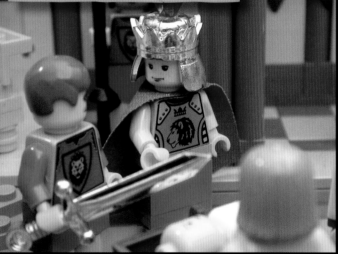

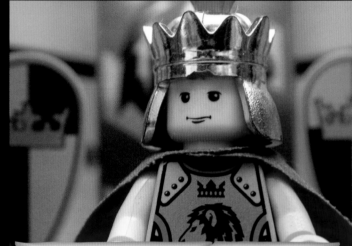

GOD GAVE SOLOMON GREAT WISDOM AND KNOWLEDGE AS MEASURELESS AS THE SAND ON THE SEASHORE. HIS WISDOM WAS GREATER THAN ALL THE MEN OF THE EAST AND ALL THE WISDOM OF EGYPT.

SOLOMON GAVE ORDERS TO BUILD A TEMPLE TO HONOR YAHWEH. THERE WERE FOUND TO BE 153,600 FOREIGNERS IN THE LAND, AND SOLOMON MADE 80,000 OF THEM STONE CUTTERS IN THE HILLS.

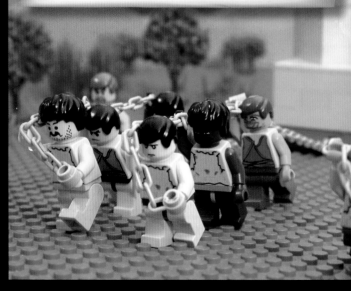

AND HE MADE 70,000 OF THEM BURDEN BEARERS.

IT TOOK SEVEN YEARS TO BUILD. ONLY FINISHED STONES WERE USED. THE SOUND OF HAMMERS, CHISELS, AND OTHER IRON TOOLS WERE NOT HEARD AT THE TEMPLE DURING CONSTRUCTION.

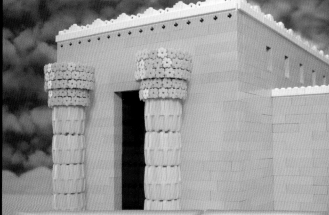

IN FRONT OF THE TEMPLE, SOLOMON MADE TWO BRONZE PILLARS, EACH 27 FEET TALL. THE PILLARS WERE SET UP ON THE PORCH IN FRONT OF THE MAIN HALL. THE ONE ON THE RIGHT HE NAMED JAKIN, AND THE ONE ON THE LEFT HE NAMED BOAZ.

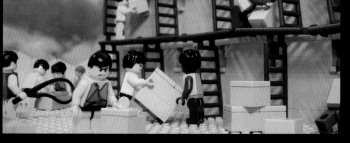

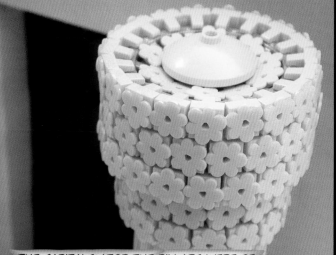

THE CAPITALS ATOP THE PILLARS WERE OF LILY-WORK AND SIX FEET TALL, HAVING 200 POMEGRANATES SET IN ROWS.

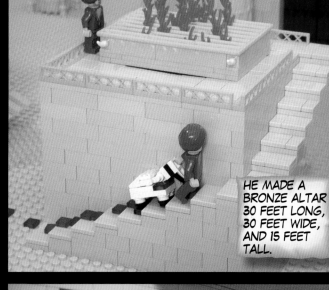

HE MADE A BRONZE ALTAR 30 FEET LONG, 30 FEET WIDE, AND 15 FEET TALL.

AND HE MADE THE BRONZE SEA. IT WAS SEVEN AND A HALF FEET TALL AND 45 FEET AROUND. IT STOOD ATOP TWELVE BULLS, THREE FACING NORTH, THREE WEST, THREE SOUTH, AND THREE EAST. IT COULD HOLD 18,000 GALLONS.

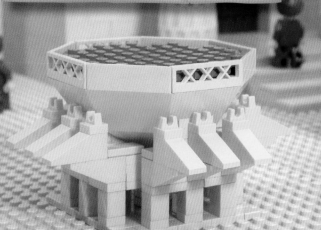

HE OVERLAID THE MAIN HALL WITH GOLD AND DECORATED THE TEMPLE WITH PRECIOUS STONES. ON ALL THE WALLS OF THE TEMPLE, HE ENGRAVED CARVINGS OF CHERUBIM, PALM TREES, AND FLOWERS.

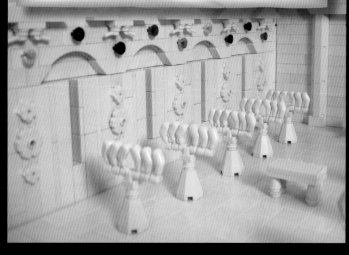

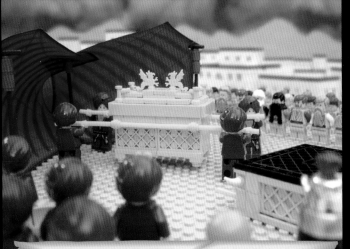

THEN, SOLOMON GATHERED ALL THE ELDERS OF ISRAEL AND ALL THE LEADERS OF THE TRIBES AND FAMILIES OF ISRAEL FOR THE TRANSFER OF THE ARK OF YAHWEH'S COVENANT FROM ZION, THE CITY OF DAVID.

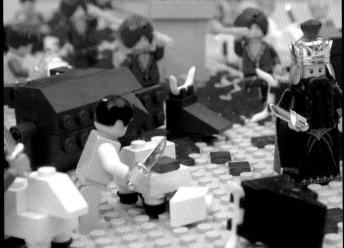

KING SOLOMON AND ALL THE ISRAELITES WERE IN FRONT OF THE ARK, SACRIFICING SO MANY SHEEP AND OXEN THAT IT WAS BEYOND ALL COUNTING.

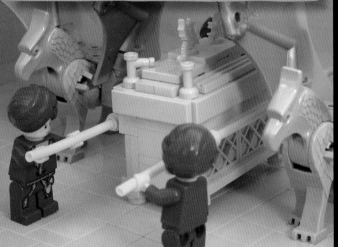

THE PRIESTS BROUGHT THE ARK OF YAHWEH'S COVENANT TO ITS PLACE IN THE HOLY OF HOLIES IN THE TEMPLE, UNDER THE WINGS OF THE CHERUBS.

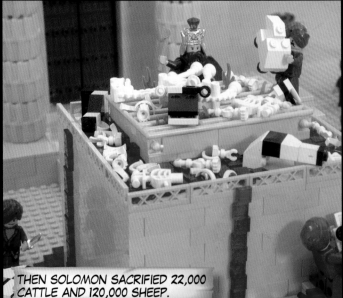

THEN SOLOMON SACRIFIED 22,000 CATTLE AND 120,000 SHEEP.

SOLOMON TOOK THIRTEEN YEARS TO BUILD HIS OWN PALACE. IT WAS MADE THROUGHOUT WITH EXPENSIVE DRESSED STONE AND CEDAR WOOD.

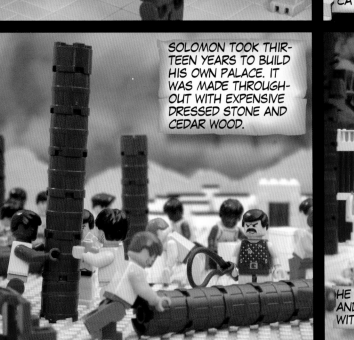

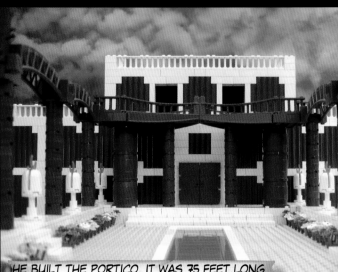

HE BUILT THE PORTICO. IT WAS 75 FEET LONG AND 45 FEET WIDE WITH A PORCH IN FRONT WITH PILLARS AND A ROOF.

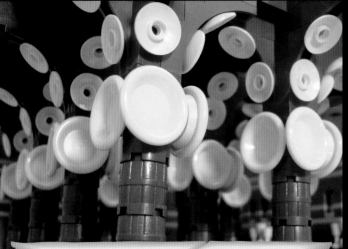

KING SOLOMON MADE TWO HUNDRED LARGE SHIELDS OF HAMMERED GOLD AND THREE HUNDRED SMALL SHIELDS OF HAMMERED GOLD AND PLACED THEM IN THE HALL OF THE FOREST OF LEBANON.

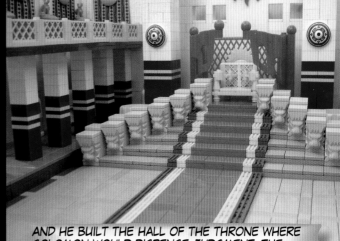

AND HE BUILT THE HALL OF THE THRONE WHERE SOLOMON WOULD DISPENSE JUDGMENT. THE THRONE HAD SIX STEPS WITH TWELVE LIONS, ONE AT THE END OF EACH STEP. NOTHING LIKE IT HAD BEEN MADE IN ANY OTHER KINGDOM.

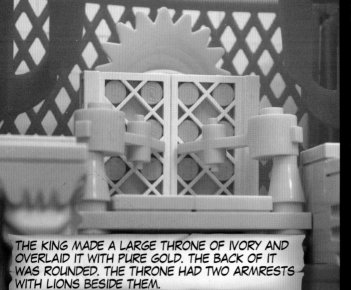

THE KING MADE A LARGE THRONE OF IVORY AND OVERLAID IT WITH PURE GOLD. THE BACK OF IT WAS ROUNDED. THE THRONE HAD TWO ARMRESTS WITH LIONS BESIDE THEM.

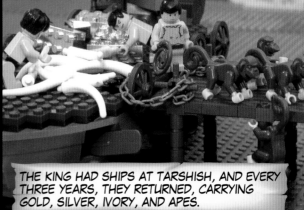

THE KING HAD SHIPS AT TARSHISH, AND EVERY THREE YEARS, THEY RETURNED, CARRYING GOLD, SILVER, IVORY, AND APES.

50,000 POUNDS OF GOLD WERE BROUGHT TO KING SOLOMON EACH YEAR IN ADDITION TO WHAT WAS COLLECTED FROM TRADERS, MER-CHANTS, ALL THE KINGS OF ARABIA, AND THE GOVERNORS OF THE LAND.

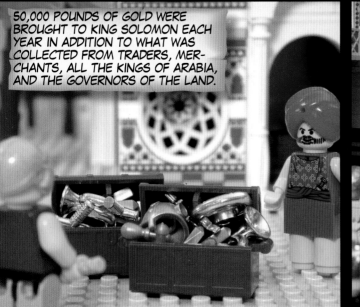

ALL THE KINGS OF THE EARTH WANTED TO VISIT SOLOMON TO HEAR THE WISDOM THAT GOD HAD GIVEN HIM.

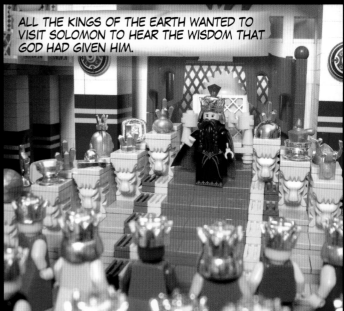

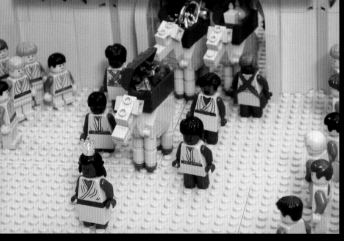

WHEN THE QUEEN OF SHEBA HEARD ABOUT THE FAME OF SOLOMON, SHE CAME TO TEST HIM WITH DIFFICULT QUESTIONS. SHE ARRIVED IN JERUSALEM WITH CAMELS BEARING SPICES, A GREAT AMOUNT OF GOLD, AND PRECIOUS STONES.

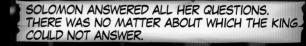
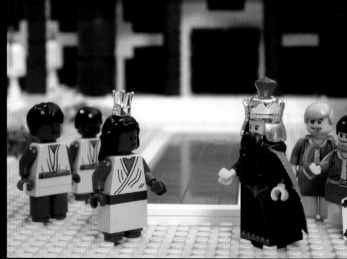

SOLOMON ANSWERED ALL HER QUESTIONS. THERE WAS NO MATTER ABOUT WHICH THE KING COULD NOT ANSWER.

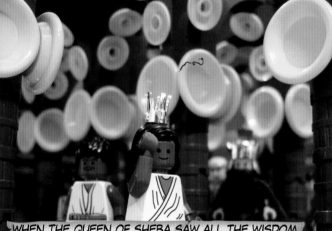

WHEN THE QUEEN OF SHEBA SAW ALL THE WISDOM OF SOLOMON, THE PALACE HE BUILT, THE FOOD ON HIS TABLE, HIS ATTENDING SERVANTS IN THEIR ROBES, HIS CUPBEARERS, AND THE BURNT SACRIFICES HE MADE AT THE TEMPLE OF YAHWEH, SHE WAS OVERWHELMED.

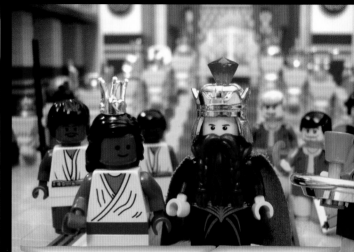

SHE SAID TO THE KING, 'YOUR WISDOM AND WEALTH ARE EVEN GREATER THAN WHAT I HAD HEARD! HOW HAPPY YOUR SERVANTS MUST BE WHO SERVE BEFORE YOU AND HEAR YOUR WISDOM!'

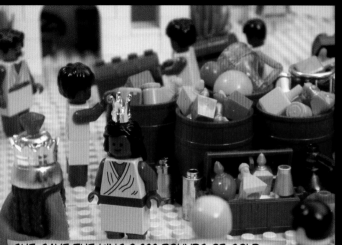

SHE GAVE THE KING 9,000 POUNDS OF GOLD, A GREAT AMOUNT OF SPICES, AND PRECIOUS STONES. NEVER AGAIN WERE SO MANY SPICES BROUGHT IN SUCH QUANTITY AS THE QUEEN OF SHEBA GAVE TO KING SOLOMON.

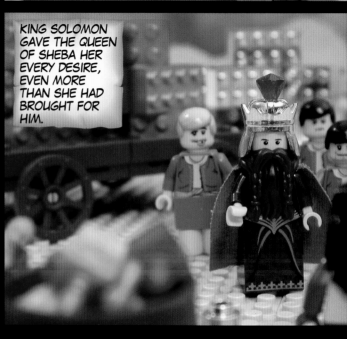

KING SOLOMON GAVE THE QUEEN OF SHEBA HER EVERY DESIRE, EVEN MORE THAN SHE HAD BROUGHT FOR HIM.

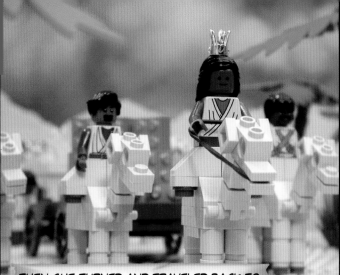

THEN SHE TURNED AND TRAVELED BACK TO HER OWN LAND WITH HER SERVANTS.

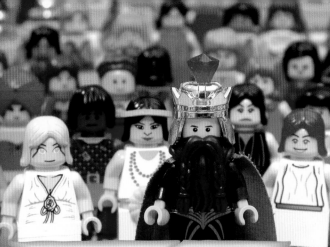

NOW KING SOLOMON LOVED MANY FOREIGN WOMEN INCLUDING MOABITES, AMMONITES, EDOMITES, SIDONIANS, AND HITTITES. SOLOMON HAD 700 WIVES.

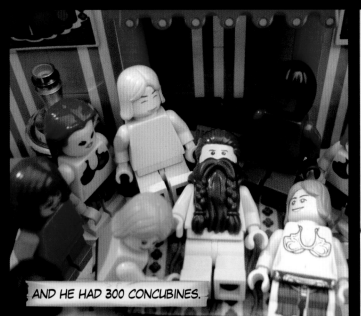

AND HE HAD 300 CONCUBINES.

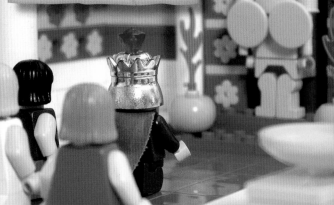

AS SOLOMON GREW OLDER, HIS WIVES SHIFTED HIS LOYALTY TO OTHER GODS. HE DID NOT WORSHIP YAHWEH EXCLUSIVELY AS HIS FATHER DAVID HAD DONE. SOLOMON WORSHIPED THE SIDONIAN GODDESS ASTARTE.

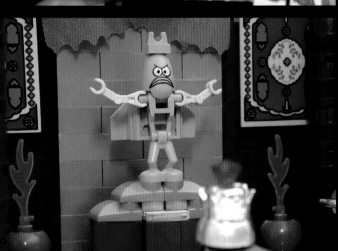

AND HE WORSHIPED THE DETESTABLE AMMONITE GOD, MOLECH.

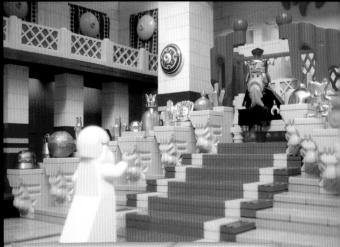

SO YAHWEH SAID TO SOLOMON, 'BECAUSE YOU HAVE NOT OBEYED MY COMMANDMENTS AND REGULATIONS, I WILL TEAR THE KINGDOM FROM YOU AND GIVE IT TO YOUR SERVANT!'

NOW JEROBOAM OF EPHRAIM WAS A TALENTED MAN, AND SOLOMON HAD MADE HIM THE TASKMASTER OF THE FORCED LABOR CREWS OF THE TRIBE OF JOSEPH.

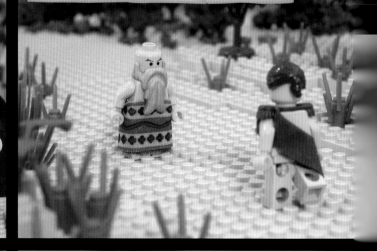

AROUND THIS TIME IT HAPPENED THAT AS JEROBOAM WAS GOING OUT FROM JERUSALEM, THE PROPHET AHIJAH OF SHILO FOUND HIM ON THE ROAD, AND THE TWO OF THEM WERE ALONE OUT IN THE OPEN COUNTRY.

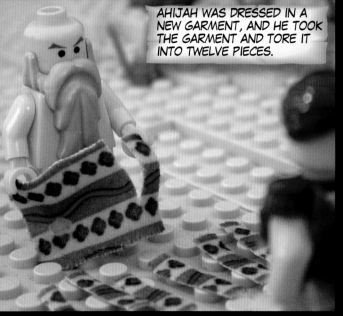

AHIJAH WAS DRESSED IN A NEW GARMENT, AND HE TOOK THE GARMENT AND TORE IT INTO TWELVE PIECES.

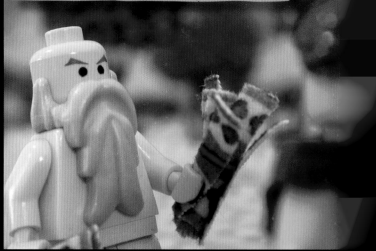

HE SAID TO JEROBOAM, 'TAKE TEN PIECES, FOR YAHWEH, GOD OF ISRAEL, SAYS, "LOOK, I AM ABOUT TO TEAR THE KINGDOM FROM SOLOMON AND I WILL GIVE TEN TRIBES TO YOU."'

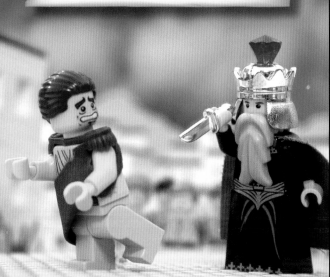

AND SO SOLOMON TRIED TO KILL JEROBOAM.

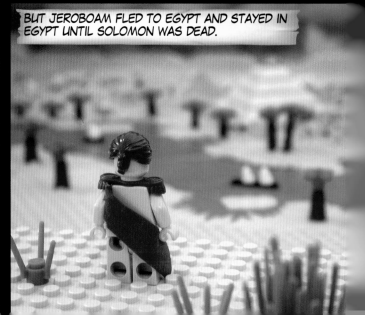

BUT JEROBOAM FLED TO EGYPT AND STAYED IN EGYPT UNTIL SOLOMON WAS DEAD.

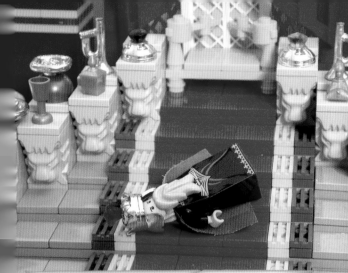

SOLOMON REIGNED IN JERUSALEM OVER ALL OF ISRAEL FOR 40 YEARS. THEN HE DIED.

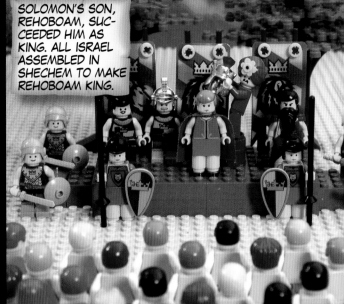

SOLOMON'S SON, REHOBOAM, SUCCEEDED HIM AS KING. ALL ISRAEL ASSEMBLED IN SHECHEM TO MAKE REHOBOAM KING.

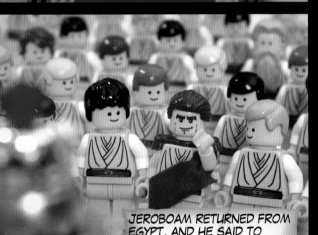

JEROBOAM RETURNED FROM EGYPT, AND HE SAID TO REHOBOAM, 'YOUR FATHER PLACED A HEAVY YOKE ON US. LIGHTEN THE HARSH LABOR AND HEAVY YOKE YOUR FATHER PUT ON US, AND WE WILL BE YOUR SUBJECTS.'

BUT REHOBOAM SAID, 'MY FATHER MADE YOUR YOKE HEAVY, BUT I WILL ADD TO IT! MY FATHER PUNISHED YOU WITH WHIPS, BUT I WILL PUNISH YOU WITH SCORPIONS!'

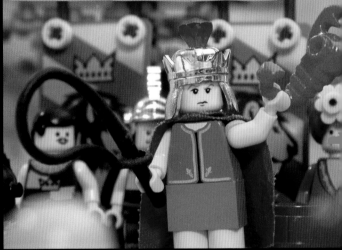

THE KING DID NOT LISTEN TO THE PEOPLE BECAUSE THESE EVENTS WERE BROUGHT ABOUT BY YAHWEH. KING REHOBOAM SENT OUT ADONIRAM, THE TASKMASTER OF THE FORCED LABOR CREWS.

BUT ALL ISRAEL STONED HIM TO DEATH.

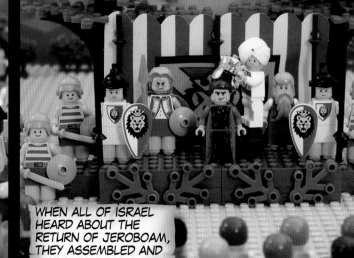

KING REHOBOAM MOUNTED HIS CHARIOT AND FLED TO JERUSALEM. AND SO ISRAEL HAS BEEN IN REBELLION AGAINST THE DYNASTY OF DAVID TO THIS VERY DAY.

WHEN ALL OF ISRAEL HEARD ABOUT THE RETURN OF JEROBOAM, THEY ASSEMBLED AND MADE HIM KING OVER ISRAEL.

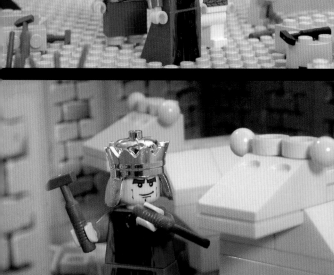

JEROBOAM FORTIFIED SHECHEM IN THE EPHRAIM HILL COUNTRY AND LIVED THERE.

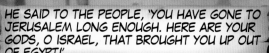

JEROBOAM THOUGHT TO HIMSELF, 'IF THESE PEOPLE CONTINUE TO GO TO THE TEMPLE OF YAHWEH IN JERUSALEM, THEIR LOYALTY WILL TURN TO REHOBOAM, AND THEY WILL KILL ME.'

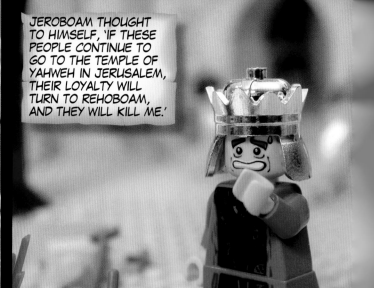

SO AFTER GIVING THE MATTER CONSIDERATION, JEROBOAM MADE TWO GOLDEN CALVES.

HE SAID TO THE PEOPLE, 'YOU HAVE GONE TO JERUSALEM LONG ENOUGH. HERE ARE YOUR GODS, O ISRAEL, THAT BROUGHT YOU UP OUT OF EGYPT!'

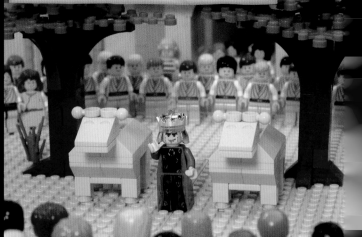

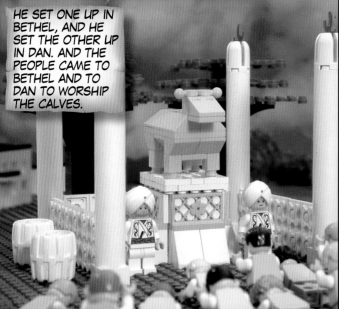

HE SET ONE UP IN BETHEL, AND HE SET THE OTHER UP IN DAN. AND THE PEOPLE CAME TO BETHEL AND TO DAN TO WORSHIP THE CALVES.

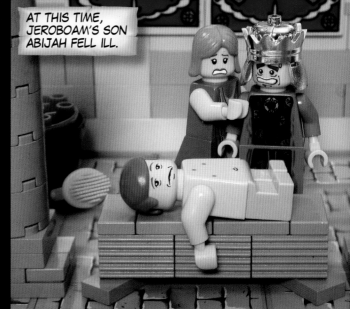

AT THIS TIME, JEROBOAM'S SON ABIJAH FELL ILL.

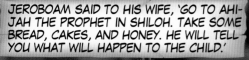

JEROBOAM SAID TO HIS WIFE, 'GO TO AHIJAH THE PROPHET IN SHILOH. TAKE SOME BREAD, CAKES, AND HONEY. HE WILL TELL YOU WHAT WILL HAPPEN TO THE CHILD.'

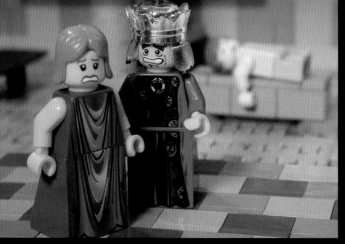

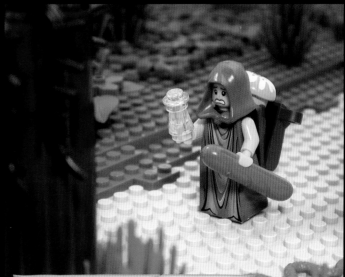

JEROBOAM'S WIFE SET OUT AND ARRIVED IN SHILOH AT THE HOUSE OF AHIJAH.

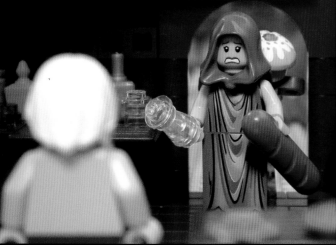

AS SHE ENTERED THE DOOR, AHIJAH SAID TO HER, 'COME IN, WIFE OF JEROBOAM, FOR I HAVE BEEN ORDERED TO GIVE YOU BAD NEWS. TELL JEROBOAM THAT THIS IS WHAT YAHWEH SAYS...'

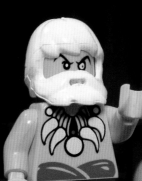

"YOU HAVE COMMITTED MORE EVIL THAN ALL WHO CAME BEFORE YOU. YOU HAVE ANGERED ME BY MAKING OTHER GODS MADE OF METAL, SO NOW I WILL BURN THE FAMILY OF JEROBOAM THE WAY ONE BURNS DUNG: UNTIL IT IS COMPLETELY GONE!"

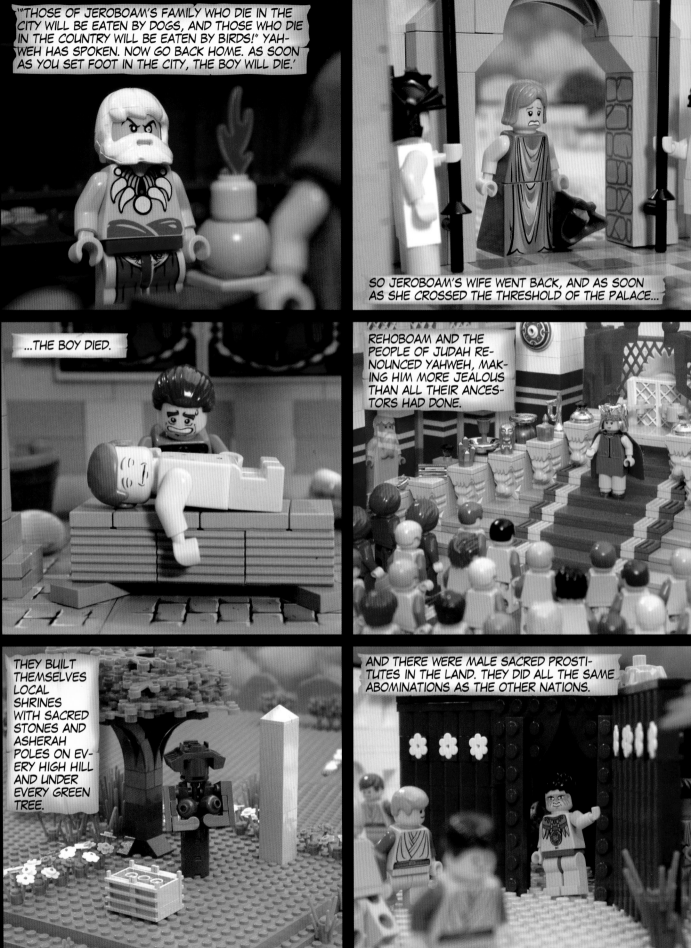

'"THOSE OF JEROBOAM'S FAMILY WHO DIE IN THE CITY WILL BE EATEN BY DOGS, AND THOSE WHO DIE IN THE COUNTRY WILL BE EATEN BY BIRDS!" YAHWEH HAS SPOKEN. NOW GO BACK HOME. AS SOON AS YOU SET FOOT IN THE CITY, THE BOY WILL DIE.'

SO JEROBOAM'S WIFE WENT BACK, AND AS SOON AS SHE CROSSED THE THRESHOLD OF THE PALACE...

...THE BOY DIED.

REHOBOAM AND THE PEOPLE OF JUDAH RENOUNCED YAHWEH, MAKING HIM MORE JEALOUS THAN ALL THEIR ANCESTORS HAD DONE.

THEY BUILT THEMSELVES LOCAL SHRINES WITH SACRED STONES AND ASHERAH POLES ON EVERY HIGH HILL AND UNDER EVERY GREEN TREE.

AND THERE WERE MALE SACRED PROSTITUTES IN THE LAND. THEY DID ALL THE SAME ABOMINATIONS AS THE OTHER NATIONS.

CHRONICLES

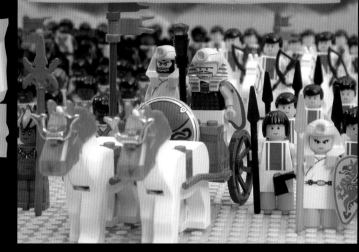

BECAUSE THEY WERE DISLOYAL TO YAHWEH, KING SHISHAK OF EGYPT ATTACKED JERUSALEM WITH 1,200 CHARIOTS, 60,000 HORSEMEN, AND COUNTLESS SOLDIERS, INCLUDING LIBYANS, SUKKITES, AND CUSHITES.

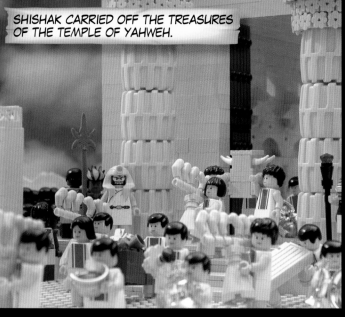

SHISHAK CARRIED OFF THE TREASURES OF THE TEMPLE OF YAHWEH.

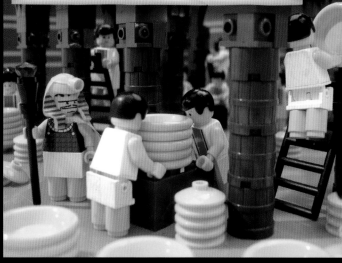

AND HE CARRIED OFF ALL THE TREASURES OF THE ROYAL PALACE, INCLUDING THE GOLD SHIELDS SOLOMON HAD MADE. HE TOOK EVERYTHING.

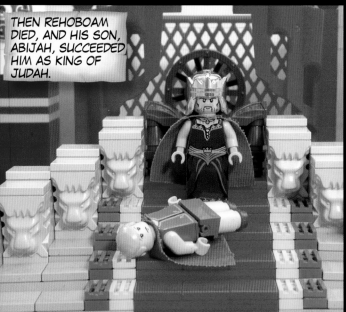

THEN REHOBOAM DIED, AND HIS SON, ABIJAH, SUCCEEDED HIM AS KING OF JUDAH.

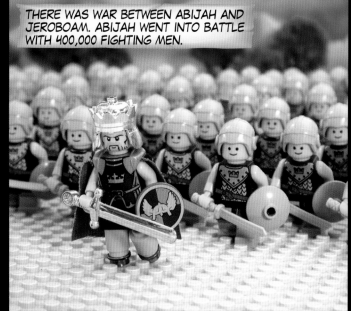

THERE WAS WAR BETWEEN ABIJAH AND JEROBOAM. ABIJAH WENT INTO BATTLE WITH 400,000 FIGHTING MEN.

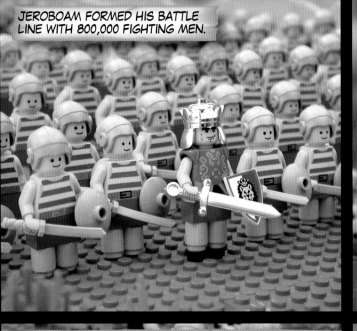

JEROBOAM FORMED HIS BATTLE LINE WITH 800,000 FIGHTING MEN.

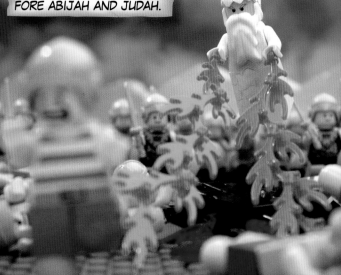

ABIJAH STOOD ON MOUNT ZEMARAIM AND SAID, 'YOU HAVE A VAST ARMY, BUT WE ARE OBSERVING YAHWEH'S REGULATIONS, WHILE YOU HAVE RENOUNCED HIM! ISRAELITES, DO NOT FIGHT AGAINST YAHWEH THE GOD OF YOUR ANCESTORS, FOR YOU WILL NOT WIN!'

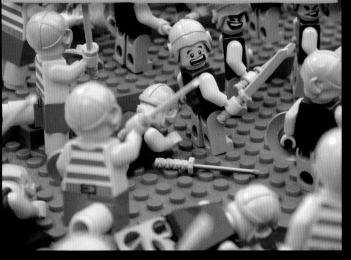

NOW, JEROBOAM HAD SENT SOME TROOPS TO ATTACK THEM FROM BEHIND IN AN AMBUSH. WHEN JUDAH TURNED AND SAW THAT THE BATTLE WAS BOTH IN FRONT AND BEHIND THEM, THEY CRIED OUT TO YAHWEH FOR HELP.

AND YAHWEH STRUCK DOWN ALL OF ISRAEL BEFORE ABIJAH AND JUDAH.

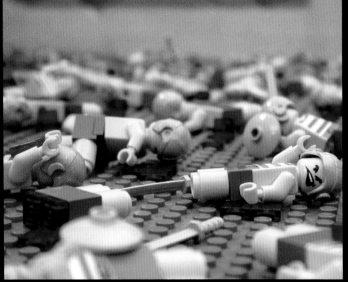

500,000 FIGHTING MEN OF ISRAEL WERE KILLED.

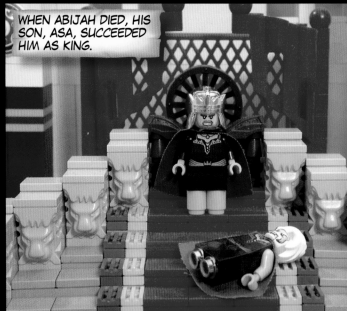

WHEN ABIJAH DIED, HIS SON, ASA, SUCCEEDED HIM AS KING.

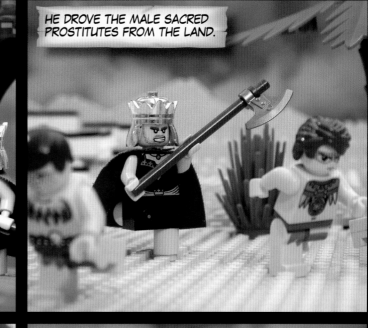

ASA DID WHAT WAS GOOD AND RIGHT IN THE EYES OF YAHWEH LIKE HIS ANCESTOR DAVID HAD DONE. HE SMASHED THE SACRED PILLARS AND CUT DOWN THE ASHERAH POLES.

HE DROVE THE MALE SACRED PROSTITUTES FROM THE LAND.

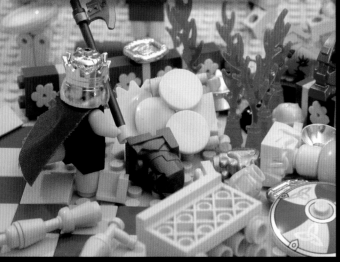

HE GOT RID OF THE LOCAL SHRINES AND INCENSE ALTARS, AND HE GOT RID OF ALL THE IDOLS HIS ANCESTORS HAD MADE.

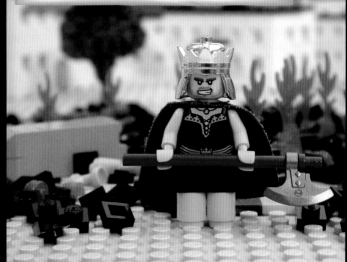

THERE WAS NO WAR DURING THOSE YEARS, FOR YAHWEH GAVE HIM PEACE.

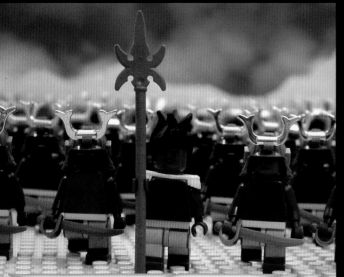

THEN ZERAH, THE CUSHITE, MARCHED AGAINST JUDAH WITH AN ARMY OF ONE MILLION MEN.

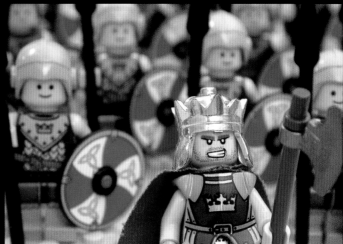

ASA MARCHED OUT TO OPPOSE HIM, AND HE CALLED OUT TO YAHWEH, 'HELP US, YAHWEH, FOR WE MARCH AGAINST THIS VAST ARMY IN YOUR NAME. O YAHWEH, OUR GOD, DO NOT LET MEN DEFEAT YOU!'

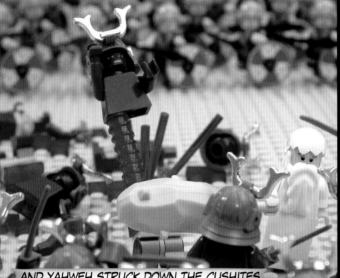

AND YAHWEH STRUCK DOWN THE CUSHITES BEFORE ASA AND HIS ARMY.

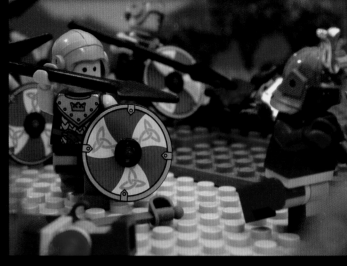

THE CUSHITES FLED, AND ASA AND HIS ARMY PURSUED THEM AS FAR AS GERAR.

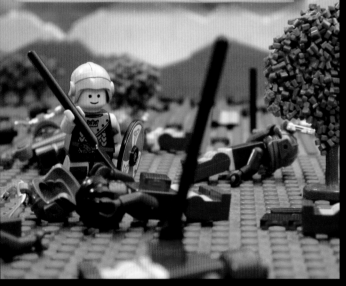

AND THE CUSHITES FELL DEAD UNTIL THERE WAS NO ONE LEFT ALIVE AMONG THEM.

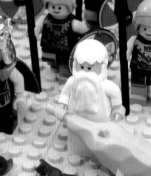

THEY WERE SHATTERED BEFORE YAHWEH AND HIS ARMY.

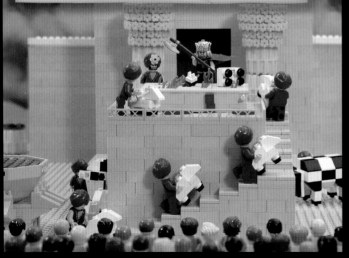

ASA ASSEMBLED IN JERUSALEM ALL OF JUDAH AND BENJAMIN, PLUS ALL THE RESIDENT FOREIGNERS FROM EPHRAIM, MANASSEH, AND SIMEON. HE SACRIFICED 700 CATTLE AND 7,000 SHEEP.

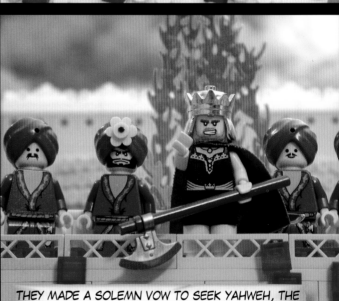

THEY MADE A SOLEMN VOW TO SEEK YAHWEH, THE GOD OF THEIR ANCESTORS, WHOLEHEARTEDLY.

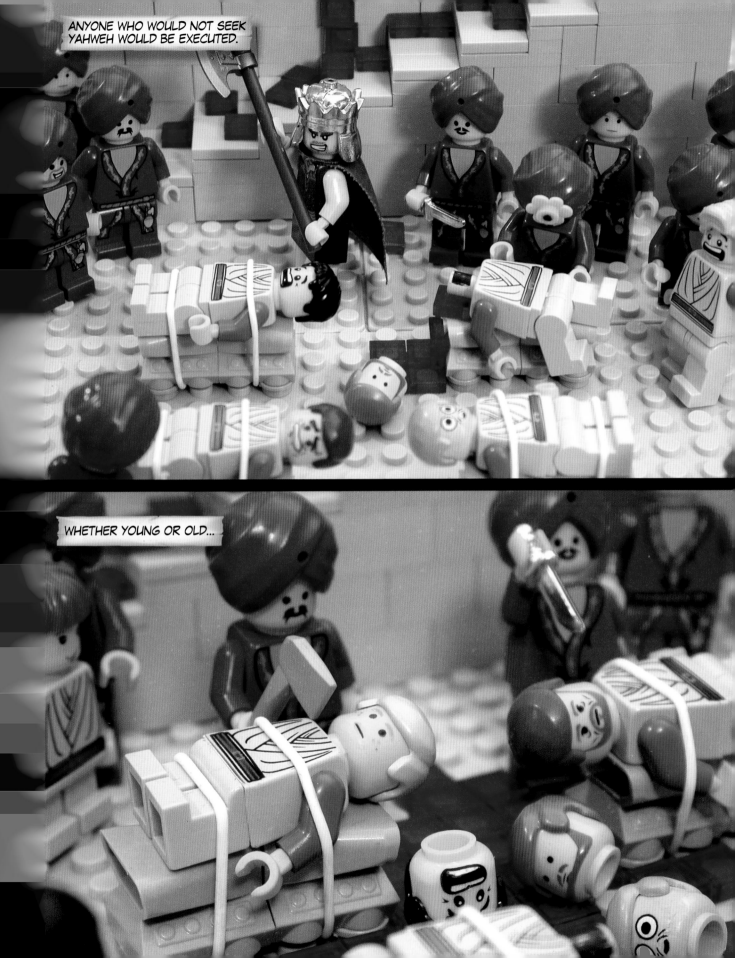

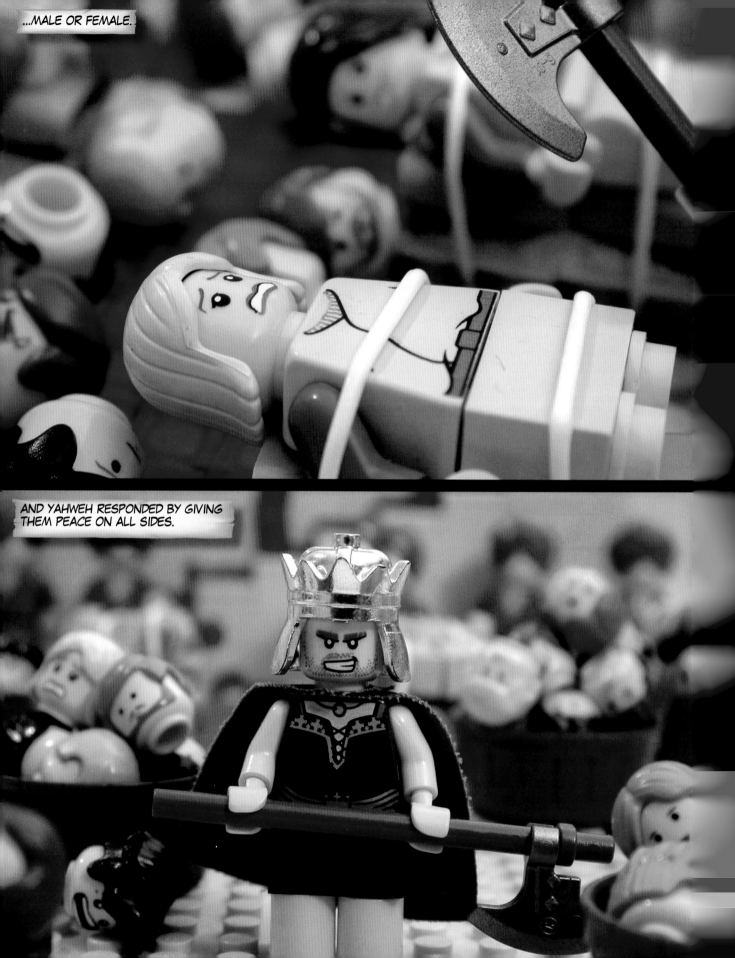

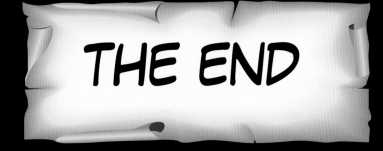